" Hello . . . Coastal "

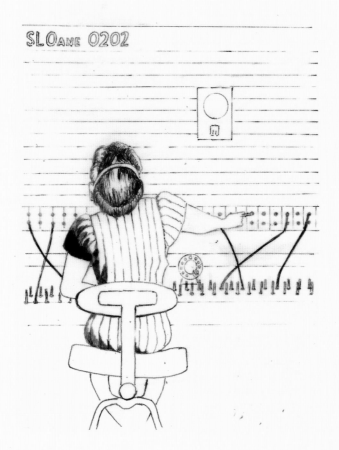

© 2007 VENTURE PUBLICATIONS LTD

ISBN 10 - 1 905304 102
ISBN 13 - 9781 905304 103

DESIGN AND COMPUTER ORIGINATION: JOHN A SENIOR

TRADE DISTRIBUTION AND SALES ENQUIRIES
MDS BOOKSALES 128, PIKES LANE GLOSSOP DERBYSHIRE SK13 8EH
01457 861508

WWW.VENTUREPUBLICATIONS.CO.UK
EMAIL INFO@VENTUREPUBLICATIONS.CO.UK

" Hello . . . Coastal "

The story
of
London's Victoria Coach
Station

Richard Paramor

Venture *publications*

Contents

A colourful scene with a selection of traditional liveries — from a painting by Paul Aitchison

Acknowledgements

If I were to express fully my appreciation of the dozens of people who have helped me to create this tribute to 'Coastal' it would need several pages, and I do not have the luxury of such space. There are several people, though, whom I must mention specifically. Chiefly I have to thank those fellow coach-people who have read, corrected, constructively criticised, and added to my manuscript as it has been developing over the months – people like Peter Scammell, John Marsh, John Walker, Don Vincent, and Ashley Wakelin. I have to thank my partner, John Reece, an avowed non-public transport (and thereby suspect) person, who nevertheless diligently read every page, pointed out several errors, and decided in the end that it was "quite interesting". Nor must I forget Glenys Lawson whose paintbrush skills produced the cover, Paul Aitchison for his nostalgia-proviking painting opposite, and, of course, Jim Russell whose collection of memorabilia was the catalyst that set off the whole project.

But most of all I have to thank Chris Nash without whose exceptional help, so freely and willingly given, this book would be a mere shadow of itself. Chris has given me enormous amounts of information about Victoria Coach Station (there can't be many ex-traffic clerks who also knew about the coach station's drains); he has checked my various diagrammatic plans; reconfirmed lots of my own memories; supplied photographs, captions, comments, and amusing anecdotes; but most of all, I am thankful that he has, through his own mad passion for 'Coastal', coaches and Victoria Coach Station, proved to me that I am not the only one with such lunatic enthusiasms.

There are so many other people who deserve a mention; the following list, which I'm sure is not without omissions, gives an idea of my indebtedness. To those I have left out – please forgive me: Mervyn Askew; Kaye Bagshaw & Jonathan Makepeace – Royal Institute of British Architects; Lyndsey Daykin – Pickfords Ltd; Alex Fairley; Professor John Hibbs; John Hillmer; Peter Jaques   The Kithead Trust; Nicholas King   Maidstone & District & East Kent Bus Club; Rory Lalwan   Westminster City Archives Centre; Garnet Langton   Paper Bygones; Liverpool University Press; Ray Le Mesurier-Foster; Steven Machell; Ray Mansfield; James Millington   Lancastrian Transport Trust; Natasha Mulder   Science Museum; Simon Murphy   London's Transport Museum; National Railway Museum, York; Alan Osbourne   Essex Bus Enthusiasts Group; Bernard Russell; Raymond Simpson; Professor Joan Skinner; The British Library; Fred Walton   Finglands Coachways Limited; Richard Waters.

Photographs

In pursuing this project, one of the most difficult jobs I have had has been tracing the origin of many of the photographs used; many of the pictures supplied were without note of the photographer or the photographic studio. I have contacted everyone whose photographs gave even the slightest clue for permission to use their pictures. For convenience London Coastal Coaches collection has been abbreviated to LCCc, and the Senior Transport Archive as STA. With some pictures, I have even tried to make educated guesses and have contacted people whose names haven't been apparent. In most cases permissions have been readily forthcoming, and I thank all those concerned. In some cases, though, the lack of replies suggests that the people concerned are no longer with us, or the photographic studios, agencies, or other publications have ceased to exist. In all these cases, and with due respect for their contribution to coaching history, I have shown where or with whom I believe the originations of the illustrations lie, but the difficulty of this task has only helped to endorse my infallibility, and I apologise for any errors or insults which I might have innocently perpetrated.

Display of modern coaches in the Coach Station in 1952

Introduction

Many, including me, would say the heyday of Coastal Coaches Limited and Victoria Coach Station was the 1950s and 1960s; but I am biased became I had the joy of working there for much of the period.

Others might say that the best times were the prewar days when advances in coach design and the public clamour to get out and about found dozens of Toms, Dicks and Harrys everywhere setting up as coach operators, with their eyes set variously on offering jolly trips to the seaside, regular long-distance services, or in the case of the truly adventurous industry entrepreneur, lengthy coach tours.

Maybe it would be better simply to call the 1950s and 1960s the settled days of the organisation – although a lot did happen in those few years.

London Coastal Coaches Limited was formed in 1925, and Victoria Coach Station was opened in 1932; these two events were certainly instrumental, if not crucial, in helping to create what was to become an important, well-organised and responsibly operated sector of the magical trade of moving people from place to place – the travel industry.

But it took time. Coaching was in a state of rapid expansion and consequent chaos until 1930 and suffered growing pains throughout the following decade. A degree of stability had been achieved by the end of the 1930s, but then came the upheaval of the Second World War. It was not until around 1947/8 that things began to return to normal on the transport front, and this is when Victoria Coach Station blossomed.

And it took some great people to set it up and keep it going: people with faith, foresight, and most of all diligence; people prepared to hitch their entire careers to this exciting industry; and it cannot be overlooked how many people lived and breathed Victoria Coach Station for most, if not all, of their working lives.

Obviously, though, if this book concentrated purely on London Coastal Coaches Limited and Victoria Coach Station, the picture it painted would be jaundiced and the story incomplete. I needed to research and describe the industry, particularly in its early days, on a much wider basis if I was to put 'Coastal' into some sort of context.

Naturally, I needed to concentrate chiefly on coaching as it affected the London area, but with that as my only restraint I started by putting together a history of how the industry began and how it grew.

I hope I have avoided presenting the historical data in a drier-than-dust manner, but have, instead, been able to describe it in an interesting way, for example, the need for licensing and legislation. I would like to think that anyone who has paid me the compliment of reading what I have written will feel, when they come to the last page, that we have merely been sitting together 'talking coaches'.

I have written about how the coach station operated in the period I knew it; I have looked at the publicity, the relationship with agents, the infighting between different factions, the routes, the tickets, the people, and a lot more . . . even including a bit of architectural detail about the building itself.

Deliberately, though, I have not written about the coaches, well except very briefly about one or two. London Coastal Coaches Limited never owned a coach of its own so, odd as it may seem, coaches don't really fit into the story at least, not in any technical or mechanical sense and there has been plenty written by people far more knowledgeable than I about the magnificent advances in bus and coach design over the years.

In Alice in Wonderland, Alice said, "What is the use of a book without pictures and conversations?" I totally agree, so you will find the pages of this book filled with dozens of pictures of coaches; there are reproductions of timetables, advertisements, posters and notices; and it is peppered with charts and diagrams intended to put forward facts and figures as interestingly as possible.

But better than all that, I have collected quotations and anecdotes from people who knew coaching in those days people who worked at the coach station, travelled on the coaches, or have been reported in the trade press and these have been dotted about on the appropriate pages.

There was a family feel about Victoria Coach Station in those days, and I have tried to recapture it in these pages.

And the title of the book. Why "Hello, Coastal"? From the time of its inception the company soon became known to coach operators, agents, and the general public alike simply as 'Coastal'; as a matter of habit, in most places throughout this book I use the familiar 'Coastal' rather than London Coastal Coaches Limited. The operators in the telephone exchange at Victoria Coach Station answered calls with a very friendly, lilting and drawn-out "Hello, C-o-oast-a-al". It was like a signature tune. How could there be any other title?

I think it is impossible for anyone to describe accurately the fascination which transport holds for the enthusiast. Whether it be buses or trains, coaches or planes, stations, airports or garages, the excitement in the pit of the stomach the result often of very simple things is beyond rational explanation. I was lucky enough to be a passenger on the first coach to travel northbound on the M1 on the day it opened in November 1959; in the early sixties I visited the new signal box at Rugby on the day it opened; I flew across the Atlantic on Concorde a few days after it started flying commercially from Heathrow; and by Douglas DC3 from Gatwick to Blackpool on the last British United flight on that route . . . and I'd love to be an early passenger to the moon. I have spent countless hours simply 'being in' bus stations, airports, and railway terminals. If I am going from A to B, I'm not happy unless I travel via Z, Q, and M.

All things old, and all things new: there is such joy to be derived from so many sources new buses, old buses; new trains, old trains; new aeroplanes, old aeroplanes. What a debt of gratitude is owed all those people who devote hours and fortunes to the preservation of old vehicles and the safeguarding of archives.

Having spent virtually all my career in the travel industry, I have done many exciting things and seen many exciting places, but I still get the same thrill as I ever did from watching the changing of a destination blind, seeing the way a coach or bus draws in to a kerbside halt, or listening to the departure announcements at railway stations.

With delight, I recall the scene as it used to be at Cheltenham Coach Station each afternoon at two o'clock, when scores of coaches poured out in a continuous flow into St Margaret's Street to places north, south, east and west; or the excitement of arriving for work at Victoria Coach Station on a busy day, seeing the long queue at the booking hall, being aware of the hustle and bustle everywhere, and knowing that a marvellously hectic and adrenalin-pumping shift lay ahead.

A great friend of mine has a wonderful collection of old and not-so-old buses and coaches housed in a huge barn in north Warwickshire. Each time I visit, I stand there amid the vehicles, enveloped in sheer, unadulterated 'coach-ness'. These marvellous machines are not inanimate objects; they are throbbing with latent life and aching to be on the move.

I hope, as you meander through this book, that some of my excitement will rub off on you, and that you will discover or rediscover the magic of Victoria Coach Station in its halcyon days.

Richard Paramor
January 2006

I know the ticket's here somewhere. Momentary panic strikes. 12th June 1952.
(London Coastal Coaches collection — LCCc)

Where did it all begin ?

Each year until 1940, upon the anniversary of the opening of Victoria Coach Station on 10th March 1932, London Coastal Coaches Limited held an open day, when guests were able to visit the offices, see how Victoria Coach Station worked, and take tea with the management. Souvenir booklets were given to the visitors, which gave details of the facilities at the coach station, listed the companies operating to this new and modern terminal, and detailed the names of the numerous tenants who were renting office accommodation on the coach station's upper floors. The souvenir booklets gave interesting statistics and a brief history of how the company and the coach station had come into existence. In these souvenir booklets, the year suggested as the foundation year for London Coastal Coaches Limited is 1919, and a journey from London to Brighton is cited as the starting point.

But our story would be woefully incomplete were we not to look back to the happenings before this trip to the seaside.

So when did it all begin? When was the common man first able to use a regular service to transport him from A to B? We must look back to days when, often, it was manpower rather than horsepower that enabled such journeys.

The sedan chair was first seen in England in 1581 but did not become a popular fashion for another 30 or 40 years; stagecoaches were operating in the late 17th century and at the same time carriers who travelled regularly to market or between towns would be happy to carry passengers or parcels upon a small payment.

Arguably, therefore, this is where we must go back to if we are to put the start of public road transport into true historical perspective. This is the time when commercially minded entrepreneurs first began to 'ply for hire': three little words that have been so crucial in the development of how people have been moved from place to place. The sedan chair was the forerunner of the taxi; the carrier provided the first local bus service; and the stagecoach provided the first long distance express coach service.

❦ ❧

The sedan chair is best described as an enclosed seat, usually with windows to the sides and front, and with a long pole on either side. With chairmen, as they were called, one at each end, the sedan would be lifted and the passenger carried to his destination. Despite the windows, one can imagine how claustrophobic these chairs were, for once the passenger was seated, the front was closed and a lid-like roof slotted into place at the top. But passengers were generally approving of sedan chairs: "The chairs, in general, are neat and clean, and free from damp; and are under the perfect controul (sic) of the corporation, from whom they receive an annual license" (*"Walks through Bath"*, *Pierce Egan, 1819*)

Sedan chairs first appeared for hire in London in 1634, when a gentleman pensioner of the King, Sir Sanders Duncombe (or Duncan as some sources quote) obtained a fourteen-year monopoly or warrant from Charles I for the building and rental-for-hire of covered 'hackney chairs' in London and Westminster. It seems that this far-sighted gentleman ran a fleet of up to 50 of these vehicles and trade was brisk for several reasons, not the least of which being that, by then, the fashions of the day included very elaborate hairstyles, with colourful and ornate clothes and shoes; the streets however remained filthy, and, particularly during wet or windy weather, elegance soon gave way to dishevelment. The sedan chair provided a reasonably sure way to achieve one's journey without too much disturbance to one's fashionable appearance. Furthermore the chairs could be taken indoors and so it was possible to travel from indoors to indoors without setting a fashionable foot in the open air.

Chairs also waited at stands in the street, and would ply for hire in the same way as do present-day taxis.

> *Two very drunk sedan chair chairmen to a passenger, Mrs Herbert, in Edinburgh: "Madam, you are so drunk, that if you do not sit still, it will be impossible to carry you". (The Age of Scandal, T H White, published 1950)*

The chairmen were licensed, and had to display a number. The numbers for London chairmen were issued by the Public Carriage Office that was for a long time at 15 Penton Street, N1. This was also the office to which the public could make complaints.

The sedan chair was cheaper than the hackney carriage, but it is interesting to note how well the method of charging had been devised. Based on distance and waiting time it is almost identical to the way taxi fares are charged today, but also took into account the terrain. One can sympathise with the opinion expressed by some chairmen that an additional charge should be made for overweight passengers.

The following is taken from a letter that appeared in ***The Rambler***, supposedly from a chairman, although one questions if a humble chairman would have had the education to write so explicitly: "It is common for men of the most unwieldy corpulence to crowd themselves into a chair, and demand to be carried for a shilling, as far as an airy young lady who we scarcely feel upon our poles. Surely, we ought to be paid like all other mortals, in proportion to our labour. Engines (public weighbridges?) should be fixed in proper places to weigh chairs as they weigh wagons, and those whom 'ease and plenty' have made unable to carry themselves, should give part of the superfluities to those who carry them".

Opposite: This poster of the 1920s shows how the extent of services by Coastal companies was still mostly confined to the South Coast and East Anglia; not then reaching as far as Bournemouth. *(Chris Nash Collection)*

The table below compiled from the information published in 1819 by Pierce Egan in **Walks through Bath** shows how precise the charging arrangements were. These happen to be rates charged in Bath in the early 1800s, but similar scales would have applied elsewhere:

Moving on to carrier services, the forerunner of local buses, it is most likely that these were started as a sideline by someone, a farmer for instance, who already had need to travel regularly to a nearby market.

Initially, the carriers would simply transport parcels and packages for other people, probably only on market days, and to start with the whole thing was a bit hit-and-miss. However, as the demand grew, it became necessary for carriers to follow set routes and set times, and people wishing to use the service would place a card or flag in their window or at their gate so that the carrier would know to call. Eventually the carriers started to carry passengers as well as goods.

The system of placing a card in the window to attract the attention of a carrier lasted for many years, and the 'CP' card in windows as an instruction to the Carter Paterson van driver to call was a familiar sight until government legislation in 1947 brought the compulsory buy-out of road hauliers and the formation of British Road Services.

Of course, licensing was unheard of in those days so carriers were not bothered by any restrictions, and could go where they wanted and when they wanted, with the only constraint on what they carried being the mail. Individual letters could not be carried, but parcels could   just as with Royal Mail today.

Gradually the carrier's horse and cart became inadequate for the increased passenger demand, and many of them acquired larger vehicles that could carry more passengers.

It was an easy and obvious step for the more successful carriers to become the forerunners in the operation of petrol and steam vehicles as they became available, and to become haulage contractors or bus operators; but to their dismay and loud disapproval, they were soon to see the introduction of licensing to help pay the cost of maintaining the roads.

It is amusing to reflect that what started as a goods carrying service with the occasional passenger as a side-line eventually became a passenger carrying service which carried parcels as a side-line, although the carrying of parcels on stage-carriage bus services has now almost completely ceased.

ଔ ଓ

Stagecoaches on the other hand were from the outset intended as a means of passenger transportation, even though they did carry unaccompanied parcels and packets.

The rise and fall of stagecoach travel fits more-or-less into four distinct periods.

Until 1662 the road network in Britain comprised mostly cart tracks across the countryside, which were often impassable in the winter and riven with deep and dangerous potholes. With the slow, but positive increase in trade in the 17th century the roads, such as they were, quickly deteriorated even further and their maintenance was still the responsibility of the parishes through which they passed. By statutes, inhabitants had to devote six days' unpaid labour to the upkeep of the roads and, to add insult to injury, they had to use their own work tools and carts. Needless to say the work was done badly and   there being then no real expertise in road making   probably only amounted to filling in the potholes. There were few, if any, attempts at building roads with hard surfaces and foundations. The roads that had originally been built by the Romans, such as the Great North Road and Watling Street, still had the original Roman paving. Stagecoach routes were few, services irregular, and travelling very dangerous indeed.

The second phase in the history of the stagecoach began in 1662 with the passing of the first act of parliament for turnpike road construction, and the setting up of 'turnpike trusts'. The act came into force in 1663, but even so it took some time for turnpikes to become established, and very few were in operation even at the end of the century. Turnpike trusts were groups of landowners and businessmen authorised by parliament to take over and rebuild stretches of road. These entrepreneurs were allowed to install toll bars (toll gates) at each end of their improved roads, and to take payments from travellers who wished to use the road.

In many cases the toll bars (or gates) were constructed with spikes on top to stop horsemen from jumping over them and thereby evading paying the toll, and it is from this that the name 'turnpike' evolved. It is an interesting throwback to those times that even in the late 1960s, and maybe even later, the first point out of London to which Maidstone and District was allowed to carry passengers on its Victoria Coach Station to Gillingham express service, was a place still called Tollgate; and Turnpike Lane is familiar to many Londoners.

To make journeying even more hazardous roads, like the fields that surrounded them, had no proper drainage. It was easy, therefore, to mistake flooded streams, flooded fields, and flooded roads. A story is told in **A History of England (Everyman -1927)** of passengers travelling through Ware in 1695 who, when their coach overturned, were forced to get out of the coach and swim.

Signposts did not become required by law until 1697, but even then were slow to appear, and there were no detailed route maps. Added to this many fields were unenclosed so it was often difficult to distinguish roads from fields, and often it was only the tracks of preceding vehicles that gave any indication of the route of the highway. It is reported that no less a person than Samuel Pepys himself, when lost on one occasion in Windsor Forest, had to navigate by the moon. (Companion volume to **'The Diary of Samuel Pepys'** by R C Latham and W Matthews**)**.

Nevertheless, we know from **Anglia Metropolis**, a publication dating back to 1690, that by then there were 118 operators providing stagecoach services from London, many of them several times a week.

At first, the building of toll roads met with a good deal of opposition, particularly from local taxpayers. The idea that new roads should be built, or old ones improved, by means of funds raised from tolls was innovative, and there were many attacks made on these new-fangled turnpike roads. Things got so bad that in 1735 an Act was passed which introduced punishment by hanging for the 'destruction of turnpike roads and property'.

However, not all roads were turnpike roads and the ever-increasing introduction of more and more stagecoaches created a need for other roads to be properly maintained; thus from 1776 owners of stage horses were taxed by the government for highway repairs.

❧ ❧

Over the years, stagecoach travel has been made to seem gloriously romantic by the many fine paintings depicting brightly painted coaches with elegant passengers and smartly uniformed coachmen. The true story is probably very different.

The stagecoach of the middle 1600s to early 1700s had seats for four or six passengers inside, with space on the roof for boxes and packages; any excess of baggage would be strapped to the back. The vehicles were totally unsprung, and were very low slung with leather-bound exteriors picked out in relief with brass nails.

Other passengers could be carried on the roof but it was very uncomfortable and highly dangerous. Apart from the risk of being knocked off the coach by the branch of a tree, people who fell asleep often fell off the coach (although one wonders how they managed to doze off in the first place), and sometimes those who had become numbed with the cold disembarked involuntarily in a similar fashion.

Although the works of Charles Dickens are mostly fictional, a good deal was based on actual events. It was not unusual for outside passengers to suffer considerable injury as stagecoaches passed through the low archways into the courtyards of coaching inns. The following from **Pickwick Papers** is apparently based on a true event that happened at a coaching inn near Charing Cross, which stood on what is now a corner of Trafalgar Square. These are the words of fictional character, Mr Jingle: "Terrible place dangerous work other day five children mother tall lady, eating sandwiches forgot the arch crash knock children look round mother's head off sandwich in hand no mouth to put it in head of family off shocking shocking".

Not only have artists glamorised the image of stagecoach travel, but so too has the image of the highwayman been

"Stage Coach". Hand coloured engraving by Dubourg from an original by James Pollard. *(John Garner Fine Arts)*

romanticised on the pages of novels and adventure stories. Attack by highwaymen was a constant threat to stagecoach travellers, and the swashbuckling Dick Turpin-like character is better seen as a cold-blooded thug or murderer. One stagecoach operator, from Leeds to London, was quoted in the **Leeds Intelligencer** of 18th July 1780, as advising its passengers that it did not travel during the night near London as that was a high risk area for attacks by highwaymen. We can assume that it is Hampstead Heath to which the stagecoach operator referred, but similar assaults were also frequent on Hounslow Heath and Shooters Hill.

But despite toll bars, turnpike roads, highwaymen and all the other inconveniences, as the improved road network became steadily more and more extended, so did the extent of

> *"The brigands fell upon us with blood curdling crys." (Royal Mail Guard on the Irish Post from London to Holyhead as it passed through North Wales)*

stagecoach routes, although journey times seem ludicrous compared with today's fast travel. One of the first regular routes, from London to Chester, and recorded as long ago as 1657, took four days, left three times a week in each direction, and cost 35/6d (£1.77½p). In 1667 the journey from London to Bath on the daringly named Flying Machine took three days, and cost £1.5s.0d (£1.25), passengers were allowed 14 pounds of baggage free of charge, with an excess baggage rate of 3½d (1½p) per pound. In 1694 the journey from Doncaster to London took four days, and even by 1750 it took two days to travel from Cambridge to London, and 16 to make the journey from Edinburgh to London. From Oxford to London it took two days with an overnight stop in Beaconsfield, although in 1669 a seasonal one-day service was introduced on three days a week that left Oxford at 6.00am and completed the journey in 13 hours. It was called the Flying Coach and operated 'if God permit' which is an interesting prelude to the many 'conditions of travel' introduced since, which begin 'this service operates subject to…'.

❧ ❧

The next, and probably most important, turning point in the history of the stagecoach came in the late 1700s when the Royal Mail began its operations and introduced the 'Mail Coach'. This brought a sophistication to stagecoach travel with greater speeds being achieved, and added safety.

The job of coachman was seen as very prestigious, and coachmen were highly respected for their skills in handling horses and coaches at high speeds. Reports both in works of fact and fiction portray the coachman as constantly cheerful, well turned out, confident, and always in perfect control. Coachmen were particularly proud of their appearance and some became so extrovert in their demeanour and style of dress that they were known as 'flashmen'. Many paintings of the day show coachmen in brightly coloured and well-tailored coats with fur hats and bright scarves or cravats.

In addition to the coachman, mail coaches also carried guards, supplied initially by the same person who supplied the horses. This turned out to be an unsatisfactory arrangement and Royal Mail (the Post Office) took over the employment of the guards, often men taken from the forces because of their presumed leadership skills and capabilities with firearms, and who thereby became 'servants of the Crown'.

The guards, in scarlet uniforms to indicate their royal appointment, were not only supplied with firearms, but also tool kits for use in the event of breakdowns. Apart from a blunderbuss and brace of pistols, guards were also supplied with a cutlass. Protection of His Majesty's Mails was the guard's prime responsibility, and should a mail coach be prevented from continuing its journey for any reason he was duty-bound to continue with the mail, on horseback to the next staging post. Furthermore, the guard on a mail coach was responsible for the timekeeping of the coach and was supplied with a watch, sealed in a case to avoid its being tampered with, and carried in a pouch that he wore throughout the journey. And this was about 200 years before the introduction of the tachograph!

Sometimes, urgent national news headlines would be chalked on the side of mail coaches, for example news of Wellington's victories over Napoleon, as this was the fastest way of bringing information to the populace.

To supplement their incomes, coachmen and guards would expect a payment from passengers for each stage of the journey, and although this was quite unofficial it seems to have been accepted as quite normal, with the employers concerned either turning a blind eye to the practice, or condoning it as a perfectly fair perk of the job.

'Besides the regular and established fare for a seat, the driver and the guard (the last of whom accompanied the mail stage only) are to be paid at the end of every stage of about twenty miles. This has been so long a custom as almost to have the force of law, and the perquisite is generally demanded as a matter of right. The usual donation, for such it is, is sixpence to each, but a shilling and even more is often given, and never refused. The sum thus annually collected by this tax on travellers is almost incredible, and the place of driver and guard to some of the coaches in the large towns is of so much emolument as frequently to considerably enrich the holders, and they are often sold at a high price.'

Joshua White, quoted in the previous paragraph from his **Letters on England** written in 1810, continued by asserting that apart from the unofficial payments to the coachmen and guards, fares were quite reasonable.

'…the travelling charges are not unreasonable or exorbitant. They are greater in the mail than in the common coaches, but the accommodations are better in the former, and the expedition is greater; hence, where this is required most travellers willingly pay the difference; and besides, there is more security from accidents and robberies.'

Nevertheless, stagecoach travel was still very much restricted to the well off. In the 1830s a ticket for a seat inside a stagecoach from London to Norwich cost £1.10s.0d (£1.50), and if one adds to this the unofficial payments to coachman and guard the total cost for the journey would be nearer £2. Comparing this with an average farm labourer, or factory worker's weekly wage of around 8/- to 10/- (40p to 50p) one can appreciate that long distance travel was way beyond the pocket of all but the reasonably wealthy. About a hundred years later, in 1937, the single fare from London to Norwich by Eastern Counties was just 9/- (45p), and even in 1968 when the National Bus Company was almost upon us it was still only 22/- (£1.10).

☙ ❧

With the introduction of mail coaches, the haphazard and often unreliable operations up to that point became better structured, and probably better coordinated. It is this point in the history of stagecoach travel that can be most likened, for its importance in its time, to the turning point in coach travel 150 years later with the introduction of the Road Traffic Act 1930, and the opening of Victoria Coach Station soon after, both of which brought in their wake similar stability and coordination of services.

In the same way that we can compare similarities in the operation of sedan chairs with modern day taxis, so we can compare stagecoaches with today's express coach services. For example, reservations were usually made in advance and tickets purchased from agents, and while a ticket guaranteed a seat it did not guarantee a specific seat. The following advice came from Joshua White writing in 1810 about his travels in England:

'The hours of departure are fixed, and passengers must be punctual to secure their seats, as this is absolutely necessary where a choice is wanted, for no one is entitled to this from his name being first or second on the way-bill. The seat may also be secured by a servant, or a cloak, greatcoat, or cane; any of which will be considered as the representative of the passenger himself'.

However, even with a seat reservation, travel could be uncomfortable. Benjamin Stillman wrote in his **Journals of Travel** in 1806 about a coach journey with several fat ladies: 'At 7 o'clock a.m. I stepped into the coach for Birmingham. It was a small vehicle, capable of carrying four passengers inside with convenience, and six with difficulty. I found five ladies already seated in the coach, and some of them were such beauties as Addison says are estimated at Haarlem by weight (presumably a reference to a comment in a contemporary satirical journal about buxom young women). Four of them carried huge band-boxes in their laps, and the fifth an infant. In so small a carriage, and under such circumstances, you cannot but suppose that an additional one must have occasioned some inconvenience. I was obliged to sit sideways, with one arm out of the coach, and I found my companions so little disposed for conversation and the situation so uncomfortable, that, before we travelled a mile, I relinquished my seat in favour of the ladies and mounted the roof of the coach".

Great care was taken to avoid overbooking, as the booking clerk making the error would be responsible for the cost of making alternative arrangements for the passenger. The provision of a private carriage or post-chaise to convey the inconvenienced passenger to his destination would be like today providing a taxi for the whole journey — a very heavy inroad into the wages of the clerk concerned.

Nevertheless, the following report, again by Benjamin Stillman in his *Journals of Travel*, seems to highlight a particularly bad case of overbooking, and relates to an overnight journey from Portsmouth to London: ' My ride was rendered uncomfortable by a very full coach, and somewhat hazardous by the numbers on the roof, where there were no fewer than nineteen grown people, which with eight inside, (two more than the stipulated number,) made twenty-seven persons for one carriage. I have never known so many to ride on the roof in any former instance, and I acknowledge the story is less credible than true. That night was very warm for the season, and the air in the coach became soon very unpleasant, so that it was necessary to keep a window open.'

Too many 'room on top' passengers, or baggage similarly stowed, could lead to other hazards, and problems with luggage in general gave rise to the following warnings by Joshua White: 'In the accommodation coach it is a good general rule to take an inside seat when the number of passengers is greatest on the outside; or the weight of baggage is such as to increase the risk of being overturned … Passengers should bestow strict attention to their baggage, for although packages are sent to every part of the kingdom with great safety in the coaches, it is not generally considered as incumbent on the coachman to attend to the baggage when the owners are present. Small trunks or bundles may be put under the seats in the coach, but larger are generally put into the boot or box behind it. Caution is particularly necessary where there are several coaches starting about the same time from the same inn, and in a country where petty thefts may be committed with so much facility and with so little danger of detection.'

☙ ❧

The emphasis with all stagecoach services was on speed, and the growth of passenger numbers was swift. By the 1830s over 1,000 turnpike trusts controlled over 20,000 miles of roads: roads that were, by then, so much improved, and stagecoaches so much better designed and built, that journey times were much reduced. Mail coaches were the fastest and, since they did not have to pay any tolls, the coachman would give a blast on his post-horn as each toll bar was neared, so that the gates would be opened in advance and the stagecoach could pass through without halting. Edinburgh to London now took just two days, and Cambridge to London seven hours. Along the route all four horses were changed at each stage (hence the name stagecoach) and the average speed reached ten miles per

hour, with one service between Birmingham and London on May Day 1830 averaging an astonishing 14 miles per hour. Little did the coachmen and passengers on the Independent Tally-Ho that day know they were the forerunners of an event about 120 years later when, in 1959, Birmingham and London were to be linked by the first motorway in Britain, and the specially built Midland Red coaches, prior to speed restrictions, reached speeds approaching and, in some cases of, 100 miles an hour on the route.

One can picture the busier roads with the mail coaches in their distinctive livery of maroon, scarlet and gold, and the regular coaches resplendently decorated throughout. The road into Bath from London was a particularly excellent Beau Nash construction planned to encourage visitors to enjoy the pleasures of the Spa Town. Supporting these early tourist promotions were The Emerald, The Shamrock, The Blue, The Regent, The Regulator, The Chronometer and many others with fanciful names and bright liveries: not so far removed from Royal Blue, Midland Red, Black and White, Red and White, the emerald of Southdown, the dark red of East Kent, and the bright red of Thames Valley and so on.

The numbers of horses needed was high. To pull a coach from London to Exeter would need around 100 horses, or twice that amount for the journey from London to Edinburgh, and sometimes, diversions were taken to avoid steep hills.

COACHES BETWEEN LONDON & BIRMINGHAM Per Week		
Year	Number of Coaches – each way	Potential no of Passengers – each way
1740	1	8
1783	30	240
1829	238	1900

Many of the services from London to the North-East and Scotland travelled out via Enfield and the Hertford Road in order to avoid Highgate Hill and Barnet Hill on the Great North Road.

Stables and coaching inns sprang up along the stagecoach routes where horses could be changed and travellers obtain refreshment. Coaching inns were open twenty-four hours a day and, as many stagecoach journeys involved overnight travel, these inns were places of continuous hustle and bustle. They were also the cause of many passenger complaints. Benjamin Stillman tells us that in 1806: 'The real test of a gentleman is his behaviour when a coach stops en route for the refreshment of its weary passengers. The journey often turned them into starving savages who would descend on the dining room, demanding service. The true gentleman would escort a lady passenger from the coach, ensure she was provided with refreshment, and pay her bill. This inevitably meant that it was impossible for he himself to eat, as time was strictly limited. The innkeepers would often exacerbate the situation by delaying the food so passengers had little time to eat their fill before having to be on the road again.'

In similar vein, passengers staying overnight at coaching inns seem to have enjoyed little comfort, and Joshua White tells us: 'Travellers in the mail and common coaches seldom meet with that polite attention at the inns for which they are generally distinguished, and which is almost always shown to those who arrive in their own carriage, or even in a post-chaise … To secure comfortable accommodations, experience taught me not to put up at the inn where the coach stopped, if I intended to remain a few days … When the coach is to set off at an early hour, the seat should be previously engaged, and the reward which the boots, chambermaid and principal expects should not be given until the morning for thus you will be certain of being called in time to take your seat; but if they receive their douceurs before you retire to bed, they will feel no interest in awaking you, and you may sleep till doomsday for what they care.'

The poet Robert Southey in his **Letters from England** dated 1802 paints the following picture: 'The perpetual stir and bustle of this inn is as surprising as it is wearisome. Doors opening and shutting, bells ringing, voices calling to the waiter from every quarter; while he cries "coming" to one room, and hurries away to another. Everybody is in a hurry here; either they are going off in packets, and are hastening their preparations to embark; or they have just arrived, and are impatient to be on the road homeward. Every now-and-then a carriage rattles up to the door with a rapidity which makes the very house shake. The man who cleans the boots is running in one direction, the barber with his powder-bag in another; here goes the barber's boy with his hot water and razors; there comes the clean linen from the washer-woman; and the hall is full of porters bringing in luggage, or bearing it away; now you hear a horn blow because the post is coming in, and in the middle of the night you are awakened by another because it is going out. Nothing is done in England without noise, and yet noise is the only thing they forget in the bill!'

But, no matter how disgruntled some of the stagecoach passengers and coaching inn clientele might have been at the time, we must not ignore the delightful legacy of those hustle and bustle days. As stagecoaches gave way to motor coaches, so coaching inns adapted to the new faster style of travel and many survived as recognised refreshment stops in the timetables of the express coach operators. Even though much of today's coaching is completed along motorways in vehicles equipped with refreshment and toilet facilities as a matter of course, many of those traditional coaching inns remain to provide comfortable accommodation and serve victuals in the traditional manner.

Looking still at the similarities of coaching in the early 1800s and the mid 1900s one is struck by the high frequency of services in the 1800s, and the already established system of en route interchange arrangements. For example, in the late 1790s no fewer than 22 services passed through Dartford, Kent, each day on their way to Dover, and in 1819, from London to Bristol there were 17 daily coaches via various routes, including five post coaches.

A number of towns became busy coaching centres with several coaching inns, including Redbourn in Hertfordshire, on Watling Street (now the A5), which in the 1830s boasted nine daily services to London and one each to Bedford, Birmingham, Derby, Halifax, Leeds, Liverpool, Manchester, Northampton and Wellingborough. It even offered one of the first road/rail connections with a daily morning stagecoach to Watford, with a return evening coach, to connect with the mainline trains to and from London and Birmingham that were introduced in 1837.

Even from more distant places services were surprisingly frequent. From Brecon, at around the same period, there were three daily services to London, and at least a dozen other daily services to various destinations.

In the same way that, from the 1930s, Victoria Coach Station was to provide not just point-to-point travel, but enormous interchange facilities, and the Black & White coach station in Cheltenham was to become the vital interchange point within the Associated Motorways network, so, as the chart below shows, Bath was a vital point on the stagecoach route map in the 1800s. There was, of course, no coach station as such, so with the high volume of interchange passengers, it involved spreading the large numbers of arriving and departing stagecoaches among several coaching inns in close proximity. This information is based on information contained in Pierce Egan's **Walks through Bath** published in 1819, and the towns of Melksham and Romsey are shown with the spellings as they appeared at the time.

There were many other similar interchange towns throughout the country which would demonstrate equally well how extensive the stagecoach network had become, how the radial route patterns then reflected those of years to come, and how the operators of stagecoaches were alert to the advantages of advertising connecting services.

Moving people about was becoming big business.

Licensing of vehicles was rather more advanced in the London area than elsewhere in the country. In the same way that sedan chairs had to be licensed, so did hackney carriages, but they were protected from too much competition, as their numbers were limited. Stagecoaches to places outside central London were not permitted to pick up passengers from other

Weekday Stagecoach Departures from Bath - 1819

6am York House *The Regent* to Chippenham, Calne, Marlborough, Newbury, Reading & LONDON.
6am Golden Lion (Mondays, Wednesdays & Saturdays) to Wells, Somerton, Langport, Ilminster, Chard, Honiton Axminster, Lyme, Sidmouth & EXETER.
6am White Hart to BIRMINGHAM *(connections to Manchester, Liverpool, and all North County coaches)*.
6am White Hart (Tuesdays, Thursdays & Saturdays) to Gloucester & CHELTENHAM.
6am White Hart to Newbury, Reading & LONDON (two day service).
6am White Hart to Devizes, Marlborough, Newbury, Reading & LONDON.
6am White Lion *Original Day Coach* to Chippenham, Calne, Marlborough, Newbury, Reading & LONDON.
6.30am Fromont & Co. *The Regulator* to LONDON
6.30am Castle to LONDON.
6.45am York House (Mondays, Wednesday & Fridays) to Evesham, Alcester & BIRMINGHAM *(connection with all North County coaches)*.
6.45am York House (Mondays, Wednesdays & Fridays) to Stratford on Avon, Warwick & LEAMINGTON.
6.45am York House (Mondays, Wednesdays & Fridays) to Redborough, Stroud & CHELTENHAM.
7am White Hart (Tuesdays, Thursdays & Saturdays) to Salisbury, Ramsey, Southampton & GOSPORT.
7am York House (Mondays, Wednesdays & Fridays) to WEYMOUTH.
7am White Hart (Tuesdays, Thursdays &d Saturdays) to WEYMOUTH.
8am White Hart to BRISTOL.
8am York House *The Subscription Coach* to Shepton Mallet, Ilchester, Ilminster, Honiton *(connection for Sidmouth)* & EXETER.
8am Golden Lion to BRISTOL.
8am White Hart to EXETER *(connections for Plymouth and Falmouth)*.
8.15am York House (Tuesdays, Thusdays & Saturdays) to Shrewsbury & HOLYHEAD.
8.30am York House to BRISTOL.
8.30am York House (Tuesdays, Thursdays & Saturdays) to Gloucester & CHELTENHAM.
8.30am Fromont & Co. to Bristol, Bridgewater, Taunton, Exeter, Tiverton, Plymouth & FALMOUTH.
8.30am Fromont & Co. to South Molton & BARNSTAPLE.
8.45am White Lion to BRISTOL.
9am Castle to BRISTOL.
9am Golden Lion to Bristol.
9am Angel *The Patent Coach* (built on Capt. Wyke's plan for safety) to BRISTOL.
9am White Hart (Mondays, Wednesday & Fridays) to Gloucester & CHELTENHAM.
9am White Hart (Mondays, Wednesdays & Fridays) to Gloucester, Worcester, Shrewsbury, & HOLYHEAD.
9am York House (Tuesday, Thursday & Saturdays) to Tetbury, Cirencester & OXFORD.
9am White Hart (Mondays, Wednesdays & Fridays) to SOUTHAMPTON.
9.30am Lamb MAIL COACH to BRISTOL connecting with WELSH MAIL.
9.30am Fromont & Co. to BRISTOL.
9.30am White Hart to Tetbury, Cirencester & OXFORD.
9.30am York House to BRISTOL.
9.45am Greyhound (Mondays, Wednesday & Fridays) to Warminster, Shaftesbury, Blandford, Wimborne & POOLE.
10am Lamb MAIL COACH to Bridgewater, Taunton, Exeter, Plymouth & FALMOUTH.
10am White Hart to Bristol and CLIFTON.
11am Lamb to BRISTOL.
11am White Lion to BRISTOL.
12noon Fromont & Co. to BRISTOL.
12noon Castle to BRISTOL.
12noon Golden Lion to BRISTOL.
12noon Golden Lion (Mondays, Wednesdays & Saturdays) to WESTON-SUPER-MARE.
12.30pm Fromont & Co. to Milksham, Devizes, Marlborough & LONDON.
1pm White Lion to BRISTOL.
1.30pm Golden Lion to BRISTOL.
2pm White Lion *Original Day Coach* to Chippenham, Calne, Marlborough, Newbury, Reading & LONDON.
2.45pm Lamb to CLIFTON.
2.45pm York House *The Regent* to Chippenham, Calne, Marlborough, Newbury, Reading & LONDON.
2.45pm Fromont & Co. to Chippenham, Calne, Marlborough & LONDON.
3pm White Hart to Bristol & CLIFTON.
3pm White Lion to BRISTOL.
3pm Golden Lion to BRISTOL.
3.30pm Greyhound to Bristol & CLIFTON.
3.45pm Golden Lion to Bristol & CLIFTON.
4pm Christopher to BRISTOL.
4pm York House To Devizes, Marlborough, Newbury, Reading & LONDON.
4pm White Lion to BRISTOL.
4pm Greyhound to LONDON.
4pm White Hart to BRISTOL.
5pm White Hart MAIL COACH to Salisbury, Southampton & PORTSMOUTH.
5pm Lamb MAIL COACH to Devizes & LONDON
5pm White Lion to BRISTOL.
5.25pm Lamb MAIL COACH to Chippenham & LONDON.
5.30pm Greyhound to Bristol & CLIFTON.
6pm Castle to TROWBRIDGE.
6pm Fromont & Co. to Bradford & TROWBRIDGE.
6pm Golden Lion TO BRISTOL.
7pm Lamb to BRISTOL.
7pm White Hart (Tuesdays & Fridays) to FROME.
7pm Golden Lion to BRISTOL.
7pm White Lion to BRISTOL.
7.30pm Greyhound to Bristol & CLIFTON.
8pm Fromont & Co. TO BRISTOL.
8pm Castle to BRISTOL.

than an authorised starting point, nor could they set down passengers within the London boundaries. For some time a paved area of central London, known as 'the stones', generally defined the boundaries; journeys took much longer in those days, so whereas places such as Clapham, Highgate or Hammersmith seem hardly any distance at all today, they were, until the latter part of the 19th century, outside 'the stones'.

This peak of stagecoach travel was, however, to last only for 50 or 60 years and the fourth period, the short, sharp decline, was brought on by the coming of the railways, which offered faster, more comfortable journeys and which soon took over virtually all long distance travel.

There had been some attempts in the mid-1800s to introduce steam coaches, but they were short lived. These heavy vehicles caused havoc to the road surfaces, and consequently incurred heavy tolls that soon made the services financially unviable.

With vast investment in railways, attention turned away from the stagecoach and road improvements. It is believed that the last regular stagecoach service in this country, or at least in the London area, was from Amersham to London and this ceased operation in 1894 with the coming of the Metropolitan Railway. A little poetic licence allows a harsh and unexpected overnight transition from stagecoach to tube train but it is not so very far from the truth.

The motorised coach followed not long after, although it was almost 25 years before long distance coaching really got under way.

☙ ❧

A faltering start was made in either 1904 or 1905 dependent on which source one is to believe. In **Victoria Coach Station – The First Fifty Years**, published in 1982, Frank Woodworth tells us that the Vanguard Omnibus Company operated double-deck buses regularly from Northumberland Avenue to the Old Ship Hotel, Brighton, from 1904, but the 1980 A McCall book **Green Line** suggests that it was the London Motor Omnibus Company operating under the fleet name The Vanguard which began the service in 1905 using double-deckers in the summer and single-deckers in the winter. The latter report is backed up in **The Moving Metropolis** (ed. Sheila Taylor and published in 2001), which suggests the change of name later than 1906, although it doesn't specify the exact date. Certainly both reports must have been referring to the same service, and whichever was correct it is certain that the service operated regularly and became quickly established, so much so that a public house in West Street, Brighton was named 'The Vanguard'.

In July 1906, a motorbus accident on Handcross Hill near Brighton resulted in the deaths of ten passengers and the enormous volume of resulting publicity concerning the risks and dangers of motorbus travel was such that the service was withdrawn immediately. The local Brighton newspaper, The Argos of 13th July 1906, reported in great length details of the accident. Certainly the bus was operating under the Vanguard fleetname, which itself might seem strange, since, as Professor John Hibbs tells us in **The History of British Bus Services**, this fleetname was not generally adopted by the company until 1907. This must surely have been one of the first ever private

hire journeys. A party of tradesmen from St. Mary Cray near Orpington had hired the vehicle from the London Motor Omnibus Company and all those killed (nine reported in The Argos, and another who died later) were shopkeepers and tradesmen from St. Mary Cray.

The Argos somewhat dramatically reported that: "The main street of the little village of St. Mary Cray was yesterday a scene of terror and desolation. At the doorway of each shop stood agonized women, many with babies in their arms, some with groups of children clustered round them. They had seen their husbands full of health and mirth start for a day's junketing in the morning. Now, with white, drawn faces, trembling lips, and streaming eyes they waited for the news which they dreaded … at last there came a telegram and there was a rush of frantic women, so that the messenger was almost mobbed. He made his way to the door of Mrs Hoar, who stood waiting with her child in her arms, her husband's sister by her side. Mrs Hoar tore open the envelope and then uttered a heartfelt prayer of thanks. The message read 'Accident, not seriously hurt' it was from her husband … other telegrams followed. There was a cry of 'Oh, God!' from one woman, who received the news she had long been dreading, and she fell back fainting".

Pictures illustrating the accident were exhibited that evening at the second performance at the Brighton Hippodrome (presumably they weren't processed in time for the first performance), and were repeated at all performances for the next two days.

Again according to The Argos, the bodies of the dead passengers were "laid out for purposes of identification" in the summerhouse at the rear of the Red Lion Hotel, Handcross "by the side of which were the remains of the bus, (and which) had become quite a meeting place for the numerous visitors who had arrived chiefly by means of the ubiquitous bicycle."

In truly traditional journalistic style, the newspaper included, further on in the same columns, details of an inquest on a boy killed by a Vanguard bus in London (although the boy, and not the driver, was to blame), and another story of a Great Western motorbus which caught fire going down Amersham Hill towards High Wycombe.

With such adverse publicity as this, it is no wonder that little, if anything, happened immediately after the Handcross Hill accident so far as long-distance coach services were concerned, although local bus services were to increase on a small scale, particularly from 1910 onwards when bus design advanced quite noticeably.

However, there were several entrepreneurial minds waiting in the wings with clear ideas about what was just around the corner, people who were to be vital in the story of London Coastal Coaches Limited and Victoria Coach Station. Notably in 1911 Maidstone & District Motor Services Limited was co-founded by a Colonel Robinson (he took over as chairman of M&D in 1924 and retained that position until his death in March 1945); in 1912 a gentleman called Leonard Turnham set up his business in Eccleston Street East and described himself as a motor trader; and hovering somewhere in the background was Mr Shirley James. These were to be three of the chief players in the story.

Progress was virtually brought to a halt between 1914 and 1918 with the onset of the First World War. The horrific loss

The report of the Handcross "Motor-Bus Disaster" in The Argos newspaper, 13th July 1906, *(British Library)*, and the remains of the Vanguard Milnes-Daimler involved in the accident. *(Author's Collection)*

of servicemen during the hostilities left the morale of the country reeling; everything was in short supply including, crucially, petrol; and large numbers of vehicles had been lost after having been commandeered for war service. But as postwar euphoria set in, more and more people wanted to forget the past few years, and enjoy themselves again; a trip by train to the seaside was the perfect answer; despite the long queues which were a normal occurrence at ticket offices.

Len Turnham, seeing an exciting opportunity, courageously decided to start a char-a-banc service from London to Brighton, and on Easter Sunday 1919 ran his first excursion from Grosvenor Gardens, Victoria; from which date coaching and Victoria became inextricably linked. Travelling at about fifteen miles per hour, it took four hours each way, and the fares at 10/6d (52½p) single and £1 return seem rather expensive when compared with the fare for the same journey by Southdown half a century later in 1969 at 12/6d single, 13/6 day return and £1.2s.0d period return (62½p, 67½p and £1.10). Although they do seem quite reasonable compared with the stagecoach single fare of 13/- (65p) in 1757.

Char-a-bancs were vehicles with rows of seats, each with its own door, running across the chassis. They were solid-tyred, and had only a canvas roof to protect the 28 or 30 passengers, so the eight-hour return journey to Brighton could not have been too comfortable.

One must assume that traffic police were thin on the ground in those days because at the time when Len Turnham was achieving an average of 15 miles per hour on his service to Brighton (even without allowing for refreshment stops), there was, and remained until October 1928, an official speed limit on char-a-bancs and coaches of 12mph. It was not until five years after Len Turnham had started his Brighton service that pneumatic tyres arrived on the scene, and even then the speed limit of 12mph remained, not being increased until October 1928, and then only to 20mph for those vehicles fitted with pneumatic tyres.

Gradually char-a-bancs were replaced by vehicles with front and rear doors, and a gangway running the whole length, thus introducing what soon became known as 'the coach', although the term char-a-banc was frequently (and still is occasionally) used for vehicles of the more modern layout.

For eleven days from 26th September 1919 the railways were paralysed by a lightning strike, giving the newly established long-distance char-a-banc industry an enormous boost, both to its popularity and its own morale. The char-a-banc operators could hardly have asked for anything better.

Apart from the hundreds of people stranded at the coast who needed to be brought home, ordinary day-to-day travel too had to be accomplished by char-a-banc. Suddenly coaching had to be seen in a much more positive light, and overnight it became a serious means of transport rather than merely an amusing way of going to the seaside. In particular, companies located outside London who had not yet been caught up in the excitement of long-distance travel were able to see the immense potential; many of them who had been involved in emergency operations during the rail strike had been shown new horizons and given added confidence. Without doubt, that rail strike, although only of eleven days duration, was of crucial importance and immediate benefit to coaching and its early progress.

With the rail strike over, and despite the comparative discomfort, char-a-banc trips to the coast became even more popular, and very quickly firms began springing up all over London, often being haulage companies who, in the tradition of the carriers before them, were looking to the transportation of passengers as well as goods as a means of income. One such company was Pickfords, a company that still holds a highly respected position as a major haulage firm for transporting goods, and a major travel agency for transporting people.

In 1920, with Mr Shirley James as London Passenger Manager, the Pickfords fleet of char-a-bancs was operating regular services from High Holborn to Eastbourne, Hastings and Brighton. Shirley James was a very astute gentleman

A Pickfords' Tilling-Stevens petrol-electric char-a-banc, with its distinctive radiator, passes one of the company's horse drawn vans as it pulls away from the loading point in Newton Street, just around the corner from Pickfords' original headquarters, in 1922. *(Pickfords Limited)*

indeed who saw the potential, not just in coach operations, but also in coach management and administration. He saw that with so many new operators coming onto the scene there could be great risks as well as great benefits. He knew that for companies to succeed and become leaders of the new industry there was need for efficient booking systems and financial and operational controls both at the London end and at distant destinations.

By then, Len Turnham had also increased the number of destinations to which his fleet of char-a-bancs was regularly travelling, and Shirley James proposed to him that they should set up a pool operation of carefully chosen members who would combine their receipts from commonly operated routes, and after deducting a minimal administrative charge, divide the balance between the members proportionate to the mileage

they had operated. Not only would this lead to savings in operation and administrative costs, but it also eliminated unnecessary competition, and participating pool members at each end of each other's routes would provide back-up facilities including booking offices, garaging, and maintenance. This was particularly important for London operators who needed back-up at the coast.

Further pooling schemes were introduced in the ensuing years, notably the Yorkshire Pool, which was formed in 1929 when the West Yorkshire Road Car Company pooled with the Yorkshire Traction and Yorkshire Woollen District companies on routes from Yorkshire to London (later to be joined by the East Yorkshire and East Midland companies), and the very important Associated Motorways network which was formed in 1934 and based in Cheltenham.

Len Turnham and Shirley James decided to call their pool London and Coastal and approached the companies whom they felt were appropriate. Initially there were nine member companies with Pickfords taking on the administrative control at their High Holborn office. Soon afterwards Turnham and Co. set up an office in a more favourable location at 7 Lower Belgrave Street, Victoria, and control of the pool moved there in 1921.

The foresight and acumen of Shirley James and Len Turnham were soon apparent. With an ever-increasing network of booking agents throughout London, and with efficient back-up services at the coast, London and Coastal services were soon well established with a reputation for efficiency.

But there was no room for complacency; many new firms were to come and go in a short period of time, others became firmly established and were to remain important cogs in the coaching industry. George Ewer brought the name Grey-Green to the

---

'LONDON AND COASTAL'
Companies in the original 1920 pool

East Kent Road Car Company Limited
Lion Cartage Company
Motor Coaches Limited
Edward Paul Limited
Pickfords Limited
Southdown Motor Services Limited
Turnham and Company
Thomas Tilling Limited
West London Charabanc & Motor Company Limited

Members who had dropped out of the pool before the formation of London Coastal Caches Limited:

Lion Cartage. *Withdrew from passenger transport to concentrate on freight.*
Edward Paul. *Withdrew to concentrate on bus operation as 'E.P.'*

Pickfords. *Withdrew from long-distance coach operation in favour of extended tours*
Thomas Tilling.

industry, and about fifty years later its coaches into Victoria Coach Station. Timpsons was another name that became established in the industry at an early date, and became heavily involved with London Coastal Coaches Limited and Victoria Coach Station.

The railway companies, too, were getting themselves organised, and in 1923, wary of the potential dangers to their profits threatened by road transport, all but two of the 122 railway concerns in Britain grouped together under the four private companies (LNER — London & North Eastern Railways; GWR — Great Western Railway; SR — Southern Railway; LMSR — London, Midland and Scottish Railways); the London Underground and the Metropolitan Railway were excluded from the grouping.

⳨ ⳩

Without doubt, the introduction of pneumatic tyres was the major improvement to coach comfort in the early 1920s, but it was just one of several improvements made as coach companies vied with each other to provide better and better facilities. Heating and ventilation still needed working out properly, and many particularly customer-conscious operators provided travelling rugs for their passengers. Travelling rugs were still provided on Southdown express services from Victoria Coach Station in the 1950s and early 1960s, as well as on the services by SMT and Western from Victoria Coach Station to Edinburgh and Glasgow, although by then coach heating systems were reliable and efficient. The word luxury appeared more and more in the names of coach companies, particularly the smaller independents, and Charles Batten of East Ham even entitled his fleet 'Batten's Luxurious Coaches'. C W Batten was a name remaining associated with coaching for many years to come.

But, with so much rapid expansion there also came a major problem: too many vehicles for the streets of London. There were no coach stations and all loading and unloading of passengers took place at the kerbside. The situation in London became chaotic, particularly for example in Eaton Square and Grosvenor Gardens where London and Coastal companies had their main loading points, and in Lower Belgrave Street where London and Coastal had a loading point as well as its operating headquarters in the offices of Turnham & Company.

In 1925, possibly in reponse to the adverse effect zealous police attention was having on coach companies but also, no doubt, in pursuance of greater efficiency, London and Coastal employed a team of paid uniformed officials, the forerunners of the inspectors who were to play such an essential part in the running of Victoria Coach Station. The cost of these officials was divided proportionately amongst the London and Coastal operating members according to the numbers of their vehicles whose departures had been supervised. By now London and Coastal members were operating 14 different routes from London to points along the east and south coasts from Great Yarmouth in Norfolk to Portsmouth in Hampshire.

The expansion of the industry was rapidly outgrowing not just the streets, but also the licensing system, such as it was, and it was clear that efficient operations were becoming hampered. Furthermore the aggravation to other road users and pedestrians around loading and unloading points was becoming

very acute indeed. Probably encouraged by the London Traffic Act of 1924, which gave the Ministry of Transport the power to declare any thoroughfare a restricted street, and certainly way ahead and in anticipation of the 1930 Road Traffic Act, the members of London and Coastal became aware that they needed to look closely, carefully and urgently at their future operations. In 1925 they made two important decisions: they would make London and Coastal a company in its own right; and they would look for a suitable off-road location as a loading point. The first Restricted Streets Order was announced on 17th February 1925; mostly affecting streets in the centre of London, it was an indication of what could happen in the near future.

London Coastal Coaches Limited was the name decided upon for the new company and, with a share capital of £1,000, it was incorporated on 30th April 1925 with the first Board Meeting being held on 5th May at 206 Brompton Road, London SW3, to where the registered office was transferred from Lower Belgrave Street soon after.

At the same time, Len Turnham was appointed as manager for a three-year period. Len Turnham's own company, Turnham and Company, ceased trading a year later in May 1926 and his position with London Coastal Coaches Limited was retitled General Manager; his appointment was regularly renewed thereafter until his death in 1944.

With Bert Smith of National Omnibus & Transport Company being the first chairman of London Coastal Coaches Limited, and National Omnibus being one of the first shareholders, it is clear that National Omnibus would always feature in the affairs of Coastal. Bert Smith started his career in the road passenger industry in 1906 when he joined the Clarkson company in Chelmsford. Thomas Clarkson was the inventor of the steam omnibus bearing his name.

It is interesting at this point to ponder, within the broadest outline, on how the National Omnibus & Transport Company developed. By the 1920s, National Omnibus had various bus interests in East Anglia, the West Country and, since the previous decade, in Nunhead, south-east London; they also had the Thomas Clarkson fleet of just over 150 vehicles, but their bus services in London were a thorn in the side of the London General Omnibus Company (LGOC) who had their eyes on total dominance of the London bus scene. It so happened that the LGOC had, before the First World War, operated buses in Bedford and although they had not resumed the Bedford area services after the war they still had their premises there. An exchange was agreed whereby, in November 1919, National Omnibus exchanged the Thomas Clarkson interests in London for the LGOC interests in Bedford, which initially they operated as part of Eastern National.

When, after grouping, the railways wanted to invest in bus companies, National Omnibus divided into three separate companies: Southern National, Western National, and Eastern National. The Southern Railway bought a shareholding in Southern National, and the Great Western in Western National — the geographical logic being easy to follow. However, Eastern National was operating both in Essex/Suffolk and Bedfordshire — virtually two different regions — and at the same time both the LMS and the LNER were also operating in each of them. The solution was for the two railway companies each to take a share in Eastern National. In due course, the Bedford area operations of Eastern National passed to United Counties, and Southern National and Western National controlled Royal Blue. Bert Smith would surely be proud of how his original National Omnibus & Transport Company was to feature in the history of the new London Coastal Coaches company that he was to chair from the date of its inauguration.

Coaching, as a trade, had been born years before with the stagecoaches and the foundations they had laid; motorised coaching began with those ill-fated but history-making trips on The Vanguard; now, coaching had truly become an industry.

It is debatable whether we should date the birth of Coastal at 1919 when Mr Turnham's excursion set off for Brighton; the point in 1920 when Mr James and Mr Turnham decided to call their pool London and Coastal; or the day five years later when London Coastal Coaches Limited was formed: whichever it was, for a long time thereafter "Coastal" was to have a great impact and its name would soon become synonymous with travel by coach.

London Coastal Coaches Limited Share Capital – First 25 Years	
Year 1925	£1,000
Year 1930	£100,000
Year 1931	£150,000
Year 1939	£200,000
Year 1950	£300,000

Coach departures from Grosvenor Gardens in the summer of 1925 with the Grosvenor Hotel in the background and stone setts still in the road. The second vehicle back on the right is a United Automobile Services Ltd AEC Y-type char-a-banc setting off for Great Yarmouth. As the Leyland S4 in front is from Cliff Garages in Gorleston we can safely assume that it is operating as a duplicate to the United vehicle. *(Motor Transport/LCCc)*

INSPIRATION

1908. Mills-Daimler early attempt at coach building. Forerunner of modern observation coach.

1910. Hallford terraced-floor development of observation coach.

1910. Straker-Squire early type single deck omnibus.

1910. Hallford early type of chars-a-bancs operated by Maidstone & District Motor Services Ltd.

IMPROVEMENT

1912 Leyland Beadle Saloon single-deck omnibus.

A.E.C. 1919. Coach. This coach actually opened the London-Brighton service. It was the first to run on this road.

1915. Daimler Chars-a-bancs with folding hood.

1915 Daimler Bus operated by Southdown Motor Services Ltd at Brighton

DEVELOPMENT

Leyland 1919. "N" type Saloon with smoking compartment.

Interior of showing compartment

A.E.C. "B" type (note windows open and close) The first attempt at adjustable windows. 1920.

1924. Tilling Stevens Petrol Electric Touring Coach with staggered seats, operated by Maidstone & District Motor Services Ltd

HEADQUARTERS

10. Eccleston Street East was the birthplace of London Coastal Coaches, for in 1919 the present General Manager commenced operations with one coach

As business increased, 7 Lower Belgrave Street was added early in 1920.

Grosvenor Gardens used for loading passengers from 1919 until Lupus Street Station opened in 1928.

In 1930 7 Lower Belgrave Street was enlarged and modernised.

From a proud London Coastal Coaches' 6th Anniversary souvenir programme. *(Jim Russell Collection.)*

Coach Stops around London *(clockwise from top right)* Heathfield Terrace, Chiswick 1940s/50s; Ealing Road, Uxbridge 1965; Jersey Road 1961; Hatton Cross 1966; Heathfield Terrace, Chiswick 1960s.
(*LCCc, John Marsh collection and Kenneth Collier.*)

The formative years

The Directors of London Coastal Coaches Limited were not the only people to see an urgent need for off-street loading. Other equally perceptive coaching men could also see the problems facing the industry, and plenty of other independent coach operators intent on benefiting from the ever-growing popularity of coach travel.

In particular it is worth turning our attention for a moment to a company that had been operating in south London from the early 1920s as Blue Bell Transport Limited and to recognise the shrewd character of Mr T Boon. Mr Boon, also, had an eye out for a suitable loading terminal, and was no doubt also looking for a good central London location.

For their part the directors of London Coastal Coaches Limited were looking at the Victoria, Bloomsbury, Charing Cross, or Marble Arch areas. It was essential for them to have a truly central London terminal if theirs was to remain a prestigious operation in the eyes of any provincial coach companies with plans for possible services to London, and who might be potential users of the terminal facilities and administrative services being offered by London Coastal Coaches Limited, or Coastal as they had by then become familiarly known.

There were already several more operators using Coastal for booking and loading control and the widespread Coastal agency network was a particular advantage. Especially notable among these additional operators was the long established family concern of Elliott Brothers of Bournemouth, who had services from London to Bournemouth, South Devon, and Weston-Super-Mare operating under the Royal Blue name. Elliot Brothers were founder members of Associated Motorways in 1934, but the following year sold out to the Tilling organisation and, strategically important from Coastal's point-of-view, most of the other companies newly allied to London Coastal Coaches Limited were either from the Tilling or BET stable.

Black & White Motorways were an anomaly, part owned by both Tilling and BET. In 1930 the shares in this company were held by Midland Red (BMMO) 40%, Bristol Omnibuses 40% and City of Oxford 20%. Thus the holding was shared 40% Tilling and 60% BET, so Black & White is probably the only instance where an actual operating link existed between the two companies.

Indeed, the list of operating companies coming under the Coastal umbrella in one way or another had grown so long that it was decided to appoint a committee made up of senior representatives of the companies concerned, to keep a close eye on anything which affected the operators, and to put forward ideas and suggestions. The industry was, after all, still very young, and lessons were being newly learned all the time. The traffic committee, as it was called, met regularly from that day almost until the date of the withdrawal of the name London Coastal Coaches Limited 45 years later.

More and more other companies, particularly in the north of England, were planning services to the capital and would soon to be in need of terminal facilities. This consideration had not escaped the attention of Coastal's directors nor had it escaped the attention of Mr Boon of Blue Bell. The race was on.

Lupus Street

Finding a site was difficult, particularly centrally. Even though Coastal had started its search in earnest in 1926, it was not until 1928 that a moderately acceptable site was found. It was not really as central as the Coastal Board of Directors would have liked, and there were several disadvantages, but the passenger-loading situation was becoming more critical by the day.

The London County Council had earmarked a two-acre site at Lupus Street, Pimlico, near Vauxhall Bridge, as a generating station for the trams. The plan was shelved and London Coastal Coaches Limited quickly came to an agreement to rent the land. One can appreciate how swiftly negotiations were hurried along knowing that the agreement was concluded on 20th March, and the coach station opened just over one week later on 1st April. But it was not an ideal situation geographically, operationally or contractually.

The best that could be said for the location was that it was off-street and on the north bank of the river. It was, though, inconvenient for passengers who had become used to the handy loading points around Victoria railway station, and so for some time it was necessary to run a shuttle service from Grosvenor Gardens to Lupus Street.

The term coach station was perhaps a little over-glamorous for the Lupus Street site as almost nothing was done to make it in any way comfortable for passengers, but nevertheless, despite its unpretentious appearance, it was the first off-street coach loading and unloading point in the Metropolitan area and so, as such, just about qualifies as London's first coach station.

Operationally, Lupus Street was extremely difficult. There was only one narrow access point so arrivals and departures had to be carefully controlled; worse still, coaches had to reverse into their stand before loading or unloading. Nonetheless, 1,250 laden vehicles left from Lupus Street coach station between the Thursday and Monday of Easter weekend, 1928.

Contractually, Lupus Street was even more of a headache for the Coastal Board because either side, at just three month's notice, could terminate the rental agreement; thus it is perhaps not surprising that Coastal did little to improve passenger facilities. Lupus Street coach station was merely a rather unsatisfactory stopgap solution to a pressing problem, and a better alternative was urgently needed.

The calm exterior gives no indication of the bustling activity inside Lupus Street Coach Station in this 1920's scene. The single access for both arriving and departing coaches, to say nothing of the lack of dedicated pathways for pedestrians, is clearly a danger. Rapid advances in coach design are now becoming apparent with the bonnetted canvassed roofed Daimler being followed by the more modern Leyland with its separate cab for the driver. Both leading vehicles have the facility to open the roof almost to the rear of the saloon, whereas the third vehicle has a fixed roof with luggage rack at the rear. The luggage boot has yet to make its appearance. *(LCCc both)*

Orange Bros. of Bedlington, Northumberland, ran this well-appointed Weymann-bodied coach on the long service between London and Scotland. Deep-backed seats were provided for the passengers, and the two doors and curtains are noteworthy. Orange Bros. business was later taken over by United Automobile Services. *(STA)*

LONDON COASTAL COACHES LIMITED

Telephones: Victoria 2766 (30 lines)
HEAD OFFICE AND MAIN DEPARTURE STATION
1a Lupus Street (near Victoria), S.W.1.
CENTRAL BOOKING AND TOURIST OFFICES
7b and 7c Lower Belgrave Street, Victoria, S.W.1.
SOUTH WESTERN DISTRICT BOOKING
AND ENQUIRY OFFICE
433 Brixton Road, Brixton, S.W.9

Associated and Operating Companies – 1930

SOUTHDOWN MOTOR SERVICES LIMITED
EAST KENT ROAD CAR COMPANY LIMITED
MAIDSTONE & DISTRICT MOTOR SERVICES LIMITED
EASTERN NATIONAL OMNIBUS COMPANY LIMITED
SOUTHERN NATIONAL OMNIBUS COMPANY LIMITED
WESTERN NATIONAL OMNIBUS COMPANY LIMITED
UNITED AUTOMOBILE SERVICES LIMITED
THAMES VALLEY TRACTION COMPANY LIMITED
ALDERSHOT & DISTRICT TRACTION COMPANY LIMITED
REDCAR SERVICES LIMITED
EASTERN COUNTIES ROAD CAR COMPANY LIMITED
NORTH WESTERN ROAD CAR COMPANY LIMITED
MIDLAND 'RED' MOTOR SERVICES
(Birmingham & Midland Motor Omnibus Company Limited)
EAST YORKSHIRE MOTOR SERVICES LIMITED
WEST YORKSHIRE ROAD CAR COMPANY LIMITED
YORKSHIRE (W.D.) ELECTRIC TRAMWAYS COMPANY LIMITED
YORKSHIRE TRACTION COMPANY LIMITED
WEST LONDON COACHES
MAYFAIR TRANSPORT COMPANY LIMITED
ORANGE BROTHERS (NEWCASTLE)
WESTCLIFF MOTOR SERVICES LIMITED
SOUTH MIDLAND TOURING AND TRANSPORT COMPANY LIMITED
BLACK AND WHITE MOTORWAYS LIMITED
ROYAL BLUE AUTOMOBILE SERVICES
(Elliot Brothers [Bournemouth] Limited)

LOADING & OVERNIGHT GARAGING CHARGES AT LUPUS STREET COACH STATION

	Loading. (per departure)	Garaging (per coach, per night)
Shareholder Companies	1s. 0d.	1s. 6d.
Non-shareholding		
Associate Companies	1s. 6d.	2s. 0d.
Outsider Companies	2s. 6d.	3s. 0d.

"The big event was the commencement of the National company's weekend service to Ilfracombe, and it must have been very gratifying to Mr Bert Smith, who was there to see the start, that it was made with two fully laden cars which, leaving Lupus Street at 9.00am, arrived at their destination about 8.00pm." (Motor Transport Magazine, June 1928)

Bessborough House, Lupus Street, the headquarters of London Coastal Coaches Limited until 1932. The notice above the London Coastal Coaches facia reads: "This site has been secured through the generosity of the public. The frontage has been given as a free gift by the Duke of Westminster. The site will be developed for building houses for Westminster workers". Obviously the chances of a permanent coach station on this site were doubtful from the beginning. *(Fox Photos/LCCc)*

To cover the cost of renting the Lupus Street site, Coastal charged a fee per departure to the companies using the coach station, and made an additional charge for overnight garaging, as shown in the tables reproduced opposite. Space was still limited when compared with demand so preference was given to associate companies, with shareholding companies given even greater priority.

A second coach station

Shortly after the opening of the London Coastal Coaches coach station in Lupus Street, a second Metropolitan area coach station was opened, by a Mr Frank Lyne, at Cartwright Gardens between King's Cross and Russell Square. Central London Coaching Station, as it was called, had greater right to use the words coach station, as it provided passengers with covered accommodation, had a single long platform with a buffet at one end and a waiting room at the other, had a separate entrance and exit, and was better located in relation to the London Underground, with nearby tube stations at

King's Cross, Euston and Russell Square. Earliest operators to use Central London Coaching Station included Finglands of Manchester, Imperial of Liverpool, Yelloway of Rochdale, Bush & Twiddy of Norwich and Crosville of Chester, and more were soon to follow.

Having then a coach station of sorts, the control and direction of London Coastal Coaches Limited was strengthened later in 1928 when the chairmanship of the company passed to Colonel H I Robinson. As we saw earlier, Colonel Robinson had been a co-founder of Maidstone and District Motor Services Limited in 1911. For 34 years thereafter he was to hold various executive positions (frequently chairman) with many other companies, both within and outside the transport industry; he served as Coastal's chairman until his death in 1945.

Also in 1928, another major player in the success of London Coastal Coaches appeared: Leonard Corbett joined Coastal as Len Turnham's assistant; he had transferred from Motor Coaches Limited (one of the original London and Coastal Pool), and remained with the firm for 42 years until retiring in 1970 from the position of Traffic Manager. In the same year, Len Corbett's wife Rene joined the company as a booking/charting clerk, a position she held until 1957.

Again in 1928, as part of the centralisation of Coastal's control into one location, the headquarters of the company was transferred from Lower Belgrave Street to Bessborough House, which stood at the entrance to the Lupus Street coach station.

And yet another station . . .

Back on the other side of the Thames, in the summer of 1929 Mr Boon and his colleague Mr Toms, of Blue Bell Transport Limited, registered a company called Coach Travel Limited described as motor hirers, garage proprietors, dealers in coaches and buses and other automobiles, and a few months later opened the third Metropolitan area coach station, Terminal Coach Station, in Clapham Road between Kennington and Vauxhall. Although south of the river and slightly further away from central London than Lupus Street, it did have the advantage of being near Oval tube station, and without doubt it was most impressive. On each side of a private approach road were the booking office, waiting rooms, a tearoom, buffet bar and shops, and within two years it was being used by more than 30 coach operators.

The majority of the earliest companies using Terminal Coach Station were operators of day excursions, but the list of long-distance express operators grew quickly and included Scout and Standerwick from Blackpool, Albatross Roadways and McShanes from Liverpool, and Greyhound from Bournemouth and Torquay.

Often the long-distance operators used two London coach stations, for example Greyhound, and Bush & Twiddy (and others) served both Central Coach Station and Terminal Coach Station, and the Empire's Best service which had already been operating three times daily to Clacton for several years was extended from Charing Cross Embankment to Terminal Coach Station. Coastal's Lupus Street coach station looked decidedly like a poor relation.

But then, still in 1929, it became known to Mr Toms and Mr Boon that a site was soon to be available for development on the corner of Elizabeth Street and Buckingham Palace Road, Victoria, and they put in a submission to the London County Council to build a coach station and hotel on the site. Certainly there was need for further hotel accommodation in the area; apart from the Grosvenor Hotel at Victoria Railway Station, the Eccleston Hotel at the back of Victoria Station,

and Ruben's Hotel between Victoria Railway Station and Buckingham Palace, there were no large hotels nearer than Sloane Square or Knightsbridge, although there were dozens of small private hotels, boarding houses and bed-&-breakfast lodgings all around. To combine a new hotel with a much-needed coach station seemed a brilliant proposition.

How anxious those times must have been for the Coastal directors. One cannot believe they could have been unaware, even if only by rumour, of what was being planned scarcely a mile away from Lupus Street, in Buckingham Palace Road although, in the circumstances, it must have come as some relief to them that they had resisted making an outright purchase of the Lupus Street lease a year before when the London County Council had found a potential purchaser and it had looked as if Coastal might lose the use of the site. The potential purchaser withdrew from negotiations and Coastal retained the site, but still on the highly nerve-wracking three-months-notice basis.

The site at Lupus Street was barely a quarter of an acre larger than the site at Buckingham Palace Road and the position of the latter was infinitely better. Had Coastal bought the Lupus Street site the previous year, it would have then been faced with the prospect of having spent a lot of money on what was, after all, still just a piece of rough, undeveloped ground, with a custom-built rival coach station and hotel going up in a superior position, rather too close for comfort. They had not acquired the site, so were not saddled with unwanted land; but they still had the threat of an adversary setting up on their doorstep. Times were not easy for the Coastal board.

However, the Toms/Boon plans for the Buckingham Palace Road/Elizabeth Street site were dropped soon after, so maybe we might surmise that the proposals, if they had come to fruition, would have risked stretching the finances of the two gentlemen to breaking point. Instead they concentrated their efforts on Terminal Coach Station, which remained and flourished for several more years, as did Blue Bell Transport Limited, which was particularly vigorous in updating its fleet with the latest vehicles.

London Coastal Coaches quickly picked up where Toms and Boon had left off, and concluded the purchase of the Buckingham Palace Road/Elizabeth Street site on 2nd September 1930. With Coastal being formed in the most part by larger operators and companies, financial restraints were probably not too problematical; however, in order to ensure that such fiscal considerations should not prevent their success, as they seem possibly to have done to Toms and Boon, the company was refinanced and acquired additional shareholders.

We should mention in passing the coach station at Hatcham Park Road, New Cross, that was opened at this time by the MT Company as a terminal for its services from Ramsgate and Margate. In the mid 1930s, however, the MT Company disposed of its operation to East Kent, and New Cross Coach Station was taken over jointly by East Kent and Maidstone & District. From then on, New Cross Coach Station was to be a point on all the East Kent and Maidstone & District routes from Victoria Coach Station, and it did not close until 28th September 1973.

A poor quality illustration of London Terminal Coach Station, but it does show its extent and comparative grandeur.
(Jim Russell Collection)

Whilst all this was going on the railway companies were keeping even more careful watch on the rapid progress being made by bus and coach companies, and were well aware of the potential effects on their own networks. They felt it prudent, therefore, to obtain interests in those road transport companies who were a possible threat to them, even to the extent that the four main railway companies applied for and eventually, in 1928, were granted authority to own and operate public service vehicles in their own right. This was the second attempt by the big four railway companies to gain interests in bus operations. In 1924 the Railway Road Powers Bill had been introduced, but did not survive its passage through Parliament. The railway companies invested chiefly in Tilling, BET, National Omnibus & Transport, and Scottish Motor Traction Group (SMT) companies, and although they never acquired controlling interests in any company, they had substantial shareholdings and also, probably more importantly, positions on company boards. There was a close association between these companies and London Coastal Coaches Limited, so the railways had cast their metaphorical shadow over Victoria Coach Station.

An advantage to passengers of this railway interest in coaching was the introduction of rail/road interchange arrangements, which enabled the holders of return coach tickets to return by rail upon payment of a supplement. Holders of return rail tickets could, if they wished, return by coach, but no compensating refund was made.

The Road Traffic Act (1930)

Probably the most vital and influential piece of legislation ever to affect passenger road traffic until the deregulation and privatisation of the industry towards the end of the 20th century, was the Road Traffic Act, 1930. Certainly it brought a semblance of order to the growing chaos of the previous decade. Companies would now have to hold licences to operate any journey whatsoever where they carried fare-paying passengers (except private hire, when it was deemed that one person, or one group, had chartered the vehicle and would not be charging individual fares). The free-for-all days, when any operator went more or less anywhere, were at an end. The act also introduced compulsory third-party insurance.

As far back as the sedan chair and the hackney carriage, London had been used to various licensing systems. In 1832, the Metropolitan Stage Carriage Act had come into force and with amendments over the years remained in use for almost a century. This was the act that affected early coach operators into and within the London area in that the Public Carriage Office in London inspected each vehicle, which, on passing the examination, was given a licence to ply for hire. An enamelled iron plate showing the licence number and the Royal Coat of Arms had to be fixed to the back of the vehicle and was valid for a year, after which the vehicle had to be overhauled, re-examined, and relicensed.

In a similar way the drivers (and conductors known then as directors) were also licensed by the Board of Stamps and needed to prove they were of good character and had been recommended by their employer. However, because of their often discourteous attitude, another Act of Parliament came into force eight years later, which dictated that they should wear a numbered oval metal badge or ticket in a conspicuous place, to which the aggrieved passenger could refer on complaint. Not until the 1st April 1991 amendment to the 1988 Road Traffic Act was the requirement for bus and coach drivers to wear a public service vehicle badge brought to an end when, under EEC regulations, the PSV classification was changed to Passenger Carrying Vehicles (PCV).

Out of London, some of the larger towns and cities introduced similar systems, with licences being approved and issued by the Watch Committee, together with similar small metal plates for fixing to the rear of the vehicle in question. Many of the smaller towns did not bother to introduce a licensing system. An operator intending to use his vehicle in several areas would need to obtain licences for each of the areas his vehicle was travelling through and where a licensing system was in force.

We can see, therefore, that in the London area, and in a good many other parts of the country, the licensing arrangements provided quite stringent controls on the maintenance of vehicles and competence of drivers: but there were no controls on where the vehicles went. Competition was rampant and on particularly busy and profitable routes led to considerable traffic congestion, particularly in towns and city centres. Central London became particularly congested. With a roadworthy vehicle and a trustworthy crew, an operator could run services where and when he liked.

At a stroke, the 1930 Road Traffic Act brought order to the confusion and introduced one licensing system throughout the United Kingdom. The country was divided into Traffic Areas, and the Minister of Transport appointed commissioners in each area whose responsibility it was to issue licences allowing operators to ply for hire. Road Service Licences applied to the routes, schedules and fares, and Public Service Vehicle Licences applied to the vehicles themselves. (For the war years the RTA was partially suspended and road service licences were replaced with Traffic Commission permits. In 1945 the traffic commissioners were known as the Licensing Authority, but in 1956 they reverted to their previous title.)

It was decided that there were to be three types of Road Service Licence: one to cover bus services (stage carriage licences); another to cover longer services where a compulsory minimum fare applied in order to discourage the short journeys rightfully the preserve of the buses (short stage express carriage licences); and a third to cover pre-bookable long-distance coach services on which tickets would not generally be issued on the vehicles (express service licences).

Companies wishing to operate services applied to the Traffic Commissioner in the area covered, and needed to support their applications with details of proposed timetables and fares, and the positioning of boarding, alighting and stopping places. Where a desired service crossed into more than one traffic area, Road Service Licence (Backing Licence) applications had also to be made in each of the other areas. The need for drivers themselves to be licensed remained, but a licence issued to a driver in one traffic area would be valid in any other, and an important effect of the Road Traffic Act was the introduction of legislation to regulate drivers' hours.

This Road Traffic Act (1930) remained in force, virtually unaltered, until 1970 when European Union (then EEC) regulations were introduced into this country.

The commissioners published regular lists of applications received so that objections to the issuing of a licence could be lodged by other operating companies, and interested parties such as the police or local authorities. It comes as no surprise that the railway companies were prime objectors to a vast majority of applications. In his book The History of British Bus Services Professor John Hibbs tells us that A F R Carling, who was later to become a director of London Coastal Coaches Limited, quoted one counsel acting on behalf of the railway companies who told the Scottish traffic commissioners that "they (the railway companies) thought they were justified in asking for the complete prohibition of long-distance services. The public would not suffer except for the higher fares they would have to pay".

Regular traffic courts would be set up in each of the traffic areas, at which the commissioners would examine details of all applications, call witnesses if necessary to support the applications or the objections, decide if the original application needed to be amended in any way in order for it to be acceptable to them, and settle on whether or not to issue a licence.

A deadline of 9th February 1931 was set for the Act to come into effect, after which no new service could start without a licence. Services which had been operated before that date also needed a licence, but operators were able to plead an established facility in support of their applications, which in most cases would override applications for similar facilities applied for by other operators. It was a system that worked well, and was for the most part very fair.

For the next few years a good deal of amalgamation and takeovers took place in the coaching industry; many smaller firms withdrew from the scene, and others expanded to become more commercially skilled and passenger-conscious. Nevertheless, there remained hundreds and hundreds of coach companies of all sizes, with various degrees of expertise and levels of professionalism.

Not all would survive.

ငာ ၏

Meanwhile, on the corner of Buckingham Palace Road and Elizabeth Street planning and building work progressed frantically.

Restricted duplication of services was frequently a problem to coach operators. The railways objected to almost every application made by coach companies to the traffic commissioners, and often vehicle duplication restrictions were imposed, one might suppose perhaps as a way of mollifying the railways. But the coach operators fought against the situation, and regularly used train overcrowding as an argument in their own favour.

(Jim Russell Collection)

The Board of Directors of London Coastal Coaches Limited, financially stable and possessed of a wealth of commercial experience, made an extremely well-considered and crucially important decision concerning the design for their new coach station. They sought the advice of the architect Thomas Wallis, and were soon to appoint his firm Wallis, Gilbert & Partners to go ahead with plans for Victoria Coach Station; in consultation with Thomas Wallis, William Lovatt & Sons Limited were appointed to undertake the building work. Coastal had, however, decided against the hotel idea, but looked to offering office accommodation instead.

It is worth spending a moment or two to consider how important and interesting Victoria Coach Station is from an architectural point of view.

Thomas Wallis, son of a bricklayer, trained in the late 1880s as an architect with the firm of Sidney R J Smith, the designers of the Tate Gallery. Much of his training would have included designing public buildings and it is not surprising therefore that he became noted particularly for his factory designs. Thomas Wallis felt strongly that workplaces should

What the Commissioners are saying—

We Commissioners are getting very concerned as to whether the railway companies are really fulfilling their obligations to the travelling public.

Mr. J. H. STIRK in the East Midland Area.

Until the railway companies can show that they can carry all their period passengers in corridor stock on long-distance journeys, without any standing in the corridors or guard's van, we shall not have very much sympathy with their representatives.

Col. A. S. REDMAN in the West Midland Area.

Stop the Restricted Duplication Scandal !

More than a year before its opening, Victoria Coach Station was attracting a lot of media interest. (*Peter Scammell Collection*)

Almost four months since the press report shown in the previous illustration, and building work has started on the "super coach station". This is how it looked on 20th May 1931. (*LCCc*)

The coach station taking shape; this picture shows the state of progress on 1st July 1931. *(LCCc)*

Three months to opening day. The art deco, and Egyptian characteristics are already very apparent.*(LCCc)*

be built with the comfort of the workforce as a prime consideration and this is particularly apparent in the detailed attention he gave to heating, lighting and ventilation in his buildings. In many ways he was ahead of his time in these respects, and had pre-empted the many new statutory regulations that were gradually introduced concerning working conditions, health and safety. Victoria Coach Station, with its bright and airy offices, is typical of Wallis's designs, although many of the public areas have needed a degree of renovation and change in recent years, either in response to the changing demands of the travelling public or, for example public toilets, where there has been a need for upgrading and improvement.

By 1900 Thomas Wallis was practising on his own account, and in 1916 he moved his practice to Caxton House in Tothill Street, Westminster, where his office was adjacent to that of an American-based firm, Trussed Concrete Steel Limited (Truscon). Truscon had developed and patented the idea of reinforced concrete, and this innovation made it possible to construct buildings with longer and better weight-carrying beams. Wallis entered into a collaborative arrangement with Truscon, whose method of concrete reinforcement became widespread in Wallis's designs, and which made it easier to incorporate the large expanses of windows or other glass decoration that are a feature of so much of the work of Wallis, Gilbert & Partners and which are seen clearly in the design of Victoria Coach Station.

There was, incidentally, no 'Gilbert' in the partnership; apparently it was a name plucked from the air and inserted with 'Partner' (originally in the singular, but eventually changed to plural) to provide a suitable name for the firm, which could remain intact irrespective of whomsoever else might be recruited *(Form and Fancy – Factories and Factory Buildings by Wallis, Gilbert & Partners. Dr Joan S Skinner, Liverpool University).*

Wallis, Gilbert & Partners moved their office to 15 Elizabeth Street (the address at that time for the offices above Victoria Coach Station), and so were one of Coastal's first tenants. From Dr Joan Skinner's investigations we learn that Marjorie Wallis, a court dressmaker and Thomas's daughter, also ran her business from rooms at 15 Elizabeth Street.

Eventually the offices above Victoria Coach Station were known more prestigiously as Coastal Chambers, and the address changed to 164/172 Buckingham Palace Road. Wallis, Gilbert & Partners remained tenants of London Coastal Coaches Limited at Victoria Coach Station until Thomas Wallis's retirement in January 1946.

But Thomas Wallis was an artist as well as an engineer, and it is the combination of his artistic and planning skills that prevails in his designs. He believed that even seemingly commonplace buildings such as factories or bus stations should be pleasing to the eye; he gave great emphasis to the aesthetic appearance of the buildings he designed. For a long period Wallis adopted an Egyptian style, which eventually gave way to a trend better described as Art Deco, with both influences being detectable in the design of Victoria Coach Station, notably in the wording London Coastal Coaches Limited on the top floor of each of the two wings, and Coach Exit above the Elizabeth Street exit.

Many of the other famous Wallis, Gilbert buildings of the same period, although basically all quite different, have a similar feel to them, both externally and internally, which is apparent also in Victoria Coach Station. The Firestone factory on the Great West Road (built 1928) and The Gramophone Company Ltd (His Masters' Voice) factory in Hayes, Middlesex (built between 1927 and 1930) are good examples, but more strikingly the Glaxo building in Greenford, built four years after Victoria Coach Station, looks very much like a straightened out version of the coach station. Likewise, although on a far less grandiose scale, one can detect within Victoria Coach Station a hint of the spaciousness and elegant design lines of the interior aspects of the Hoover Building in Perivale (built 1931), and the GEC Building in Whitton, Birmingham (built between 1918 and 1922).

A particular feature of many of Thomas Wallis's designs is the use of oak panelling in boardrooms and other prestigious executive locations. This is seen in several of the rooms in Victoria Coach Station, and great emphasis was made of the oak panelling in Coastal's publicity, in particular the annual souvenir programmes published during the 1930s on each anniversary of the opening of the coach station.

One cannot but admire the awareness and foresight of the Coastal directors in choosing Wallis, Gilbert & Partners to design Victoria Coach Station. The design was totally contemporary and to a high quality both visually and in its construction methods. It is probably fair to compare the social significance, design and construction impact of Victoria Coach Station in the 1930s with those of such terminals as St Pancras railway station in the previous century.

The construction of transport-related buildings was not new to Wallis, Gilbert & Partners. As early as 1917 Thomas Wallis had designed the Tilling-Stevens factory in Maidstone (from early pictures it is easy to detect the design lines which were eventually to develop and influence the design of Victoria Coach Station), and ten years before designing Victoria Coach Station he had designed the Reigate garage of East Surrey Traction. Wallis, Gilbert & Partners then went on to design the Swanley, Crawley, Dorking, Dunton Green and Windsor depots of the same bus company, and during the four years following the opening of Victoria Coach Station, the firm designed the LPTB (London Passenger Transport Board) garages and offices at Epping, Hemel Hempstead, Luton, Tring, Addlestone, St Albans, Staines, Tunbridge Wells, Northfleet, and Leatherhead, as well as the extensions or reconstructions of the tram and trolleybus depot in Wood Green, and the tram depot in Hanwell.

Another Wallis, Gilbert & Partners building which became a coach terminal, although in fairness it was never planned as such, was the Avon India Rubber Company depot at Mabledon Place, London. The building was completed in 1931, and used by the tyre manufacturers until the mid-1960s when it became the air terminal for Sky Tours.

What cannot be disputed is that the impact, and modern image, of Victoria Coach Station in the early 1930s gave an immense boost to the overall representation and respectability of the rapidly emerging and developing coaching industry. There have been periods, notably in the late 1970s and throughout the 1980s, when one might have justifiably and sadly protested at the shoddy, down-at-heel appearance of the public areas compared with the way they had been fifty or so years before, but the refurbishments of 1992 brought the terminal up to date, made the best use of the available space, and provided quality refreshment facilities and toilets, as well as reasonable seating. Importantly, and one wonders why this had not been a feature in much earlier years, glass screens separated waiting passengers from the coaches.

Even today, or maybe especially today, almost three-quarters of a century since its opening, the prospect of Victoria Coach Station as one approaches it along Buckingham Palace Road is still very arresting.

So it was that on 10th March 1932, less than thirteen years after Len Turnham's char-a-banc had made its momentous first excursion from Grosvenor Gardens to Brighton, Mr P J Pybus, CBE, MP, the Minister of Transport, opened Victoria Coach Station. A Maidstone and District Leyland Tiger was the first coach to enter, driven by Foreman Driver C W J Cliff Hill of Maidstone. The 250 guests had luncheon in the restaurant that was an integral part of the splendid new building. The Chairman, Colonel Robinson, proposed toasts to His Majesty the King and to the Ministry of Transport, and Shirley James proposed another to the architects and contractors.

And just to finish off that memorable day on yet another high note, the night service to Glasgow was operated with a diesel-engined AEC Regal coach of Midland Bus Services. It was the first long-distance journey by bus or coach on public service to be operated by other than a petrol-engined vehicle.

The anxieties, careful planning, difficult decision making and unfaltering enthusiasm of everyone involved with London Coastal Coaches Limited during the decade just past had then been justified and rewarded in a superb and magnificent fashion.

ও ৪০

The two wings of Victoria Coach Station were designed to stand almost at right-angles to each other on the 1 ¾ acre site, with the shorter wing facing onto Buckingham Palace Road, and the impressive main passenger entrance at the junction of the two wings leading into the booking hall with its ten ticket windows. Lifts serving all floors were installed at both extremities of the building.

Drawing of Victoria Coach Station as at the time of its opening in 1932. *(Bus & Coach)*

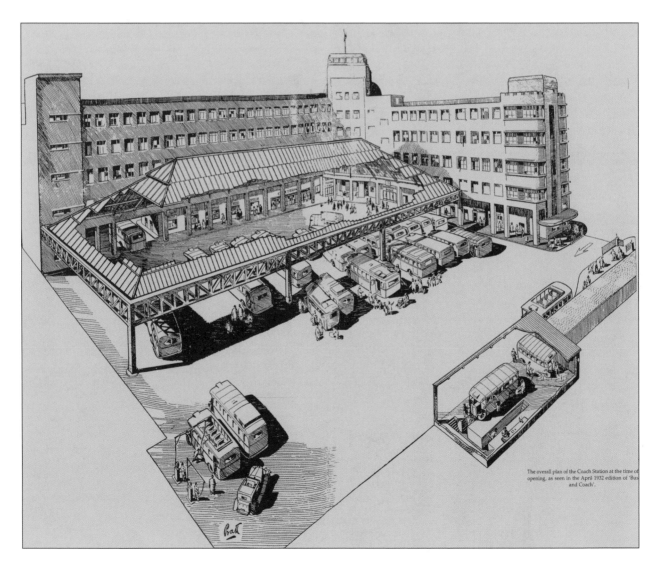

The overall plan of the Coach Station at the time of opening, as seen in the April 1932 edition of 'Bus and Coach'.

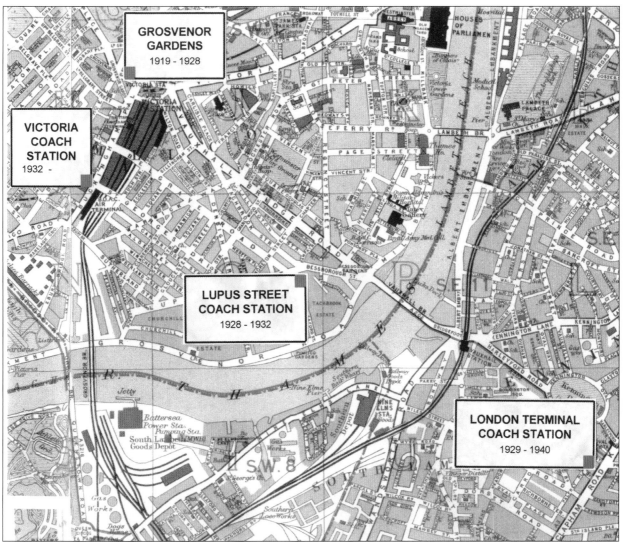

GROSVENOR
GARDENS
1919 - 1928

VICTORIA
COACH
STATION
1932 -

LUPUS STREET
COACH STATION
1928 - 1932

LONDON TERMINAL
COACH STATION
1929 - 1940

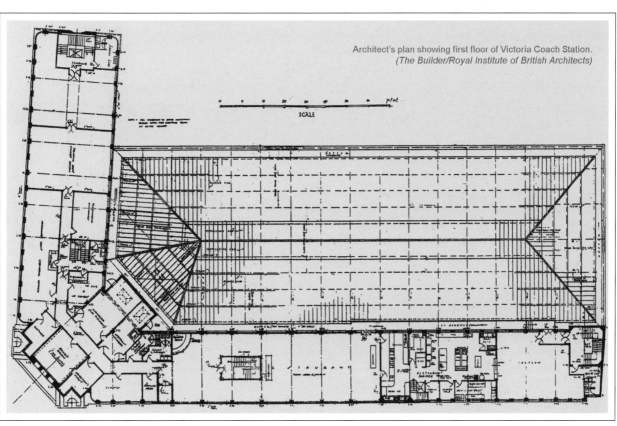

Architect's plan showing first floor of Victoria Coach Station.
(The Builder/Royal Institute of British Architects)

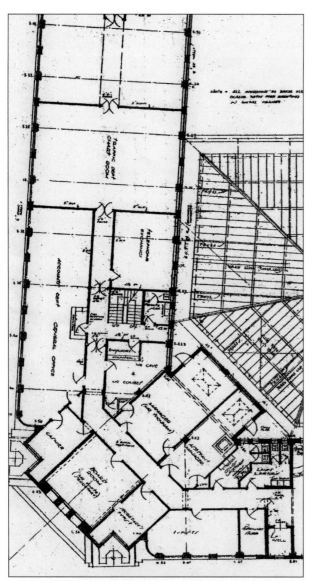

Below: The Opening Ceremony on Thursday 10th March 1932. Those indicated are: 1. Mr P J Pybus, Minister of Transport; 2. Revd E St George Shomberg, JP, Mayor of Westminster; 3. Colonel H I Robinson, Chairman, London Coastal Coaches Limited; 4. Mr W White, Secretary, London Coastal Coaches Limited; 5. Mr L M Turnham, Manager, London Coastal Coaches Limited; 6. Mr L E Corbett, Assistant to Manager, London Coastal Coaches Limited.

At street level along the Buckingham Palace Road wing were several shops, and a hairdressing salon on a mezzanine floor. After the war and until the 1960s, this mezzanine floor accommodated Coastal's tours department. There were more street level shops along the Elizabeth Street wing together with a buffet bar, and a lounge bar on a mezzanine floor, above which, on the first floor, was a large 200-cover restaurant with dance floor, and extensive kitchens.

The executive offices and oak panelled boardroom were located on the first floor, above the main entrance. Along the Buckingham Palace Road wing, on the first floor, were Coastal's administrative offices and 62-line telephone exchange.

The remaining three floors were designed as office accommodation for letting to outside tenants and these were quickly snapped up. Furthermore, the influx of tenants had a beneficial effect on Coastal's extensive catering facilities, and the restaurant and lounge bar were always busy at lunchtimes with staff of the tenant companies. One wonders why, though, just one year after the opening of Victoria Coach Station, it was decided to redecorate the restaurant. Interior designers Mollo & Edgar were chosen for the work, and with (according to Mr W White, the Secretary and Estate Manager of London Coastal Coaches Limited, in February 1933) "a view to restfulness of the eyes after a long journey" the colour scheme decided upon was pale green and pink with a gold spray.

Strangely though, the buffet, redecorated at the same time, was described as having 'a bold, futuristic wall design that is distinctly novel' which doesn't really seem to show the same respect for tired eyes.

At the same time, 1933, Coastal had a staff restaurant where employees could obtain a square meal for 1/- (5p), and a staff recreation room at the top of the building was nearing completion.

In the 1950s when Coastal needed more office space for itself, the accounts and ticket audit department and the agency administration office took over part of the second floor, and the recreation room became a workshop for the publicity department whose very active team constructed a good many of their own window display units for agents offices.

A new coach station with all its facilities needed a lot more staff. Booking clerks and uniformed officials were able to transfer from Lupus Street, but many more were to join. This was an exciting time and massive steps forward were being taken in the coaching industry. As the story of Coastal and Victoria Coach Station evolves one realises what a surprising number of people, both executives and staff, remained with the company for the whole or most of their careers. Then as now, for so many people, once travel was in the blood they became willing captives for life. The saying "once a railwayman

Facing Page Upper: London Coastal Coaches Ltd Board Room at Victoria Coach Station. *(Sperryns Limited/LCCc)*
Left centre: The Restaurant, Victoria Coach Station. *(LCCc)*

Driver Hill of Maidstone drives a Maidstone & District Leyland Tiger with Harrington coachwork into Victoria Coach Station – the first ever arrival. *(LCCc)*

"Buildings for manufacture and transport may be said to be special to this age, and they will be the ultimate evidence on which the architectural intelligence of our time will be judged."
(J Dixon-Spain, 'Factory Design • the opportunity of our time' in The Architects Journal, 13th January 1932)

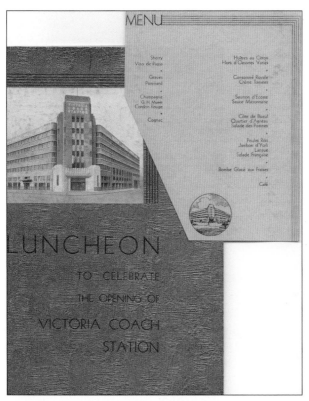

The celebration luncheon menu. *(Author's Collection)*

The first diesel-engined coach to operate a long-distance service journey; a Midland AEC Regal, enters Victoria Coach Station on its opening day, in readiness for the journey to Scotland. *(Author's Collection)*

always a railwayman" applies equally as "once a coachman always a coachman", and can include everyone from the lowliest employee to the man at the top.

In 1931, 18-year-old Marjorie Robbins had joined Coastal as a booking clerk at Lupus Street, and was one of the first people to work in the state-of-the-art booking hall at Victoria Coach Station when it opened the following year. In January 1971, Mr T Gailey, Coastal's chairman at that time, presented her with a tea and coffee set to commemorate her 40 years' service with the company. Most of that time had been spent controlling and developing the operation of the booking hall — no mean feat when considering the varying levels of demand not just from season to season, but from hour to hour. At the end of April 1971, 'Robbie', as she was known to everyone at the coach station, became seriously ill, and she died the

"When the history of the industry comes to be chronicled, there will be no more romantic chapter than that describing the growth of London Coastal Coaches Limited." (Bus and Coach Magazine, April 1932)

following year having devoted vitually her whole life to Coastal.

To those members of Coastal's Lupus Street staff already mentioned can be added others who were to join the awesome new Victoria Coach Station and remain on the payroll often until retirement. In 1932, Frank Garman joined Coastal as a

post boy almost immediately upon the opening of Victoria Coach Station, and quickly moved on to the agency accounts department. At the outbreak of the Second World War in 1939 he was the first member of Coastal's staff to go into the services — he joined the army — and when the war was over he returned to Victoria Coach Station to take over agency administration. He retired from the position of Agency Superintendent in 1978.

In 1936, Charlie Howard, a railway clerk from Suffolk, joined Coastal as a ticket clerk, and after his war service he returned to take over the ticket audit department, introduce the punch-card accounting system and control ticket supplies and refunds. He remained with Coastal for 34 years until his retirement in 1980.

Another long-serving stalwart joined Coastal in 1937 as a shorthand typist. At various times during her 40 years with Coastal, Olive King was secretary to George Newman, Fred Robinson and Len Corbett. Particularly in the early postwar days of the 1940s and 1950s when the industry was growing at such a hectic pace, a strong and dependable secretarial back-up was essential. Retiring in 1977, Olive King, who by marriage had become Olive Staples, was yet another example of the long-term devotion that so many people gave to the company.

London Coastal Coaches Limited was now a very strong component indeed in the coaching industry, even though it didn't own a single coach. It had by far the best coach station and a strong network of agents throughout London and the suburbs. The major coach operators who were either shareholders or associate companies now moved their services to Victoria Coach Station and it would not be long before other operators would transfer their allegiance to Coastal. Until then, several of the provincial operating companies had their own offices in London, sometimes just as booking and control offices, but often as central London loading points, particularly if they were also using the rather less conveniently located Terminal Coach Station. However, as many of them gradually joined the Coastal fold and, benefiting from the efficiency of the London Coastal Coaches arrangements, began to close their own London offices, so for a while Coastal opened its own satellite offices away from Victoria Coach Station. McShanes to Birmingham and Liverpool and Standerwick's to Blackpool, for example, shared a London

> *"Those who predicted a 'white elephant' will have to try again." (Coaching Journal comment when reporting successful letting of Victoria Coach Station office accommodation, February 1933)*

Opening Day, March 10th 1932, and a Daimler from the West London Coach Company fleet arrives at Victoria Coach Station at the start of a journey to Aylesbury – a route that was soon to pass to Green Line. Mr P J Pybus, the Minister of Transport, having performed the opening ceremony just a short while before, stands with the Revd E St George Shomberg, the Mayor of Westminster, doing some coach-spotting. *(LCCc)*

Three pictures showing alterations to the western wall of Victoria Coach Station (backing onto Peabody Buildings). The first, taken in 1932 soon after the official opening of the coach station, shows the small undercover arrivals or service area almost as originally planned; the second shows how much provision had been made for arriving passengers, including an adequate area for meeting and greeting; and the third shows the original service area having been converted into inspectors' offices – the arrivals platform remains unchanged, but obvious advantage has been taken of advertising potential. *(LCCc)*

office in Woburn Place, Bloomsbury, but this closed in 1933 and London Coastal opened a booking office almost next door, in the Royal Hotel Building. The Lower Belgrave Street office was still in operation at that time and both offices came under the supervision of Len Turnham. By 1936 Coastal had offices at 7 Lower Belgrave Street, Victoria; 1 Terminus Place, Victoria; 47 Woburn Place, Russell Square; 7 South Side, Clapham Common and 299 Hammersmith Road, Hammersmith; some lasted for only a short time and the Brixton office which had been listed in the timetables of the Lupus Street period seems to have long-since gone. By 1937, as publicity of that year shows, only the Lower Belgrave Street and Clapham Common offices remained.

Black & White of Cheltenham had an office in Hammersmith Bridge Road, Greyhound of Bristol in Hammersmith Road, Imperial Motor Services of Liverpool in Southampton Row and Fingland's of Manchester operated a full travel agency service from prestigious offices at Fingland House in Southampton Row having appointed Mr I Benjamin as their overall London manager. Mr Benjamin had transferred from the Bush House booking office which had been run on a cooperative basis by Finglands, John Bull, Birch Brothers, Batten's and Farnham Blue.

☙ ❧

The relationship between the Coastal operators and the Coastal agents was simple. The agents directed all booking requests through Coastal, issued a Coastal ticket and made payment for sales, less their commission, to Coastal who, after deduction of administration fees, apportioned the receipts among the operators. In the London area, the Coastal operators would recognise only Coastal agents, and would not appoint agents independently or accept the tickets of other booking organisations.

Elsewhere, though, the situation became more and more confused and acrimonious. The independent operators in a few cases issued ticket books directly to agents, but it was more usual for main agents   so called   to set themselves up in business as booking agents (and sometimes control agents) with their own ticket books which they would issue to appointed sub-agents. The result was that independent coach operators would accept the tickets of several main agents who were each vying for the business of the sub-agents.

Then came 1933, a year that was to see the start of a great deal of activity and change.

In February, General Travel Agency (London) Limited (GTA), which was described in Coaching Journal of that month as being intimately associated with Red & White Motors Limited, and their associated companies, took over the London Terminal Station and booking facilities of Coach Travel Limited. (As we have seen, Coach Travel Limited was the company set up originally by Messrs Toms and Boon and

The cigarette salesman seems more keen to take advantage of this photo-opportunity than to sell his wares to the passengers boarding the Southdown Leyland Tiger TS2 on the London to Brighton route – 1933. *(LCCc)*

was the first contender for the site by then occupied by Victoria Coach Station; and Red & White was already operating services into London Terminal Station). GTA was also a main agent of some importance, and had sub-agents who issued GTA tickets.

In the meantime Central London Coach Station had got into financial difficulties and Yelloway, Fingland's and the landlord of the Coach Station site had planned a rescue package. However, Charles Fingland died unexpectedly, so plans had to be changed rapidly. Charlie Fingland, as he was known by all, although in the coach business for only four years (since 1929 when he bought a coach and operated between Manchester and Blackpool) was a far-seeing character of some importance in the coaching industry during those days of rapid growth. A tester with Rolls Royce, he started Fingland's Hire Cars, a luxury private car hire company in Rusholme, before setting up Fingland's Booking and Coach Stations Limited in Manchester.

A new company, Central London Coach Station (1933) Limited, was formed by, among others, Yelloway, Varsity, Underwoods and Red and White! They were also joined by Motor Coach Ticket Clearing House Limited, but the Central London ticket (famously known as the Gold ticket) and booking organisation was maintained, although reorganised. But the end was in sight for Central London Coach Station and although it remained active for a little longer, within three years the only major operators still using it were Yelloway and Empire's Best.

At the same time, came a new purpose-built coach station just around the corner from Central London Coach Station on a site almost opposite King's Cross and St Pancras railway stations. It too had a separate entrance and exit for the vehicles, one being on Belgrove Street and the other on Argyll Street, and was the first of the coach stations to be called King's Cross Coach Station (King's Cross Coach Station No. 1). Several of the operators that, until then, had been using Central London Coach Station, transferred there. However, the life of this coach station was also very short as it more or less closed at the outbreak of war in 1939. A few services continued until the government ban on services in 1942, and it was used again for a short while from 1946 until being closed in September 1947 when the lease ran out.

An atmospheric mid-1930s glimpse of Victoria Coach Station, on the facing page, with passengers waiting to depart and some early transport enthusiasts who had come on their scooters. They are looking away from the Maidstone and District Leyland Tiger, has something even more up to date just arrived to hold their interest? *(LCCc)*

Or were they perhaps watching this Southdown departure, above, another similar Leyland but in the operator's green livery rather than Maidstone's green. The Associated Daimler on the right was a much rarer model than the Leylands, and represented an association between the AEC and Daimler companies which lasted only from 1926 to 1928. *(LCCc)*

In the view below another Maidstone vehicle seems to be taking on board a good load of passengers, and the luggage racks are about to be well-filled judging by the hand luggage in view. The advert for AEC vehicles in the background was a familiar sight for passengers, but how many of them would have known if their coach's chassis was actually from the Southall factory? *(LCCc)*

Confident in the knowledge that Coastal arrangements were so straightforward and efficient by comparison, the management of London Coastal Coaches Limited were, no doubt, looking on with sardonic amusement and self-satisfaction.

However, by then many of the independent coach firms had realised that the situation was becoming unsatisfactory and Mr F A Flin, together with numerous independent operators, set up a new company called PSV Operators Limited to perform a service for the independent companies similar to that which Coastal was performing for its associated companies. They proposed that one ticket only — the PSV ticket — should be solely accepted by their members to replace all the various other main-agent tickets, and a similar payment

scheme to the Coastal system should apply (i.e. between agent and PSV Operators, and between PSV Operators and the independent coach companies). This was clearly a sensible arrangement, and from the list of original PSV Operators Limited board members — most to remain substantial personalities in the industry for a long time — one can see the strength of the emerging organisation. PSV Operators Limited acquired comfortable offices in First Avenue House, Bedford Row. The offices had originally been part of the First Avenue Hotel, but because of the slump in the tourist trade at that time were converted into well-appointed offices with central heating and luxurious heavy carpets. The coaching industry was, indeed, taking on an impressive air.

Some years before, the agents had very wisely formed the Booking Agents Association of Great Britain Limited, which already had a strong voice in discussions, and many names appeared on the BAA committee in those early 1930s years that were to remain well respected within the travel trade for many years to come. (The BAA continued to be the agent's voice in the industry until it was eventually superceded by the

A mid-1930s departure scene – with drivers loading luggage on coach roofs. Keith & Boyle would soon revolutionise this activity with their patented drop frame extension to the coach chassis, enabling a commodious luggage boot to be provided and thereby keeping passenger's effects safe and dry. *(LCCc)*

coach travel section of ABTA [The Association of British Travel Agents]. Notable among the original committee is Mr F Phipard Shears, whose office in Chiswick was one of Coastal's busiest agencies. Despite being fiercely critical of the industry at times, Mr Phipard Shears was well respected by everyone; in typical fighting spirit, at the Coastal Conference at the Kensington Close Hotel in 1972, when the new NBC symbol was being launched, he said "we need timetables and brochures not signs".)

Discussions were often quite heated, but on the whole members of the BAA committee were in favour of the PSV Operators Limited one-ticket scheme, although it took some time to agree an agency contract, and not surprisingly one of the sticking points was the rate of commission to be paid to agents. Apparently it had been usual for some coach operators to offer agents higher commission rates than others in order to divert passengers to their services; with PSV Operators setting down a maximum 10% to ordinary agents and 15% to control agents, the PSV Operators set rates were bitter pills for some ordinary agents to swallow. Furthermore, agents in close

proximity to pick-up points, who often acted as unofficial information offices or waiting rooms, felt that they should be paid more. At one stage during the initial discussions the BAA even advised its members to accept the ticket book but not to sign the Agreement. Thus the confusion in the industry, or to be more exact the independent sector of the industry, was to continue for a little longer.

Judging by a committee meeting of the BAA, it can be assumed that a certain coolness also existed between the BAA and Coastal, as it is reported that: "Mr Bailey pointed out the occasion 'might' arise when, in the interests of members, it 'might be advisable' to confer with the board of London Coastal Coaches Limited".

For a while PSV Operators Limited held back on their stipulation that operators within their group should recognise only PSV tickets and not those of any other main agents, for (again in 1933) we learn from an announcement to agents that Orange Luxury Coaches (not then part of George Ewer, but a fleet name of Keith Boyle Limited) would accept General Travel Agency, King's Cross, Motor Coach Ticket Clearing

During the early 1930s the motor coach was evolving from the erstwhile bus shell into the luxury coach, as seen in the illustrations on this page and opposite. Low-backed seats gave place to luxury cushion seating, but one bugbear of the industry during this time was, as illustrated previously, the question of where to accommodate all the luggage. The drop-frame chassis extension was not in use yet, and so all the vehicles shown here, with one exception, utilised roof racks. Bromilow & Edwards, of Bolton, well-known as builders of tipper lorries, found an early solution to this problem by constructing what became termed an 'observation coach' body. The design necessitated the removal of the entrance door to the front of the body, a feature that was soon taken up by other builders. The Standerwick and John Bull coaches also display a feature that was becoming increasingly common, that of the fitted toilet compartment, clearly indicated by the opaque stylised window with its leaded-light pattern in the bay behind the door. The use of Empires Best and Yelloway vehicles on this page to illustrate these developments is doubly interesting, as by 1936 these were the only two major operators using the Central London Coach Station, such was the impact of Victoria Coach Station. *(STA; Dave Haddock collection)*

The three examples of coaches from official photographs all taken by body maker Duple of Hendon, opposite, show the gradual development of the marque. One of a great number of London's coachbuilders be found in the late 1920s Duple was, by the mid-1930s, one of the few survivors. *(STA)*

John Bull of Blackpool later passed to Standerwick, also of Blackpool. Standerwick became a Ribble subsidiary. (*STA both*)

South Midland eventually became a subsidiary of City of Oxford Motor Services Ltd. (*STA*)

House and Rickards tickets, as well as PSV. However, circular letters were sent out to agents in February 1933 by Timpsons, United and George Ewer announcing that from a certain date only their own and the new PSV tickets would be accepted by them, and it is at this point we begin to see the gradual dissolution of main agents, some of which went into liquidation. Within just two or three years London agents had only London Coastal Coaches Limited and PSV Operators tickets to issue.

But there was another difficulty about to raise its head. Coastal had already warned its less enthusiastic or less efficient agents that they could lose their agency appointments in favour of more productive agents. At the same time, PSV Operators Limited were planning to increase the number of agents in the London area to more than 2,000 (then, more than three times the number of Coastal agents) but were also intent on getting rid of worthless agents, and, indeed, the agents themselves were aware that there were some of their number who were deadwood.

Understandably, agents holding Coastal agencies began to worry about the attitude Coastal might take if they also held a PSV agency. Clearly, though, PSV Operators Limited seemed to think themselves the equal of London Coastal Coaches Limited and took the lead in the matter by writing to all their agents saying that the holding of Coastal tickets "would not debar them" from holding PSV tickets. The anxiety of the agents, of course, was the other way round. Coastal, on the other hand, felt that the statement by PSV Operators could be misinterpreted, and might seem to imply that there was some common agreement between the two organisations, so it hastily retaliated with an announcement to its agents that the PSV ticket book "has nothing whatsoever to do with London Coastal Coaches; that they have not co-operated in its production, and that the tickets cannot be accepted or bookings effected on any charts held by London Coastal Coaches Limited".

By then many of the PSV agents were afraid that too many new agents would open in close proximity to themselves, so they proposed, unsuccessfully, a distance limit as protection against such competition. They certainly had good cause for concern, as eventually there were a great many extra PSV Operators agents in the London area; maybe not two-a-penny, but by comparison a Coastal agency appointment was thought of as being very prestigious, at least by the agents concerned.

The year 1933 had certainly been one of considerable upheaval in many ways.

ⓒ ⓑ

Also in 1933 came the legislation that resulted from enquiries set up by the Minister of Transport the previous year under the chairmanship of Lord Amultree, and concerning the rapidly worsening state of traffic congestion in London. Briefly,

These two Southdown advertisements clearly show the alternative coach styling mentioned earlier. In the example below the driver now has his own compartment, separated from the distractions of the passengers, but taking away some of the atmosphere and removing any possibility of commentary on the passing scenery or other information until the advent of on-board radios with microphones arrived. The bonnetted Leyland was unusual by the time of the other advert, dated 1936, but Southdown obviously found them suited to the task. Note that the word 'tour' is nowhere to be seen. For fear of being mistaken for a "fantail" holiday operator, *Southdown* used the term 'coach cruises'. *(Jim Russell collection)*

SOUTHDOWN
MOTOR SERVICES LIMITED

THE SERVICES FOR

**BOGNOR REGIS
BRIGHTON
CHICHESTER
EASTBOURNE
FAREHAM
GOSPORT
HORSHAM
LITTLEHAMPTON
PORTSMOUTH & SOUTHSEA
WORTHING
and all Parts of Sussex**

PLEASE NOTE! Improved services King's Cross, Victoria, etc., to HINDHEAD AND SOUTHSEA.

Publicity Supplies, and Particulars of Through Bookings, Local Connections, etc. from the Victoria Coach Station

Main London Agents: **LONDON COASTAL COACHES LIMITED**
VICTORIA COACH STATION, BUCKINGHAM PALACE ROAD, S.W.I. Sloane 0202

the various 1933 legislations included the formation of the London Passenger Transport Board (LPTB) with the operation of all bus and coach services within approximately a 30-mile radius of central London being transferred to the new board, and the introduction of restrictions on the cross-London routes to be taken by provincial coaches operating to London coach stations, which would keep them away from the most heavily congested central London streets.

Most of the longer-distance services (within that 30-mile radius) became LPTB Green Line routes. Green Line had been in operation since 1930 and had been formed from the services of several independent operators in the London area and the suburbs.

The new LPTB arrangements affected Victoria Coach Station very little. It lost a couple of services and gained a couple. Redcar, who since 1928 had been operating from Lupus Street to Tunbridge Wells and had transferred to Victoria Coach Station in 1932, became part of Green Line and transferred its terminal to Eccleston Bridge; and West London Coaches, who had operated from Lupus Street and later Victoria Coach Station to Aylesbury, also transferred to Green Line. Additionally, some of the services from Victoria could not now carry passengers within the London area; Maidstone & District, for example, could no longer carry passengers to Wrotham on its Victoria to Maidstone service, or to Gravesend on its Gillingham service.

Services eventually gained by Victoria Coach Station were generally to places in south-east England, but beyond the 30-mile radius from central London.

Farnham Blue had been operating from Farnham to Aldwych, and Aldershot & District's service was from Farnham to Great Scotland Yard. Aldershot & District bought out Farnham Blue in October 1934, and transferred the services to Victoria Coach Station.

The other route gain for Victoria Coach Station took longer to come into effect. Thackrays Way and Ledbury Transport, with services from Oxford Circus to Reading, transferred their London terminal to King's Cross Coach Station on the introduction of the new 1933 legislation. They were sold to Thames Valley in 1934, but did not transfer to Victoria Coach Station until 1946, upon resumption of their services after the war.

Inevitably, though, many of the long-distance operators were to amalgamate their services, and this inevitably resulted in independent operators being taken over by the big companies who were already operating into Victoria Coach Station. Gradually throughout the 1930s fewer and fewer long distance services were available to PSV Operators agents.

The PSV Operators vs Coastal situation became almost a David and Goliath relationship, and one can sense the animosity in the following editorial from the PSV News of April 1936, and punctuated exactly as it appeared:

"THE P.S.V. – COASTAL AGENT"

Since 1935 some changes have introduced themselves into the trade. Fingland, Charlton, Fleetways have 'gone over.' As regards the first, they have sold out to the Ribble group who are 100 per cent Coastal. Not that it matters 'a damn' as far as the P.S.V. agent is concerned, because he has Yelloways to book on for Manchester, and Scout for intermediates such as Coventry, Birmingham, Newcastle-under-Lyme, Knutsford etc. a prominent display of Yelloway and Scout's posters outside the agent's shop will quickly produce the 'goods.'

The services to Cheltenham and South Wales were generally provided by Black & White and Red & White, which despite the similarity in titles, were two very distinct and each in their own ways, very individual companies. Both were founder members of the Associated Motorways pool.

Black & White Motorways Ltd was unusual in that from 1930 it was jointly owned by Birmingham & Midland Motor Omnibus Co (Midland Red), Bristol Tramways & Carriage Co (later owners of Greyhound) and City of Oxford Motor Services.

Later in the opening day on March 10th 1932, above, and with the official opening ceremony now over, and the crowds dispersed, a *Black & White Motorways* departure awaits its passengers. (LCCc)

Red & White, based at Chepstow, was owned by the Watts family and the company were staunch Albion supporters, frequently fitted with bodies from Northern Counties of Wigan, but in this case by Duple. The company remained independent until 1950 when it was purchased by the British Transport Commission. (Richard Waters collection)

TRAVEL THE
KING'S HIGHWAY
BY
BLACK & WHITE
RED & WHITE
SOUTH MIDLAND
ALDERSHOT & DIST.
THAMES VALLEY

BOOK THROUGH
LONDON COASTAL COACHES LTD
VICTORIA COACH STATION S.W.I.

In the case of Charlton who have joined the United-Majestic-Orange Group, P.S.V. agents already enjoy booking facilities on this group. Fleetways, taken over by the Lincolnshire Road Car Company will also continue present booking arrangements, so that the P.S.V. agent has actually lost nothing by the taking over of these three companies. It all depends on him, however, how long he will enjoy these faciltites.

To be perfectly frank. At the present moment there are four associate, i.e. Coastal groups, who accept P.S.V. bookings, namely United Automobile, United Counties, West Yorkshire, and Lincolnshire Road Car. These four have faith in the non-Coastal agent with the publicity he can display, the bookings he can account for, the passengers he can produce, (there used to be five but Red and White Services, persuaded by Black and White Motorways, have thought fit to spurn all independent bookings).

A number of these P.S.V. agents hold also Coastal ticket books and we gather they are being persuaded (a mild term) to use the Coastal book when booking on United Automobile, United Counties and West Yorkshire – shortly, no doubt, the same will apply to the Lincolnshire Road Car Co. Such agents are, of course, free to follow their own inclinations. But will they be wise in obeying such pressure? We doubt it. On the contrary, they should make every effort to put as many bookings on the P.S.V. ticket as possible, and not only qualify for the retrospective (extra?) commission, but also prove that long-distance bookings cannot be a monopoly of any given group of agents, but should be open to all if the machinations of the railways are to be countered.

We, therefore, hope that every booking agent will, in the interests of the industry, use his P.S.V. ticket only for booking a United Automobile, United Counties, West Yorkshire and the Lincolnshire Road Car Co."

The acceptance of P.S.V. Operators tickets on these Coastal services lasted for only a very short time.

Possibly the rancour within the trade is, to a large extent, understandable. If we are to think of Mr Turnham's trip to Brighton in 1919 as the starting post for the coaching industry, it had been in existence for a mere decade and a half. Companies and personalities were still flexing their muscles and weighing each other up; it was an industry growing at a remarkable rate and the pecking order amongst the players was not yet properly defined. Clearly Coastal was somewhere near the top of the pile, but it could not afford to be complacent.

Charles C Knights, FSMA, a highly respected commentator of the time, said in May 1936: "The word 'co-operation' is so freely used these days in the trade that one would get the impression that in the Road Passenger industry real efforts are being taken to co-operate. It is to be regretted, however, that in this respect no signs of improvement are made. The Combine (presumably London Coastal Coaches Limited) and the independent groups are as far apart as the poles, showing not the slightest inclination to get together".

With great initiative, and no doubt to combat the disadvantage of not having resort-based members, in 1936 PSV Operators opened offices or kiosks at most of the seaside resorts to offer information and help to passengers of any of its operator members. Mostly these were in coach parks but in Clacton the nominated office was the Eastern National garage in Wash Lane, so maybe there was a little co-operation after all.

☙ ❧

From all the reports of the time, it would be very easy to believe that bad blood existed throughout the whole of the industry: Coastal vs PSV Operators Limited for supremacy; agents vs Coastal and PSV Operators for more commission; PSV Operators and Coastal vs unproductive agents for more business; and PSV Operators vs deserting coach companies. It is quite extraordinary therefore to discover an active social side to the business, which spread happily into all quarters and through all factions of the trade; it was even suggested at one point that a social club should be formed somewhere in the London area for the entire coaching industry that was to be called The Coaching Club. It didn't happen, but dinner dances, football matches, and other social gatherings were frequently held.

So prevalent was this bonhomie that during the first quarter of 1933, a period of apparently severe in-fighting within the business, Coastal decided it needed a Company Social Secretary to promote its social activities and added the job to Len Corbett's position of Traffic Manager. A whole series of Coastal Dances was held, with an announcement that "undoubtedly the last of the season" (presumably the socialising, not the coaching, season) was to be held at Caxton Hall, Westminster on Monday, 27th March, with dancing until 1.30am when coaches would be available to take the revellers home. And all for the cost of 2/6d (12½p).

PSV Operators produced a series of pamphlets featuring independent services from 16 different locations around London, which were available free to PSV agents so long as they would guarantee a door-to-door distribution. The industry was lively and competitive and the number of coach operating companies huge, so promotional gimmicks and plentiful publicity supplies were vital if success was to be achieved and maintained.

Advertising styles soon become dated, but they capture the spirit of the times. Coaching industry advertising is no different, and trade advertisements in particular go a long way in portraying the mood of the business at that moment. But in some ways poster design for the coaching industry was a little disappointing although colourful, it tended too often to be wordy and insufficiently pictorial. One of the major obstacles to good poster advertising for coach services at this time was the continuing emergence of superb railway posters; as chalk and cheese is probably the best way to compare them. The railway companies were contracting some of the best professional artists, and the railway poster had become an art form in itself. Furthermore, many of the local authorities joined forces with the railway companies and shared in the cost of promotion, often taking the lion's share of the expense; there are few if any examples of similar cooperation with coach companies.

☙ ❧

In the same three-month period, the Booking Agents Association held a dinner dance at the Imperial Hotel for 9/

6d (47½p) with dinner, or 3/6d (17½p) dancing only, and a Grand National Sweep; the Croydon & District Motor Coach Owners Association held a dinner-dance at the Greyhound in Croydon; Highway Coaches held their second dance of the season at Porchester Hall; Timpsons, who by then had their own social and athletic club, held a dance at Woolwich Town Hall; Southdown held a Carnival Dance at the Regent Dance Hall Brighton and arranged coaches to take everyone home afterwards including a large contingent from London Coastal Coaches Limited; and there was a Coaching Trade Night at the Versailles Club in Regent Street. The BAA proposed forming a football club, but Timpsons already had one and played a match versus Agents/Operators whose team included staff members from Finglands, Standerwicks, MacShanes, Coaching Journal and London Coastal. Coaching Journal arranged a return match in Eltham, and to ensure that plenty of supporters were there to support them, coaches were provided free of charge by Orange Luxury and United Service Transport.

As the years passed, the frivolities went from strength to strength and at the start of 1936 PSV Operators held a dance at the Porchester Hall with a massive guest list which included representatives from London Coastal, and a month later London Coastal held a Grand Carnival Ball, also at the Porchester Hall. Grey-Green had just set up its own Football and Social Club; the Booking Agents Association couldn't decide whether their official outing should be to Southend on Eagle Steamers, or by coach to Windsor followed by a boat trip on the Thames, and a dance at a wayside river-house; and Red and White fixed their first annual staff outing from anywhere on their network via Cheltenham to London with one night's accommodation, three meals and a London sightseeing tour all for 26/- per head (£1.30p).

The unexpected spirit of friendship that had been unleashed so lavishly in those early days was to continue for many decades, and still exists, although there is probably a lot less jollification now.

☙ ❧

Throughout the industry, attitudes to publicity had been acute, even from the very early days, and by the 1930s it had in many ways become quite sophisticated. Every coach operator produced literature to promote his **or her** services, and it was essential to keep agents supplied promptly with up-to-date information and publicity materials. (There were many ladies involved in the industry as agents and coach operators: Mrs Fingland was appointed managing director of Fingland's Booking and Coach Stations Limited upon the death of her husband Charles in 1932; and it would be particularly remiss not to mention Miss Culverhouse of Venture Transport in Hendon   respected by everyone, she was a stalwart in the business for many years).

Coastal, being by then such a large organisation and acting on behalf of its associated companies, already had a publicity department under the control of Mr Lambert and a publicity van which made regular monthly calls on agents; it was less easy for independent operators in the provinces or for smaller operators in London who lacked the manpower to ensure regular agency visits   they relied on Royal Mail, which was expensive for bulk supplies of leaflets and unsatisfactory for the distribution of flimsy posters. One admires, therefore, the enterprise of a firm that set itself up in Alexandra Mews, Paddington as the London Publicity Distributing Company and took over the distribution needs of many of the independent operators. More and more, there was room in the growing industry for far-sighted entrepreneurs.

Roadway Publications, with their Roadway Motor Coach Timetable for Great Britain, was another firm quick to benefit from the network of express coach services. It retailed at 6d (2½p), but agents were able to buy it at one-third discount and the publishers supplied plenty of supportive display materials. London Coastal Coaches had produced a comprehensive timetable much earlier, in 1926, but it would be unfair to compare this with the Roadway publication, which covered the whole country. Coastal's innovative first timetable included only the details of its associate companies' routes into Lupus Street and was a 20-page booklet; in 1930 it was issued for the first time in ABC format, reverted to standard timetable in 1932 and eventually appeared in loose-leaf form.

From the 1930s Coastal produced each year a booklet Coach Travel   which listed all the destinations available from Victoria Coach Station together with all applicable fares including seasonal variations. It was fully illustrated, and included a good deal of promotional editorial. On average during the 1930s, 250,000 copies were produced each year, which were distributed free of charge both at Victoria Coach Station and through Coastal agents. Coach Travel was still being published in 1970.

One of the many coaching industry dances held at the Porchester Hall in 1933. *(Jim Russell collection.)*

THE GREAT NORTH ROAD

SCENE 2: *A "pukkah" Motor Coach Agency.*

AGENT: Good evening, Sir. Did you enjoy your journey to Glasgow?

CUSTOMER: Yes, very much so. But—I say—how on earth do you remember me? This is a flourishing business, and you must have seen thousands of people since you booked me to Glasgow by

ORANGE BROTHERS

—five months ago—and yet you recognised me the moment you saw me, and even remembered the town to which you booked me.

AGENT: That is true, Sir. Of course it is good business for any salesman to remember every little detail regarding each of his customers. But in your case—I was expecting you.

CUSTOMER: Expecting me?

AGENT: Yes, Sir. You see, I have found from experience that passengers booked on

ORANGE BROTHERS'

Services invariably return to me to let me know how they appreciated the journey. In fact, to such an extent is this so, that it has become quite an axiom with agents in the trade.

CUSTOMER: I understand now. "Axiom" is the right word to use in my case, anyhow, because I want you to book me two period returns to South Shields by **ORANGE BROS.**, leaving King's Cross Motor Coach Station at 11.30 a.m., next Wednesday.

AGENT: That's the kind of appreciation we like to receive, best of all, Sir.

Hullo, Exchange. Give me **TERMINUS 6185.**

An Orange Brothers mid-1930s departure for Newcastle with connections to Edinburgh and Glasgow. The service, operated jointly with United Automobile Services one of whose vehicles is seen at the foot of the page, provided through bookings to many of the border towns by changing coaches at Newcastle. Sportingly, the timetable provided to agents pointed out that direct services to Edinburgh and Glasgow were available by SMT and Western – and even told them from which leaflets to find the details. (LCCc)

Typical of many 1930s coach booking offices, J. Ridd was both tobacconist and booking agent, although judging by his window display, he seemed to consider cigarette sales merely a sideline. Before the pattern of services to and from London became more settled after the introduction of the 1930 Road Traffic Act, there was competition on many of the routes, as the above advertisement demonstrates. Majestic eventually became part of the North Western/Midland Red provision (see page 58) whilst South Wales Express was taken over by Associated Motorways. A Majestic coach is shown below. *(LCCc both)*
Facing page:
A selection of advertisements from the trade press of the early 1930s. Clearly the Advertising Standards Authority has not yet come into existence with adverts such as that from MTC on the top right being published in *'PSV News'*. *(Jim Russell collection)*

The changing 'thirties

Although this book is not primarily concerned with the vehicles themselves, there were occasional advancements in passenger comforts that are, if nothing else, amusing to dwell on for a moment or two. In 1932 coaches were first equipped with radios, and Fingland's Radio Coaches were seen on the road. It was commented in **Coaching Journal** in February 1933 that "this obviously is where wireless entertainment will be appreciated at its fullest". It is hard for us now to realise the novelty of radio in those days, but in the early part of the 1930s to have coaches with radio gave operators a strong promotional advantage. The following account from a correspondent to Coaching Journal highlights the wide-eyed wonder of it all at that time: "Accepting Duple's invitation to a private view of the wireless sets being installed in a number of their latest coaches, I went down to their works at Hendon last week and my eyes and ears were opened. The demonstration I witnessed was on one of Fingland's five new and really 'splendiferous' AEC Regals. The reception was perfect — as clear as any set I have heard, and absolutely unaffected by the running of the engine or when passing anything electrical, such as tram wires, generating stations etc. This is due to suppressors, which are placed on the sparking plugs, magneto, cut-out, dynamo, etc. A double aerial runs around the top of the coach, and the set is placed under the driver's seat with the switching in a convenient place in his cabin so that there is no need for him to take his eyes of the road when switching on or changing stations. The receiver, in the form of a neat cabinet, is inside the coach. The wonderful 7-valve super hetrodyne set — for it is wonderful — costs about £50 for the complete installation, and apart from Fingland's coaches, Corona are having them fitted, and Standerwicks and a number of other operators are favourably considering the matter. Quite obviously they have come to stay — to be an added attraction for road travellers. Operators and agents please note."

∞ ∞

The efficient and professional approach by the whole of the London Coastal management is apparent from the outset, and is particularly noteworthy when it is recalled that they had to accommodate the different operating practices of many coach companies into one smooth-running function. This not only involved the actual movement of the coaches into and out of Victoria Coach Station, and the safe handling of ever-increasing numbers of passengers, but also the accurate recording of reservation details, and the speedy dissemination of information to the network of agents.

An important early Coastal innovation was to assemble all the timetables of the services from Victoria Coach Station, organise them into logical order, produce them numerically on standard octavo pages and supply them in punched-hole spring binders for use by coach station booking and enquiry clerks, and agents. These binders had additional pages giving an index of all the places served from Victoria Coach Station; general information about luggage, dogs, refunds, lost tickets, etc. and information about getting there by bus or tram. The timetable binder was invaluable to the booking clerk, and with ticket book and telephone formed the essential three Ts.

Most of the London Transport bus routes to Victoria in the 1930s remained to a large extent unaltered until the 1960s, although services 10 from Abridge and 134 from Potters Bar then ran beyond Victoria Railway Station to Victoria Coach Station, and from south London there were no fewer than six tram routes terminating in nearby Vauxhall Bridge Road.

Coastal's loose-leaf timetable for staff and agents continued until late in the 1960s, and although the leaflet numbering system was revised after the war, and the page size eventually increased to quarto, the operating companies and the routes operating from Victoria Coach Station at the end of the 1930s remained, just like the bus services bringing passengers to Victoria Coach Station, almost unaltered until the 1960s.

PSV Operators also regularly produced an agents' timetable during the 1930s, which covered the services of its operator members, but this was not continued after the war.

Reflecting what was becoming an acceptable common practice in other areas of retail commerce — payment by instalments — at the start of 1936 Coastal introduced a coach tickets by instalment plan under the name Travel Club. This was simply a savings stamps scheme, with the stamps being bought at Victoria Coach Station or from Coastal agents; ahead of its time though it was, the scheme did not achieve the success it deserved. One stumbling block seems to have been that it was not received very enthusiastically by the agents with only 1 in 10 showing any interest in the bold new idea when it was first introduced. It was not really a credit or hire-purchase scheme but merely a savings plan and was another significant first for Coastal.

By the end of 1937 the industry had settled down. For several years lots of big fish had been swallowing smaller fish and many of the provincial companies that had been operating into London had been taken over by various of the bigger concerns, so that by then the majority of the principal long-distance express services to London operated to Victoria Coach Station. Several independent operators were using King's Cross Coach Station, but any other coach stations, like the new Grey Green example at Mile End Road, were chiefly to service the express services and excursions of the coach company owning them.

But one strange anomaly did arise. In that same year, 1937, Red and White acquired London Terminal Coach Station and Blue Belle Coaching Services (which somewhere along the line had added the 'e' to the word Bell) with hopes of creating an interlinking facility between its own services from South Wales, and the Blue Belle services to the south coast resorts. (It is believed that Mr Toms and Mr Boon left the coaching industry upon the sale of Terminal Coach Station to Red and White. Terminal Coach Station was completely destroyed by bombing in 1940, and Blue Belle was acquired after the war by United Service Transport Limited.)

This latter financial move created a truly extraordinary situation which did not sit too well on the Coastal vs Independents landscape. Red & White services to London were by then operating as part of the Associated Motorways network (a Coastal-related organisation) and for a while Associated Motorways services operated via Victoria Coach Station (strictly Coastal) and then continued south of the river to terminate at Terminal Coach Station (a diehard independent stronghold).

❧ ❧

Another aspect of coaching to flourish in the 1930s was the **tour**, in which several highly professional companies specialised; in addition many operators of express coach services also ran (so called) coach tours. Anomalies soon became apparent and disagreements arose. The chief problem seemed to be in deciding exactly what the word tour meant and what constituted a coach tour.

It was obvious that, when a coach took a specific circuitous route, staying overnight at different points en route, with the specific and sole purpose of enjoying the various amenities and scenery in an area, it was quite correctly a tour. How, though, could one describe a holiday where passengers travelled by a regular express service to one specific destination, stayed in one hotel for the entire holiday, and were provided with local sightseeing trips during their stay? Surely this could not be termed a tour   it was just a coach journey, a hotel booking, and a handful of day or half day trips. Soon the term fantail tour was used for the latter, and eventually centred holiday or inclusive holiday.

Some of the earliest firms to offer coach tours in the true sense of the term from London were Glenton, Southdown, SMT (Scottish Omnibuses) and Wallace Arnold, but virtually every other firm with an express service to anywhere offered the fantail type holiday, with Black & White dabbling in both (it had tours through the West Country and South Coast, as well as holidays centred in Cheltenham with day trips to South Wales, the Wye Valley and the Cotswolds). With an 8-day tour of Devon & Cornwall averaging eight guineas (£8.40) or a 12-day tour of Scotland averaging twelve guineas (£12.60), it is easy to understand why agents were keen to sell these holidays; and as the whole concept of seeing the country and taking holidays became more a part of everyday life for an increasingly large part of society, coach operators were very happy to cater to the demand. (For the adventurous and wealthy, a 15-day tour through France in an 8-seat Rolls Royce was available for £29.)

Crosville combined both express service and coach tour, and issued a programme of conducted tours in Scotland and Yorkshire from London. This was disingenuous, for the tours started in Chester, and passengers from London joined them by using the company's regular London to Liverpool express service from Victoria Coach Station. Nevertheless, at £20 for a 14-day holiday these were very popular and, as the programme stated, a deposit of 10/- (50p) secured a seat.

Coach tours were very important for Coastal too, as they were selling the tours and holidays of their associated companies; indeed, so important was this business to Coastal that any bona fide agent, whether Coastal or non-Coastal, could book on tours and holidays from Victoria Coach Station and be paid full commission.

Soon the when-is-a-tour-not-a-tour situation became more acrimonious and the coach tour business very divided. Firms operating proper touring holidays began calling their holidays coach cruises in order to differentiate them clearly from the fantail arrangements. Coach cruises represented the superior side of coaching, and without doubt offered a very high measure of service and luxury. Many, but not all, of the fantail holidays were of poor standard and badly organised, and it is

understandable that the coach cruise operators were reluctant to be seen in the same light. Fantail operators of dubious character were relying on the expression coach tour to imply a degree of quality.

Initially, fantail holidays involved the long-distance express coach operator transporting the passengers to and from a resort, and using a local coach firm to operate the excursion programme; hotel accommodation was of reasonable standard, and with the total arrangements (the expression package holidays had not yet been introduced) generally offering value-for-money. They were popular with travellers who could not afford the luxury of the coach cruise. But soon more and more less-scrupulous coach firms jumped on the bandwagon armed with an express licence to a resort and a contract with a cheap boarding house; they would keep their own vehicle at the resort and operate the local excursions as well. The fantail holiday market became very cut-throat; such activities caused a loss of revenue to local coach firms and further jeopardized the reputation of this type of holiday.

Eventually several test cases were heard in the licensing courts and sometimes this led to interesting conflicts of interest between major operators who otherwise enjoyed cooperative relationships. A 1936 case heard in the South-Eastern court by Sir Henry Piggot involved no fewer than 43 applications from various coach operators in the North-West who wanted to operate fantail tours to Eastbourne and Bournemouth. Although most of the applicants were small companies, there were some heavyweights amongst them, including Ribble, Yelloway, Midland Red and Crosville. Opposed to the tours were local operators including Southdown, Hants & Dorset, Southern National and Western National. The Traffic Manager of Southdown, Mr H Bowman, was chief witness for his company and gave evidence of the dramatic decline of its local excursion traffic in Eastbourne; in the other corner Mr R Cope of Midland Red and Mr E Johnston of Crosville admitted that until competition had forced them to reduce the price of their holidays to Bournemouth and Eastbourne they had always used local operators, but this was no longer possible at the cut inclusive fare.

The whole situation concerning fantail holidays rambled on unsatisfactorily and virtually unresolved for several years and the coach cruise increasingly established itself and was considered a sophisticated pastime indeed by wealthier clientele.

The railway companies, too, had their eyes on the touring market, and as early as 1927 Land Cruises had been introduced by Great Western, which included first-class rail travel, meals and accommodation. The railway companies had the advantage of owning many of the best and biggest hotels in the popular coastal and inland resorts as well as in London. In the true character of competition, these Land Cruises were promoted as a way of avoiding long, fatiguing road journeys.

A far-reaching occurrence in 1936 that did not work in favour of Coastal was the refusal of the Metropolitan Area Traffic Commissioners to allow R Barr (Leeds) Limited to make Victoria Coach Station the London terminal for Wallace Arnold Tours, who as a result remained associated instead with PSV Operators Limited, with the latter's agents issuing PSV Operators' tickets to cover reservations in the London area for this well-respected company.

Mid-1930s hustle and bustle at Victoria Coach Station (below) with a vehicle prominent whose route board clearly shows it to be operating on the Yorkshire Services Pool. Maybe the demand had been stimulated by advertisements of the type shown above for these services which served a number of destinations, and under whose umbrella the 'Yorkshire Services' title was used from 1930, the principal partners being West Yorkshire Road Car, Yorkshire Traction (only recently then renamed from Barnsley & District) and Yorkshire Woollen District. *(LCCc)*

Before the days of the present motorway network, journeys to London were often lengthy outings and necessarily involved breaks for comfort and refreshment. Coaches from two of the operators who formed the Yorkshire Pool Services are seen in the view above, taken in Nottingham in 1936, where such facilities were available. On the left are two Leyland Tigers of East Yorkshire; to the right is similar Leyland belonging to Yorkshire Woollen. The lower picture shows a close-up of the front of an earlier Leyland of East Yorkshire. (*Both: GHF Atkins © John Banks collection*)

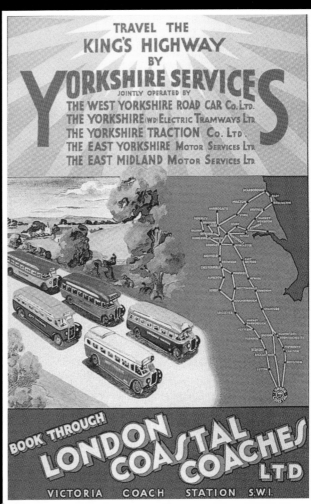

TRAVEL THE
KING'S HIGHWAY
BY
YORKSHIRE SERVICES
JOINTLY OPERATED BY
THE WEST YORKSHIRE ROAD CAR Co. Ltd.
THE YORKSHIRE (WD) ELECTRIC TRAMWAYS Ltd.
THE YORKSHIRE TRACTION Co. Ltd.
THE EAST YORKSHIRE MOTOR SERVICES Ltd.
THE EAST MIDLAND MOTOR SERVICES Ltd.

BOOK THROUGH
LONDON COASTAL COACHES LTD
VICTORIA COACH STATION S.W.I.

LONDON

OXFORD
BANBURY
COVENTRY
BIRMINGHAM
WOLVERHAMPTON
STAFFORD   NEWCASTLE
MACCLESFIELD
STOCKPORT

MANCHESTER.

NORTH WESTERN
ROAD CAR CO. LTD.

Services from London Victoria to Birmingham and Manchester were generally provided jointly by BMMO (Midland Red) and North Western Road Car Company, who were both part of the extensive BET empire, the former based in Bearwood, Birmingham, and the latter based in Stockport, Cheshire. Only the latter tended to operate north of Birmingham. This fine, if slightly stylised advertisement from the pre-war period, presumably aimed at the northern end of the market, in fact makes no reference to the joint partner, but illustrations of that company's coaches will be found on page 66. North Western's coach illustrated below was new in 1936 and was a Harrington bodied Leyland TS7. It is seen at Victoria that year, having just completed a trip from Manchester, in the course of which it traversed the route shown in the diagram. (STA; GHF Atkins © John Banks collection)

A 1937 evening scene. The *Crosville* vehicle in the foreground is, no doubt, the overnight service from London to Liverpool which in those days left at 11.00pm, so the *Southdown*, *Maidstone & District*, and *East Kent* departures were probably the 11.50pm to Brighton, the 11.35pm to Maidstone or Gillingham, and the 11.30pm to Ramsgate – all but *Crosville* calling additionally at Horse Guards Avenue for the benefit of homeward bound theatregoers. *(Fox Photos/GEC/LCCc)*

The poster, left, advertises tours of Scotland and Yorkshire despite Crosville's home territory including Snowdonia, the Menai Straits and many other 'local' scenic attractions. But trips to Yorkshire and Scotland involved travel from London which was, of course, the name of the game.

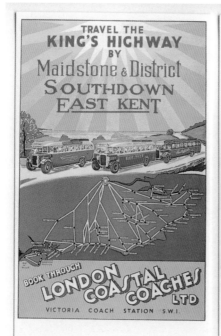

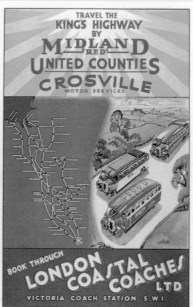

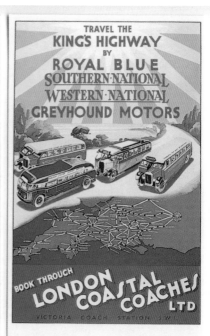

A variety of publicity material was produced by London Coastal Coaches as shown on this page to promote the services that utilised its facilities, of which the examples shown above are only a small selection of what was on offer. Anniversary programmes were also produced, pre-war. Some 30 years after they were originally issued, the upper posters were produced as a limited edition postcard set for collectors. (*Dalkeith Publishing Company/Paper Bygones,Bournemouth*)

LCC were of course up against the far greater publicity machines of the four mainline railway companies, who themselves were not above copying each other, as seen on the opposite page. The famous Southern railway poster dates from 1936 but was based on a snapshot taken in 1924 at the end of one of the platforms on Waterloo Station by Charles E Brown. The poster was designed by Cassandre. The LNER did have the grace to offer a friendly apology at the bottom right hand corner of their poster, which had been designed by AR Thomson. Whether the left-hand view of a young child posed with a friendly Southdown driver and his Leyland Tiger TS7, part of a series which also included the right-hand view, were influenced by the railway posters we shall never know! (*The National Railway Museum, York/Science and Society Picture Library; London Coastal Coaches Collection*)

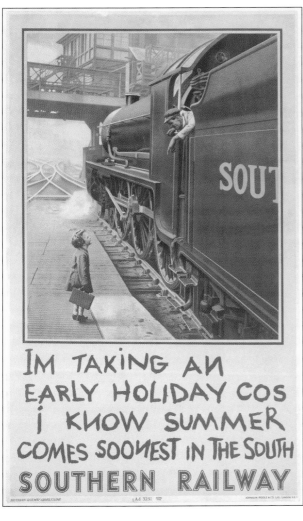

Returning to the previously mentioned problem relating to the accommodation of luggage, Red & White's solution was the fitting of full depth doors at the rear of the coach to access the luggage compartment, which was still at this stage supplemented by a roof rack. (STA)

It was not only coaching that had become a rapidly growing method of travel at this time; there was also aviation, and a great deal of close cooperation between the two industries already existed. By the end of 1932 a ferry service was being operated between Cardiff and Bristol using three-seat Fly Moths and taking 25 minutes. The service was a joint venture between Red & White and Norman Edgar Limited; coach tickets were issued (crossed "Air Service") and agents earned normal coach travel rates of commission. The headquarters of the operation were at the Red and White office in Wood Street, Cardiff, but the somewhat obvious opportunity of through coach/air bookings from Victoria Coach Station to Cardiff via Bristol was impossible because, although the London to Bristol route was operated almost entirely by Greyhound Motors, Red & White were still not associated in any way with London Coastal Coaches Limited.

But Red & White's part ownership of an air service was small fry compared with the railway companies' advances at the same time. With crew and aircraft in Great Western Railway livery supplied by Imperial Airways, the GWR operated a service from Bristol to Plymouth in 1933. Then in the following year, Imperial Airways, together with all four major railway companies, set-up Railway Air Services an airline that continued until 1939 when it passed into government ownership.

In the early 1930s the three local authorities of Ramsgate, Margate and Broadstairs were looking into the possibilities of providing an Isle of Thanet Civil Air Port, and Hillman Airways were trying to agree a contract with the Royal Air Force to use Manston aerodrome. In 1936 the Court of Common Council of the City of London was considering a new airport for London to be sited at Fairlop, near Chigwell, in Essex, which it was estimated would cost £600,000. For this second project a lot hinged on the proposed London Passenger Transport Board extension of the Central Line underground, but whatever the outcome, there was apparently a growing urgency for a more accessible and central aerodrome than Croydon and Heston.

PSV Operators managed to steal a march on Coastal so far as air travel was concerned, when PSV Agents were able to make reservations for the services of British Airways and several other airlines, and issue PSV coach tickets to cover them. There was, however, no exclusivity in these arrangements, as airlines were already making direct agency agreements and, as is shown in this extract from an agency agreement dated 25th July 1936 between Jersey Airlines Limited and J Russell of Pavilion Booking Office, Hackney, N9, instructing them to: "Issue to the passenger your own voucher or receipt showing the date and time of the passage booked, together with the passenger's name in block letters. This voucher will be exchanged for one of the Company's tickets either at one of the Company's control offices or at the aerodrome of departure". Jim Russell was later to become Traffic Assistant to Len Corbett at Victoria Coach Station.

Such rapid progress inevitably brought some silly suggestions or comments, although these often sprang from sensible issues not properly thought through. A contributor to the Leyland Journal and reported in PSV News in April 1936 said: "It is really important that stops should be made on long-distance services at the right times and at good restaurants for meals…it is not a bad idea to arrange for the restaurant menu to be passed around in the coach half-an-hour before the meal stop…passengers can make up their minds what they want and this makes the essential saving of delay in serving".

Admittedly there might have been a slight saving of the time taken as people in the queue made up their minds, but what happened if the menu changed, items became unavailable, or the driver handed out the wrong menu? And who would drive the coach while the driver was distributing the bills of fare half-an-hour before the meal stop?

The railway companies were constantly trying to prevent coach operators securing new licences, and traffic congestion was often cited as a reason for objection. The following exchange ensued: "With a view to reduce congestion of traffic, elevated roads should be built on top of the permanent way of the railways" *(source unknown)*. "This would completely obscure the view from railway carriage windows. It is vandalism" *(various letters in the press from un-named correspondents, but suggested by Commentator in PSV News to be from the publicity bureau of the Big Four railway companies)*. "Dear me, but do not railway travellers already travel with blinkers in the nature of tunnels, interminable cuttings, and the backyards of miles of grimy slum areas? Another blinker or two will not do us any harm" *(Commentator PSV News, April 1936)*.

Evidence of growth in the taking of regular holidays and the popularity of coach travel over train travel is emphasised when it is considered that by the end of the 1930s, despite the fact that the number of people travelling to their holiday destination by rail had more than trebled, the share of the traffic by coach operators increased considerably and consistently, year-on-year, probably because of the sizeable financial savings offered.

By 1939 the coaching industry had found its feet, and following a sometimes fretful but always very exciting childhood and adolescence would, the next year, come of age. Coaching had become a way of life for many and an accepted means of transport for many more; route structures, operating procedures, public acceptance, passenger comfort and so much more were now securely in place in readiness for a healthy and confident future.

However, war with Germany was declared on 3rd September of that year.

A 1936 Coastal trade advertisement promoting everything – regular services, tours, private hire *and* the 'Coastal' travel club. *(Jim Russell collection)*

CHRISTMAS DAY
(FRIDAY, 25th DECEMBER).

SERVICES FROM LONDON
(Victoria Coach Station).

MAIDSTONE & DISTRICT MOTOR SERVICES, LTD.

	a.m.	a.m.	a.m.	a.m.
MILTON, HALFWAY and SHEERNESS				9.15 Only
TOLLGATE, ROCHESTER, CHATHAM and GILLINGHAM... ...		9.0	10.30	12.0 noon
SITTINGBOURNE and FAVERSHAM				9.0* Only
(* Change at Chatham.)				
WROTHAM, BOROUGH GREEN and MAIDSTONE	9.0	9.30	10.30	11.30
PEMBURY, GOUDHURST, HAWKHURST, NORTHIAM and RYE				9.30 Only
STAPLEHURST, CRANBROOK, BENENDEN and TENTERDEN				9.30 Only
SUTTON VALENCE, HEADCORN, BIDDENDEN and TENTERDEN ...				9.0 Only
HURST GREEN, BATTLE, HASTINGS and BEXHILL				9.0 Only

EAST KENT ROAD CAR CO., LTD.

	a.m.	a.m.	a.m.	p.m.
ASHFORD, HYTHE, FOLKESTONE and DOVER			9.15	1.15
DOVER—Direct Service (Via Bridge)			7.30 Only	
MARGATE, BROADSTAIRS and RAMSGATE			9.0	2.0 p.m.
HERNE BAY (Change at Canterbury)			9.0 Only	
BLEAN and WHITSTABLE (Change at Canterbury) ...			9.0 Only	
LITTLEBOURNE, SANDWICH and DEAL			9.0	1.45 p.m.
CANTERBURY	9.0*	9.0†	1.45* p.m.	2.0† p.m.
(* Via Chilham, † Via Boughton.)				

THAMES VALLEY TRACTION CO., LTD.

	a.m.
SUNNINGDALE, ASCOT, BRACKNELL, WOKINGHAM and READING ...	11.15 Only

THACKRAY'S WAY.*

	a.m.	a.m.	a.m.	a.m.	a.m.	a.m.	noon	p.m.	p.m.	p.m.	p.m.
SLOUGH, MAIDENHEAD and READING	8.30	9.30	10.0	10.30	11.0	11.30	12.0	12.30	1.0	2.0	6.30	9.30
(* From King's Cross Coach Station.)											

EASTERN NATIONAL OMNIBUS CO., LTD.

	a.m.
BRAINTREE, HALSTEAD, BOCKING, WETHERSFIELD, GT. BARDFIELD	10.30 Only
(From King's Cross Coach Station. No connection for Hedinghams.)	

With the Season's Greetings to all our Passengers

FOUR-IN-HAND, 1836

CHRISTMAS HOLIDAY ARRANGEMENTS, 1936

TRAVEL BY MODERN LUXURY COACH

MODERN LUXURY COACH, 1936

LONDON COASTAL COACHES, Ltd.
VICTORIA COACH STATION, S.W.1
Phone : SLOANE 0202

Christmas 1936, with services operating every day; including departures on no less than 32 routes on Christmas Day itself. It is interesting to note from the cover of this leaflet that London Coastal Coaches Limited were happily acknowledging the stagecoach as the forerunner to the modern coaching industry. *(Chris Nash collection.)*

In 1936, Coastal's innovative Savings Stamp scheme , promoted as 'Coastal' Travel Club, involved buying stamps for use in payment or part-payment of an eventual ticket purchase. (*Chris Nash collection*)

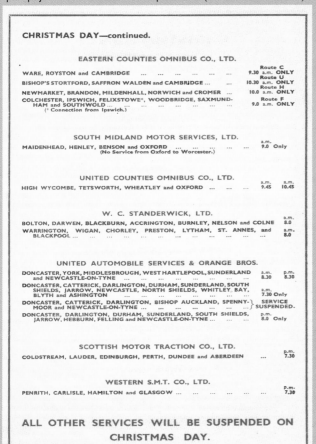

GO BY

EASTERN NATIONAL

DAILY SERVICE

LONDON

(VICTORIA COACH STN.)
TO AND FROM

CLACTON AND JAYWICK SANDS

2 JOURNEYS EACH WAY
(6 JOURNEYS SATURDAYS)

THROUGH BOOKINGS TO
FRINTON, WALTON, etc.

Also Between

LONDON

(King's Cross Coach St'n)
AND

Maldon

Burnham-on-Crouch*

Braintree

Halstead

Gt. Bardfield

Hedinghams, etc.

* Change Coaches at Maldon

FOR FULL DETAILS SEE
"**EASTERN NATIONAL LONDON SERVICE FOLDER**"

Containing Times and Fares of ALL London Services. (March Issue current until July 1st.)
From LONDON COASTAL COACHES LTD.

Head Offices:
New Writtle Street, CHELMSFORD
Phone 1031 (3 lines)

EN. AD. /436

EXPRESS COACH SERVICES DAILY
Between Liverpool and London

FIRST CLASS COMFORT
FARES LESS THAN A PENNY A MILE

HEAD OFFICE
CRANE WHARF
CHESTER

DETAILS FROM
ANY LEADING
TOURIST AGENCY

The degree of comfort provided by some operators is self apparent from this view of the interior of a Crosville coach. It will be seen from the publicity that utilised this picture that the Company was well aware of the luxury travel it was supplying. What was termed 'two and one' seating was by no means common, either before or after the war. *(STA)*

Crosville operated bus, long-distance express and excursions services with a fleet of modern buses and coaches. Based in Chester it ran throughout north Wales into Cheshire and on Merseyside. Buses, as this one crossing the river Conway, were maroon, harking back to its LMS ownership from 1929, but its coaches, of which a Harrington example is shown, were green and grey. The company became part of the Tilling empire in 1942, having previously been in the TBAT group. *(STA both)*

67

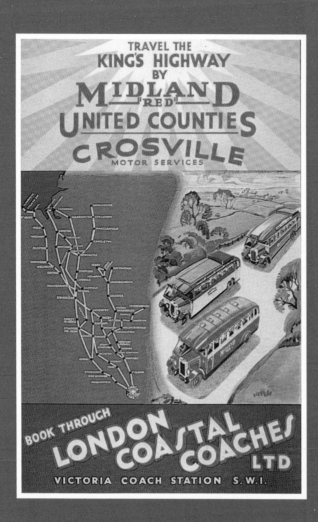

The Birmingham and Midland Motor Omnibus Company (BMMO – or Midland Red to its many passengers) held a unique position in the British bus industry; it was the biggest bus and coach operator outside of London and it continued to build its own vehicles and engines when all other operators purchased from the manufacturers, even to the extent, as shown later in this story, of producing high-speed coaches exclusively for the first motorway service to be operate. Pre-war it produced its SOS LRR model in 1933 (above), whilst the final SOS design was the full-fronted ONC type of 1939, seen below. Their distinctive black and red livery was an instantly recognisable feature to intending passengers.
(*Both: GHF Atkins © John Banks collection*)

The Associated Motorways network was based on Cheltenham as this poster clearly shows. *(LCCc)*

Long distance services between the capital and Scotland were pioneered by the Midland Bus Service in 1928 from Glasgow four years before the well-known Western SMT company came into existence as this illustration (left) from the Senior Transport Archive shows. Western SMT had the distinction of operating brand new coaches into the Coach Station on its opening day fitted with the then relatively untried diesel engine. Above we see a pair of Leyland-bodied Tiger TS7 coaches, new in 1935. Note the unusual window frame embellishment. Below a later TS7 carries Burlingham full-fronted bodywork, built in Blackpool. *(Both: GHF Atkins © John Banks collection)*

Services to the south east of England were almost entirely in the hands of three companies, all of them BET subsidiaries and all of them shown on the cover of the 'Kings Highway' leaflet on this page. Representatives of the pre-war rolling stock from two of the operators are shown here. Prominent in the top picture is a pair of Park Royal-bodied Leyland Tigers of East Kent, based in Canterbury, whilst below is yet another brace of Tigers, this time belonging to Southdown Motor Servies of Brighton and built in 1936. That on the left is bodied by Harrington whilst its companion, with revised livery, is another example from the Burlingham factory. All three companies were staunch Leyland users at this time, though their body orders were placed amongst the many principal coachbuilders of the day, including Beadle, Harrington, Park Royal and Weymanns – all of whom were also based in the south east of England. Leyland were based in Lancashire, of course, whilst the nearer AEC London-based factory, surprisingly perhaps, was not favoured at this time.

(Both: GHF Atkins © John Banks collection)

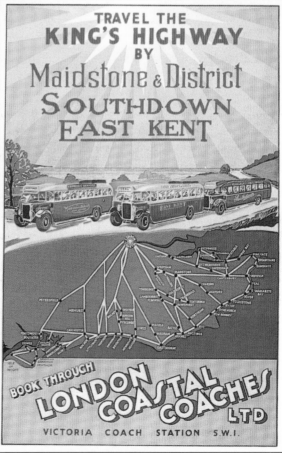

Low days and heydays

Long before Neville Chamberlain's chilling words on September 3rd 1939 when he announced to the nation that "this country is at war with Germany", plans and preparations were being made for the anticipated hostilities.

Most Green Line routes around London were withdrawn as each 'last coach of the day' reached its depot during the night of August 31st 1939, and a great many of the vehicles were converted into ambulances in readiness to evacuate patients from central London hospitals. As it transpired, several Green Line routes, or parts of routes, were subsequently reintroduced at various times during the war years depending on various and varying situations, or alternative London Transport 'bus routes were introduced to cover lost Green Line mileage.

At the same time an evacuation programme was put into action involving hundreds of thousands of children who were moved out of London by train to the presumed safety of towns and villages away from the metropolis.

In the event, the air raids, which the Ministry of Defence had anticipated as imminent, did not materialise for several months, and, unlike Green Line, express coach services and Victoria Coach Station did not suffer any immediate adverse effects. Indeed, for a short while there was a marked upsurge in coach travel with families making as many visits as they could afford to their evacuated children.

Although petrol restrictions were introduced, together with severe blackout regulations that involved streets being unlit and the headlamps of vehicles being masked, probably the greatest problem that winter was the severe weather conditions. Maybe the true impact of being at war had not yet been fully felt, and possibly a false sense of security had crept in, but certainly there was a great spirit of 'soon everything will be back to normal', as the programme of Victoria Coach Station's Eighth Anniversary celebrations on April 10th 1940 confidently implied:

"On this Anniversary, it seems that we must definitely look forward to better times, better understanding and eventually, better coaching business."

So confident were the operating companies that the war would come to nothing, that at about the same time as the Eighth Anniversary celebrations, a meeting was held at Victoria Coach Station to plan some very extensive publicity activity, and to push forward their promotional ideas, which had become even more innovative in 1938 and 1939.

The previous decade had witnessed a good deal of close, and growing cooperation between the companies using Victoria Coach Station, and a new professionalism was apparent in much of the coaching industry. Noticeably, the executives of the companies operating into Victoria Coach Station together with Coastal's own board were by then able to look at the industry on a nationwide basis rather than in

Autumn 1939; war had already been declared, but for a few months Victoria Coach Station enjoyed a period of heavy demand. *(LCCc)*

Three interesting coaches from the United Counties fleet on the Oxford loading bay during the early days of World War Two, whilst express services were still able to operate. The nearest is a Leyland TS3 with Eastern Counties bodywork formerly belonging to the Aylesbury Omnibus Company. A newer Leyland Lion with bodywork from the Blackpool factory of HV Burlingham is parked behind, with an ECW-bodied Bristol L at its side. Headlamp masks and white-edged mudguards have been fitted as part of wartime regulations. *(AE Jones)*

Wartime photographs such as the one above are rare, partly because the coach station was out of use for such purposes between September 1942 and March 1946. Whilst white edging might have seemed a little unneccessary on a cream coloured coach there is no doubt that on a dark red vehicle such as the Midland Red example seen below, it made a significant difference. Examples of this type of vehicle would still find their way into Victoria on occasions. *(GHF Atkins © John Banks collection)*

purely localised ways, and they had gathered sufficient trading and operating records between them to enable promotional and development plans to be evolved based on actual information, rather than guesswork. Unmistakable and consistent patterns were becoming easy to detect, and in 1939, for example, it had become evident to all that whilst Friday to Monday business was very satisfactory, there were too many vehicles sitting idly in garages in the middle of the week; so it was that plans were made during that 1940 meeting to promote, amongst other things, mid-week travel and in particular cheap day return tickets. By persuading some of the weekend passengers to travel on Tuesdays, Wednesdays or Thursdays instead, better vehicle utilisation would ease fuel shortages.

Certainly the enthusiastic attitude abounded. Reviewing the year 1939/40 Coastal reported in its eighth anniversary programme:

"We are fortunately able, in reviewing the past year, to say again, that in the face of the difficulties of the past few months,

including petrol restrictions, black-outs, and the worst weather in history, the coaching industry has progressed. Coach design, mileage, agencies and, above all, passenger figures, have been extremely satisfactory. It is very pleasing to think that, despite all our trials and tribulations, everyone has carried on with good will and efficiency"

But had a shadow of doubt crept in further on in this annual review? It continued:

"Let us hope, too, that the restrictions on the operation of road vehicles will be made as easy as possible for the industry, and that the necessity of keeping in a state of full efficiency and readiness the long distance passenger side of road transport, which may be called upon to fill a gap should any serious hold-up be caused to other means of transport, will be realised by those in authority".

Sadly, within a couple of months the bubble of enthusiasm was burst with the German attacks on the Netherlands and Belgium, followed by the collapse of France in June, and the bombing raids on London in August that heralded the Battle of Britain. Now we knew we were at war.

∽ ∾

The bombs began dropping on London in August 1940. Between September 7th and November 2nd there was heavy bombing every single one of those 56 nights and it continued persistently until May the following year and intermittently thereafter, with the added terror of Germany's V1 and V2 rockets, the latter arriving with absolutely no warning.

Considering the huge amount of bomb damage suffered by properties in the maze of streets all around Victoria it is a wonder that Victoria Coach Station, and the brand new Imperial Airways terminal opposite, which had opened in 1939, didn't suffer any serious structural damage. Any damage that was sustained was chiefly broken glass, of which Victoria Coach Station had plenty.

From the City of Westminster Civil Defence Records we know that within just a few days at the beginning of October 1940 a great many nearby properties in Claverton Street, Denbigh Street, Alderney Street, Charlwood Street and Belgrave Road were razed to the ground and the Grosvenor Hotel at Victoria Station suffered damage on October 9th. Then in November, Eaton Square, Ebury Street and Chesham Street suffered particularly severe bombing, with a direct hit on Sloane Square Tube Station at 10pm on November 12th hitting a Circle Line train and causing 79 injuries, but thankfully no deaths. December 21st was to see a lot of damage to Victoria Railway Station and Ebury Bridge, and bombing was again particularly horrific in the Lillington Street and Sutherland Terrace areas on April 16th 1941 as well as in Ebury Street and Semley Place. The next day an incendiary bomb landed on the Buckingham Palace Road Library, one of Coastal's next-door neighbours. All this wreckage and devastation within a mere half a mile or so of Victoria Coach Station.

SNOWED UP!

With road transport practically at a standstill all over the Country, what would happen to the Nation's vital food and fuel supplies if the RAILWAYS could not carry them as they are doing at this very moment?

THE RAILWAYS ASK FOR A SQUARE DEAL

THE NEED IS URGENT

ISSUED BY THE RAILWAY COMPANIES' ASSOCIATION.

SNOWED UP?

Notwithstanding statements to the contrary, the passenger road services operating from and to VICTORIA COACH STATION to all parts of the country are being maintained.

Bookings as usual at

VICTORIA COACH STATION
and Usual Agencies

ISSUED BY LONDON COASTAL COACHES LTD

Points scoring by the railway companies was an accepted sport, but swift responses from Coastal and its associated companies were usually short, sharp and to the point. *(Jim Russell collection)*

The sandbagged front of Victoria Coach Station during the first years of the war. *(Jim Russell collection)*

Typical of the wartime devastation on the doorstep of Victoria Coach Station. On July 28th 1944 a German flying bomb caused major damage to Ebury Buildings in Semley Place. About 50 flats became uninhabitable, whilst in the remainder of the building, a further 70 flats, suffered severe blast damage. The Westminster City Council incident report listed further severe blast damage in the area bounded by Pimlico Road, Buckingham Palace Road, Elizabeth Street and Ebury Street. In this picture Semley Buildings are in the foreground, Peabody Buildings is to the left in the middle ground and the Elizabeth Street wing of Victoria Coach Station is in the centre distant ground. The distance from the trees in the foreground to Victoria Coach Station is only a few hundred yards. *(City of Westminster City Archives Centre)*

For the first three years of the war coach companies struggled to provide services, although there was an understandable drop in demand. Obviously fewer and fewer people wanted to visit London, and visits to the coast became impossible as more and more coastal towns became barred to visitors. A dramatic and worsening shortage of vehicles placed immense strain on those operators who tried to maintain regular services, and this was made even more difficult as staff members were recruited into the forces. Fewer drivers were driving fewer coaches.

Heavy shipping losses were drastically affecting fuel supplies and, despite the stringent fuel restrictions that had been imposed, by 1942 stocks throughout the country were down to dangerous levels. Tyres were by then in very short supply because of Britain's loss of Malaysian rubber plantations.

Although, itself, not directly relevant to Victoria Coach Station operations, a Green Line traffic circular dated 1st May 1942 emphasises the situation that all operators were then facing. In this, it was pointed out to drivers that a serious shortage of both fuel and spare tyres was being experienced, and that effective measures must be taken to ensure economies. Staff were asked to avoid driving at excessive speeds, making unnecessary brake applications, striking kerbs and pavements

Victoria Coach Station yard, requisitioned during the war for the parking and repair of military personnel cars and other vehicles – chiefly from the U.S. Army, and the Supreme Headquarters Allied Expeditionary Force (SHAEF). There were by now, no coach services operating so the clearly visible *Samuelsons* Leyland Tiger, was no doubt on contract work, as would have been the independent operators vehicles in the distance. The other parked cars most likely belonged to National Fire Service staff working in the newly requisitioned, and otherwise temporarily unneeded Coastal chartroom. *(LCCc)*

with their tyres, or leaving engines idling at terminals *['Green Line' A. McCall].*

In September of that year the Minister of Transport gave an order that all but absolutely essential express coach services were to be discontinued.

And what did the Coastal booking agents do? Not surprisingly, within less than three years from the outbreak of the war almost a third had closed down completely. The situation was probably worse with the P.S.V. Operators agency network because a great many of those agents were reliant chiefly on local operators and the seaside day-trip market, which of course had come to a standstill. At least, for a couple of years, Coastal agents still had the, albeit dwindling, long distance express services from Victoria Coach Station on which to make bookings.

Four important activities enabled London Coastal Coaches Limited to remain buoyant during the remaining war years,

not least of which was the income still being generated from the letting of the office accommodation at Victoria Coach Station. Further very valuable income resulted from the continued operation of the coach station restaurant and bar.

With the withdrawal of coach services much of the office and administrative accommodation that Coastal itself had been using on the first floor of the coach station had become redundant; there was no longer need for a chartroom, and hardly any need for an accounts department. As a result, these areas were released to the National Fire Service for the remaining war years.

By September 1942 coach operations had come to a complete halt at Victoria Coach Station, and within a couple of months the War Office had requisitioned almost all of the departure area, always referred to, then and now, as 'the yard', for use by various forces units, including many vehicles belonging to General Eisenhower's Supreme Headquarters of

Only the suspended bay numbers give the clue that this photograph was also taken inside the coach station duing the war years. *(LCCc)*

the Allied Expeditionary Force. In a similar way the Canadian Army authorities acquired the use of Samuelson's garage on the other side of Elizabeth Street, in Eccleston Place. Of course, wartime security measures, and limited post-war availability of information prevent us from knowing in anything more than scant detail or conjecture, exactly which, what, and whose military vehicles were garaged or maintained at the coach station, but it was certainly of great benefit to the War Office to have such spacious, ideally located and almost purpose-built facilities so readily available and, what's more, **vacant**.

Probably, though, one of the most interesting and far-reaching results of wartime arrangements at Victoria Coach Station following the withdrawal of coach services in 1942 concerned the enquiry office, which one might have suspected would also have been made temporarily redundant. Until then, Coastal's central enquiry office had only involved itself in giving information about express coach services from Victoria Coach Station, but rather than letting the lack of coach services cause its closure it was to discover a new raison d'etre, and became an information centre for local 'bus services throughout the country. This was an enormously

important new service, particularly as there were so many people doing war work in places previously unknown to them, or servicemen and women moving to new locations, and as the information provided by the Coastal office was constantly updated with the latest and unceasingly changing details it was a vital source of accurate advice concerning public road transport throughout all of Britain.

Although this information centre was originally intended only to operate as a wartime provision, in fact it created an ongoing service that continued after the hostilities, and from then on both the public enquiry office, and the telephone enquiry section at Victoria Coach Station held full sets of local 'bus timetables in addition to express coach service information. With most local 'bus companies being part of either the B.E.T. or Tilling (later B.T.C.) groups, the majority of these 'bus timetables were conveniently of identical page size, and could be stored very tidily in both the public and telephone enquiry areas in smart heavy duty covers, on bookshelves that surrounded a large map of the United Kingdom, which had been overdrawn to show the operating region of each 'bus company and the area covered by each timetable book. Whether or not the covers, shelves and maps in use after the war were those in use during the hostilities is uncertain, but without doubt they were based on the easily retrievable information systems developed during that period. Additionally

The now less than impressive front of Victoria Coach Station seen in a wartime picture taken after coach services had been suspended for the duration. With ground floor windows boarded up, a newsvendor in residence in the main doorway, and the lettering at the top of the main block showing superficial damage, the building still retains its original sphinx-like Egyptian style front decoration. *(LCCc)*

in post war years, copies of timetables and information leaflets of almost every other independent 'bus operator in the British Isles, no matter how small, were held in the Post Bookings department, which also had responsibility for answering enquiries received by mail. All-in-all Coastal's immediate post-war information service was very comprehensive indeed, probably the best in the country, and a good foundation for the service which was to be introduced years later in Ramsgate.

Return to Peacetime

The German surrender on 7th May 1945 ended the war in Europe, 8th May being declared VE Day, and the capitulation of the Japanese on 14th August following the dropping of atom bombs by the Americans on Hiroshima and Nagasaki brought the Second War to its close.

An immediate return to peacetime conditions, however, was impossible and would be long delayed. Petrol, although more plentiful, was still rationed and remained so for licensed services until 1948; there was a drastic shortage of vehicles and until demobilisation could take effect there was a continuing shortage of staff. Furthermore, Victoria Coach Station, or to be exact, the yard, was still officially a requisitioned area and remained so until early 1946.

Coach services were gradually resumed from March 1946 and by the end of that summer a fairly comprehensive pattern of routes had been built up. The route network from Victoria Coach Station was complemented by the Associated Motorways network from Cheltenham, which restarted on 3rd June. The reopening and re-establishment of services from these two important coaching hubs within such a comparatively short time was helped by the organisational strength so well established during the 1930s.

PSV Operators Limited, too, were quick in re-establishing their successful prewar foundations, and must have particularly welcomed the useful fillip to their efforts when, through the offices of the Passenger Vehicle Operators Association (PVOA), they were appointed as a clearing house to obtain the services of London-area independent coach operators to undertake many peak-period operations for London Transport. This arrangement involved the provision of vehicles and drivers, with London Transport providing the conductors, and ran for almost two years from October 1947.

It was now time to build on these foundations and to look forward to the better coaching business that the Eighth Anniversary programme had prematurely heralded six devastating years earlier.

ᘉ ᘍ

Three of London Coastal Coaches' pioneers died before the new era of coaching could begin in earnest. In July 1944 Len Turnham, who had been Coastal's Manager then General Manager since its inception (and joint founder of London & Coastal in 1920) died after a short illness; William White, who had been the Company Secretary for 15 years took over as General Manager but became ill during 1946 and died the following year; and 1945 was to witness the death of Colonel Robinson who had been the Chairman of London Coastal Coaches Limited since 1928.

There were people available to step into the roles left by these forerunners: people with skills and experience, or at least determination and enthusiasm, to build Coastal into an even more prominent element of the coaching industry; and noticeably, people who were to uphold the tradition set by earlier Coastal staff and remain with the company until their retirement.

Having been invalided out of the Royal Air Force at the end of 1943, George Newman joined Coastal as an assistant to the Company Secretary, William (Willie) White. In 1948 he became Assistant Secretary to F W J (Fred) Robinson, who had joined Coastal as Secretary the previous year, and who was to take on the role of General Manager in Len Turnham's place. Bert Smith, the original Chairman of London Coastal Coaches in 1925, who had been forced to stand down in 1928 because of ill health, was now in much better physical condition and returned to the chairmanship of Coastal in 1945.

Jim Russell also joined Coastal in 1945. Russell had become involved with the coaching industry in 1929 when he extended his confectionery and tobacco business in Morning Lane, Hackney, and set-up the Pavilion Booking Office, soon becoming a well-respected Coastal booking agent and an influential member of the Booking Agents Association. In 1940 he closed down the business to join the army. Very soon after being demobbed in 1946 he unexpectedly met Ken Gray, then and throughout the 1930s Coastal's Agency Superintendent, who invited him to join the staff at Victoria Coach Station. He started work with Coastal as a £3 per week

Mr W. White, Colonel Robinson, and Mr L.M. Turnham. *(Jim Russell collection)*

Opposite: While the photographs of Jack Wheeler, the ever-attentive and ever-patient Station Master, were undoubtedly taken to promote the friendly image of coach travel, one could well imagine that, despite his reassuring words to the elderly lady, at the back of his mind he was quietly wondering how the enormous pile of luggage on the trolley behind her was going to be accommodated! *('John Bull'/LCCc)*

chartroom clerk, became chartroom supervisor in 1950, and then in 1952 Traffic Assistant to Len Corbett, the Traffic Manager. In addition to the chartroom, his new position brought with it overall responsibility, among several other things, for the booking hall, and for resolving passenger complaints. Doris Russell, Jim's wife, joined him for many years as his secretary. He retired at the end of February 1975 after 29 years with Coastal, and was without doubt instrumental in bringing into effect many of the advances made at Victoria Coach Station, particularly during the 1950s and 60s.

The Station Master at Victoria Coach Station until 1948 was Jack Eggleton whose near neighbour, Jack Wheeler, had spent his war years serving in the Royal Air Force. Upon Jack

Wheeler's return from the forces in 1946, Jack Eggleton suggested he might like to consider being a Coastal inspector. Wheeler took the advice and two years later, when Eggleton emigrated to Australia, he took over his job as well. Jack Wheeler is probably best known for his unflappability and the kind way in which, over many years, he helped solve the problems of so many of the travelling public who passed through the coach station. His team of inspectors emulated his example, thus creating the often-unappreciated smooth running of this busy terminal, particularly at peak times when the inevitable chaos of any transport terminus demands cool heads and calm temperaments. In October 1974 Jack Wheeler visited Lancaster House to receive the British Empire Medal

The London Coastal Coaches stand at the 1950 Daily Mail Ideal Homes Exhibition. *(Jim Russell collection)*

that he had been awarded in the Birthday Honours List for his devoted services to coach passengers. He retired in 1981 after 35 years at Victoria Coach Station.

Another of Coastal's long serving staff to receive an award also started in 1947. Mary Lambourne joined Coastal as a booking-hall clerk, becoming supervisor in 1973 (having by then married Bill Dare, a senior Thames Valley inspector). In the Birthday Honours List for 1976 she was awarded the MBE.

London Coastal Coaches built up a strong team in the immediate postwar years; a team that could hone prewar systems and experience into a continuing, professional and efficient operation. The Board's executives fulfilled the need for clear and positive direction, and the staff at every level was enthusiastic and flexible, whether it was in the booking hall, the yard or at any other administrative level. It was as if the halt that the war had forced upon the coaching industry in 1942 had been, for Coastal at least, an opportunity to draw a deep breath, take stock, and then press forward with renewed enthusiasm. The urge to pull together in this exciting, and for many captivating, adventure created close cooperation among everyone and a family feeling soon developed, probably aided unintentionally by the notable husband and wife partnerships of Len and Rene Corbett, Jim and Doris Russell and Cuthbert Embleton and his wife. The inexplicable "magic" of the travel industry as a whole, and coaching in particular, was the life-blood of Victoria Coach Station; it was predominantly powerful then and throughout the two decades to come. Undoubtedly, Coastal's zenith.

ᜃ ᜂ

In the late 1940s the country was finding its feet. Art treasures that had been removed from London during the war were brought back and museums and exhibitions were once again giving visitors a reason to come to the capital. (The Elgin Marbles and many other British Museum items remained in London through the war years stored in the tunnels of the London Underground Holborn/Aldwych branch, which was closed during the war.) As early as 1947 the Victoria and Albert Museum held a particularly successful exhibition of French tapestries, and in the same year the National Gallery

bravely exhibited the Munich Collection of Pictures. Radio Olympia was staged with demonstrations of the latest wonder television; the Ideal Homes Exhibition became one of

1948 London

London's major attractions again; and the Olympic Games were held in Britain in 1948.

As an understandable release from the traumas of war, people wanted to get out and enjoy themselves again and, apart from traditional day-trips to the seaside, more and more were taking holidays away from home. In the country generally there was a feeling of elation; the National Health Service had already come into being in 1948, and the future looked brighter than it had for many years. British seaside resorts began to enjoy unprecedented visitor numbers and with the cost of rail travel being beyond the pockets of many people, the coach journey became part of the holiday. The coaching industry throughout the country was buoyant and growth in demand was widespread.

In February 1949 the Booking Agents Association called a meeting at Victoria Coach Station, which included addresses by both Fred Robinson, the General Manager of Coastal, and Mr W F French, the Chairman of PSV Operators. It was an achievement by the BAA to have both groups under one roof at the same time and not even on neutral territory.

Fred Robinson reported that London Coastal Coaches ticket sales in 1948 had increased by 49% over 1947, and while it was expected that demand in 1949 would remain steady, the old problem of insufficient midweek travellers was becoming more than a mere irritation. Furthermore, the railways had introduced a new cheap-day excursion policy that was bound to have an adverse effect on coach travel.

Mr French highlighted slow delivery of new vehicles and the inadequate supplies of timetables because of paper shortages as two key problems, and was rather pessimistic about improvement during the next year. But it was the impact of the so-called peak period that was creating the major difficulties; despite a lot of talk about staggered holidays, nothing had been forthcoming to relieve the demand during the fortnight from the last weekend in July, which in many cases could not be satisfied. No doubt the fact that August Bank Holiday had not then been moved from the first to the last Monday in August had also exacerbated the situation.

Passengers travelling from Victoria Coach Station increased at a terrific rate. Coach departures during 1947 totalled 100,000; during 1948 this had increased to 148,000, and in 1949 had reached 160,000, an increase of 60% in just two years, although it is worth remembering that Coastal were claiming 100,000 coach departures from Lupus Street in 1930, and around 135,000/150,000 per year from Victoria Coach Station during the middle 1930s. Then in 1950 the number reached almost 200,000, with 3,140 over the Easter period (Thursday to Monday) alone. These were pleasing results with which to celebrate Coastal's 25th Anniversary, and the Board of Directors (which still included four of the original members) were no doubt content.

Intended to mark the centenary of the Great Exhibition of

Intended to show the art deco style lettering above the coach exit, this post-war picture of a *Crosville* departure to Liverpool, shows that the signage was already in need of some maintenance. *(LCCc)*

Coastal's Directors in 1950: Standing *(left to right)* Shirley H. James, F.P. Arnold and C.E. Holmes.
Seated: R.P. Beddow, Bert Smith (chairman) and A.E. Cannon. *(Jim Russell collection)*

June 1950 advertisement in 'Coaching Journal' – the 25th Anniversary of the formation of London Coastal Coaches Limited. *(Jim Russell collection)*

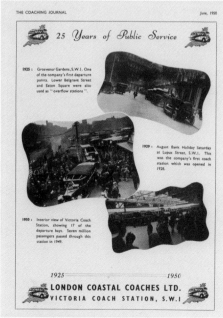

Victoria Coach Station on an averagely busy day in the early 1950s. By now coach services had resumed after their wartime suspension and passenger numbers were increasing rapidly. Underfloor-engined coaches have made their appearance, in particular the distinctive Royal Tiger from Leyland Motors. *(Jim Russell collection)*

1851, the 1951 Festival of Britain focused on the arts, architecture, science, technology and industrial design. It was held for the most part on the south bank of the Thames on a site between Waterloo Station and County Hall. The Royal Festival Hall was built and opened at the same time and was one of the country's finest contemporary concert halls. Although the Olympic games had brought many thousands of visitors to London, it was the Festival of Britain that really marked the upswing of Britain's postwar recovery a recovery mirrored in the coaching industry. Two years later the Coronation of Queen Elizabeth II brought a huge influx of visitors not just to London, but also to the whole of Britain.

These, and many other events, all had beneficial effects on coach services to London, and as private car ownership was to remain for a few years the exception rather than the rule, travel by public transport, whether for long or short distances, was part of everyday life.

But a spectre had appeared on the landscape, which, although not to become fully manifest for just over twenty years, was a forewarning of the dire threat to the coaching

> *"I remember being able to get on and sit in the coach well before the departure time; the driver going off for his break and leaving the door open. This was much more pleasant than the present procedure. When the driver returned he would go round the coach collecting the tickets."*
>
> *Alex Fairley*

industry as it had by then become. At the end of 1946 the Labour Government under Clement Attlee introduced a Transport Bill, which led, on 1st January 1948, to the formation of the British Transport Commission (BTC), which took responsibility for all the interests of the newly nationalised railways, including the railway hotels; the docks and inland waterways. Soon after, all the Tilling's road passenger interests (including all the Tilling companies who operated into Victoria Coach Station), together with their substantial share holdings in London Coastal Coaches Limited, were voluntarily sold to the BTC. (The only road-passenger transport operators to be truly "nationalised" were Midland General, Notts & Derby and Mansfield District, owned by Balfour Beatty, who were nationalised because of their electricity generating interests. A sidelight on this unusual situation was that those three passenger-transport operators were for a time administered by the British Electricity Authority.)

This did not affect London Coastal Coaches or Victoria Coach Station to any great extent at the time, because the share-holding by BET companies counterbalanced that of the newly formed BTC, so equity of control between the two groups was preserved.

By now the coal industry had been nationalised, and the BTC anticipated that eventually the whole of the country's passenger transport system, both road and rail, should be nationalised also. It suggested that this nationalisation should be initiated on an area-by-area basis; the first proposed region being the Northern Area, which was to comprise the counties of Northumberland and Durham, large parts of the North Riding of Yorkshire and the County Boroughs in the area. The BET Group was aghast and promptly produced and published a list of 136 north-country independent operators and BET operating companies that would be "doomed if the BTC's profligate, cumbersome scheme is adopted" *(Coaching*

Journal – October 1949*).* Mr J S Wills, the Managing Director of BET, outlined the scheme in the following concise summary: "The scheme (a) Proposes, without attempting to give a reason, to acquire compulsorily all passenger road transport undertakings belonging to private enterprise in a large area of the country, and to confiscate similar undertakings belonging to the municipalities. (b) Suggests a very top-heavy form of administrative machinery and pays lip service to various forms of consultation with Committees whose advice may be completely disregarded.

The persons or bodies responsible would be: (1) the Minister of Transport; (2) the Transport Tribunal (on fares policy); (3) the Commission; (4) the Road Passenger Executive; (5) an Area Board; and (6) a General Manager.

Advising the Minister and the Commission would be the Central Transport Consultative Committee; advising the Commission, an Area Transport Users Consultative Committee; advising the Area Board would be district Consultative Committees; and advising the district Consultative Committees would be sub-division Consultative Committees.

The scheme makes it quite clear that the Commission, subject to the absolute and over-riding authority of the Minister, is to decide all question of even minor policy, and it is difficult to see what use the Area Board is to be, except as a letter-box.

> "The company is not prepared to negotiate in any shape or form with the British Transport Commission for the voluntary sale of any of its undertakings."
> Major H.C. Drayton, Chairman of B.E.T. Limited to a group of operators in Newcastle – February 1949

> "In view of the many rumours which one hears on this subject, I wish to make it quite clear that your company has not been nationalised, neither is nationalisation of the passenger road transport industry a certainty, for despite the acquisition of a number of undertakings by the British Transport Commission, by far the greater part of the industry is still in the hands of municipal and company operators."
> Mr J.M. Womar, MinstT, chairman of Trent Motor Traction Co. Ltd at the 36th AGM of the company.

Possibly its inclusion is intended to salve the feelings of local councillors whose buses are being taken over without compensation, by trying to make nationalisation look more like socialism."

Nor were fears much assuaged when in 1950 the entire, and until then somewhat maverick, Red & White bus and coach conglomeration, which at the end of the war had also taken over South Midland, was acquired by the BTC. Particularly since there was no way anyone could consider Red and White a Northern Area operator.

However, the BTC produced a remarkably dismal first year Annual Report for 1948, which showed a loss of almost five million pounds. The Commission, with delightful understatement, described the situation as unsatisfactory, but the report continued by saying: "Unfortunately, the trends of traffic receipts and of expenditure in 1949 hold out no hope that the immediate future is likely to show better results, at any rate, with the existing levels of fares, rates and charges…the net result is that a further marked deterioration of the working results is inevitable in 1949".

This gloomy report, which certainly did not seem to reflect the reports of Messrs Robinson and French at the Booking Agents Association meeting in February 1949, ran to 424 pages and included the suggestions that "the charges policy is the key to effective integration" and "the Commission have to face the great disparities between the level of rail fares and charges on the one hand, and road fares and charges on the other".

YEAR 1948 DIVIDENDS PAID TO BRITISH TRANSPORT COMMISSION BY B.E.T GROUP AND OTHER COACH COMPANIES

B.E.T. Companies	£
Aldershot & District	22,748.00
Birmingham & Midland "Red"	324,000.00
City of Oxford	30,818.00
Devon General	23,869.00
East Kent	38,701.00
East Midland	56,818.00
East Yorkshire	67,892.00
Hebble	15,000.00
Maidstone & District	66,498.00
Northern General	91,778.00
North Western Road Car	135,757.00
Ribble	132,686.00
Southdown	60,698.00
Trent Motor Traction	67,745.00
Western Welsh	59,977.00
Yorkshire Traction	78,781.00
Yorkshire Woollen	96,000.00
Other Coach Companies	
Black & White Motorways	1,900.00
Blackpool omnibus Stations	320.00
London Coastal coaches	5,509.00
Omnibus Stations	450.00
Timpsons	20,677.00
TOTAL	**1,398,622.00**

Euston Square Coach Station with a busy departure of *Standerwick* coaches. *(Fox Photos/LCCc)*

The map opposite shows the coach stations in the Kings Cross and Euston areas. *(Harper Collins Publishers/based on Bartholomews Reference Atlas of Greater London 1961)*

> *"This body is not concerned with the coach and 'bus operators' viewpoint, but with that of the travelling public. The contention of this association that road transport is to be linked with 'bankrupt railways' with the merging of fares, is not denied by supporters of nationalisation, who frankly forecast the curtailment of long-distance coach services and the raising of coach fares."*
> Omnibus Passengers Protection Association at their inaugural public meeting – February 1949

> *"When restored to power, the Conservative Party will restore the 'bus and coach services to the local authorities and companies"*
> Sir David Maxwell Fyfe. March 1949

and by Standerwick, whose timetables referred to it as New King's Cross Coach Station. Less flatteringly, but probably more accurately, it has also been called "an open air sort of bomb site operation" (John Walker transport enthusiast and historian, ex-employee of London Coastal Coaches, and subsequently proprietor of John Walker Travel Limited, Kings Road, Chelsea, SW3. c1960).

Judd Street Coach Station lasted until 1954, when yet another King's Cross Coach Station (King's Cross Coach Station No 3) appeared in Pentonville Road, between Killick Street and Northdown Street. This was a PSV Operators Limited initiative, and although the coach station was purpose built, and admirable in many ways, it was much less convenient geographically than either Central London Coach Station, the original King's Cross Coach Station (No 1), or Judd Street (No 2) had been, so at about the same time a new coach station was opened in front of Euston station, staffed by London Coastal Coaches, and called Euston Square Coach Station.

In the meantime, at Victoria Coach Station, barely twenty years after its opening, a similar problem was raising its head to that which had faced London Coastal Coaches in the 1920s; not enough room to accommodate the number of vehicles needed to satisfy demand. Thus, at the start of the 1950s, Coastal's directors were not, as they had been at the start of the 1930s, looking for a site on which to build a coach station; now they were working out how to enlarge the coach station they already had.

The problem was twofold. More space was needed for arrivals and departures, and there was a growing need for parking space, particularly for those vehicles that had come into London as overnight services, and needed to park for the day before returning as overnight services the next night. The coach station yard could not accommodate all-day parking, and parking space in Samuelsons garage was equally in demand.

For a while casual parking was available on several bombsites in the vicinity, at Battersea Wharf and on the vacant ground facing the River Thames alongside Chelsea Bridge and in the

Reading between the lines it is obvious that the BTC intended that road transport should subsidise rail transport.

It is interesting to note that in the year in question the net profit from the BTC's road transport interests (mostly the original Tilling companies and the Scottish Motor Traction group) was just over four million pounds. Added to this the Commission's shareholdings in BET companies (from the 1930s when the railways had invested in coach companies), added almost £1.4 million more to the BTC balance sheet. And yet they still showed a loss of £4.7 million. Road transport certainly had subsidised rail travel that year.

The brouhaha became more and more heated during the next two years, and the BTC nationalisation plans for the entire public transport industry did not come into effect at least, not then.

☙ ❧

Meanwhile in the King's Cross area, and with the closure in 1947 of the coach station almost opposite King's Cross and St Pancras main line stations (King's Cross Coach Station No 1), a coach station of sorts was operated in Judd Street (King's Cross Coach Station No 2) and used for a while by, among others, Yorkshire Services and North Western, and shown in their timetables as King's Cross Coach Station, Judd Street;

As services gradually got back to normal after the war, many services were undertaken by independent operators on behalf of Coastal's associated companies.   Here we see several Lansdowne Coaches of Leytonstone. *(LCCc)*

St. Phillips Church (the 'Russian' church), with Flask Lane and the Grosvenor Club to the extreme left in this picture. The Buckingham Palace Road entrance to Victoria Coach Station is at the extreme right. At the time of this photograph – February 1956 – the church was being demolished in order to extend the coach station. Flask Lane was closed soon after, and eventually the Grosvenor Club was also demolished. *(Howard Photographic Service/LCCc)*

shadow of Battersea Power Station. However, in the summer of 1950 permanent parking became available in Lombard Road, Battersea. Although it would have been more convenient to have had a coach park closer to Victoria, the dead mileage involved by vehicles shuttling between Victoria and Battersea was acceptable.

Enlarging the coach station itself, or the yard at least, took longer to resolve. Vehicles entering the coach station still had only the entrance in Buckingham Palace Road opposite the Imperial Airways (by then BOAC) terminal, and the only exit from the coach station was at the other end of the yard, through the archway by the Station Master's office, and into Elizabeth Street.

At the far end of the coach station on the north side of the yard (the side furthest away from the Buckingham Palace Road wing of the coach station) was a long two-storey building accommodating a bakery, and in the north-west corner was a large ventilator shaft from the District Line underground railway between Victoria and Sloane Square stations. In effect these two constructions would seem to have prevented any coach station development in that direction.

To the west, in Buckingham Palace Road and just beyond the coach entrance, stood St. Phillip's Church, which although having been used temporarily as a Russian Orthodox Church, still remained within the auspices of the Ecclesiastical Commissioners; and beyond that a very narrow roadway called Flask Lane, which led into Ebury Square and Semley Place. On the other side of Flask Lane was the Grosvenor Club, owned by Grosvenor Estates and used chiefly as a social club by staff of the Duke of Westminster, the owner of Grosvenor Estates. Without the acquisition of the Russian Church at the very least, it was difficult to see how expansion in that direction, either, would be possible.

Negotiations were put in place for the purchase of the property at either ends of the yard; the bakery, the Russian Church, and the Grosvenor Club.

Buying a church, or a church site, is not a straightforward procedure. The Ecclesiastical Commissioners needed to obtain authorisation from both Parliament and the Bishop of London before the sale could go ahead, and although the Commissioners had agreed to the sale in March 1953, completion took a further three years. There had been no difficulty in obtaining permission to close Flask Lane, and in March 1956 a frantic demolition programme began and within eight or nine weeks the Russian Church site was available for coach parking and unloading.

In the same month, March 1956, the purchase of the bakery building was completed, and a refurbishment programme started that involved providing an improved staff canteen on the first floor; with a much-needed Continental Terminal and passenger waiting rooms on the ground floor. By converting the original staff canteen into enhanced offices for the operating companies' inspectors, the original and unsuitable inspectors' offices could be demolished to allow access to the Russian Church site.

London Transport helped the situation through their agreement to the closing of the original District Line ventilator shaft, and its replacement with a smaller and better-located one. This made it possible to provide a second coach exit into Semley Place and Ebury Street   thereby, to a large extent, resolving the critical congestion problems in Elizabeth Street. Thus by the summer of 1957 the overcrowding situation

With the demolition of St. Phillips Church and the Grosvenor Club in 1956, and the closure of Flask Lane, a good deal of space became available for parking and coach movements. The area on which St. Phillips Church had originally stood was designated arrivals Bays 1A and 7A, although they were often used for departures – particularly at busy times. It was not until 1965 that redevelopment took place to double the length of the Buckingham Palace Road wing, and completely reshape this corner of Victoria Coach Station. (LCCc)

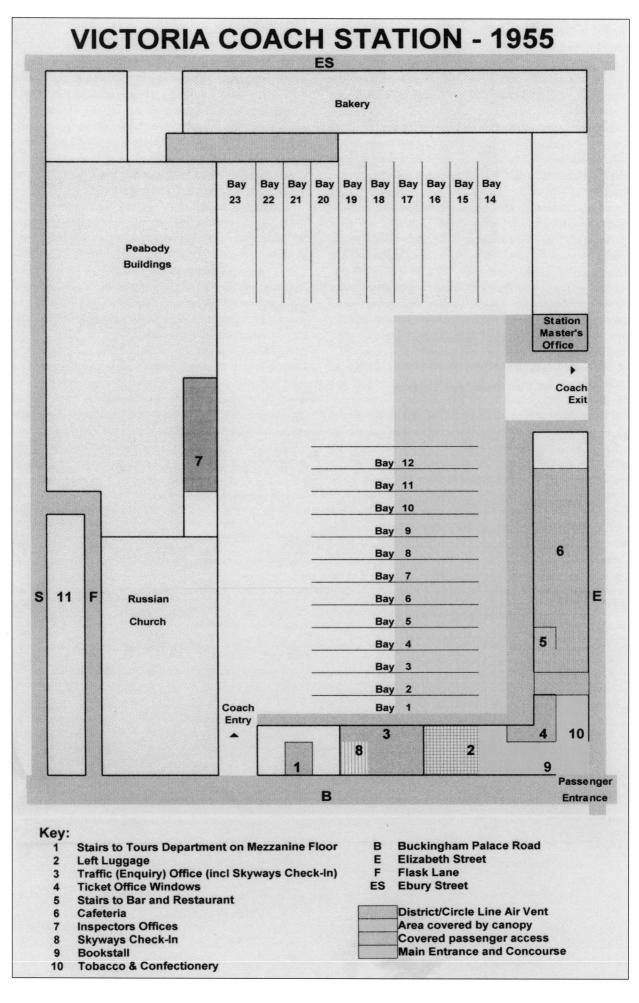

VICTORIA COACH STATION - 1955

ES

Bakery

Peabody
Buildings

Bay 23 | Bay 22 | Bay 21 | Bay 20 | Bay 19 | Bay 18 | Bay 17 | Bay 16 | Bay 15 | Bay 14

Station Master's Office

► Coach Exit

7

Bay 12
Bay 11
Bay 10
Bay 9
Bay 8
Bay 7
Bay 6
Bay 5
Bay 4
Bay 3
Bay 2
Bay 1

6

S | 11 | F

Russian

Church

E

5

Coach
Entry
▲

3

8

1

2

4 | 10

9

B

Passenger

Entrance

Key:
1   Stairs to Tours Department on Mezzanine Floor
2   Left Luggage
3   Traffic (Enquiry) Office (incl Skyways Check-In)
4   Ticket Office Windows
5   Stairs to Bar and Restaurant
6   Cafeteria
7   Inspectors Offices
8   Skyways Check-In
9   Bookstall
10   Tobacco & Confectionery

B   Buckingham Palace Road
E   Elizabeth Street
F   Flask Lane
ES   Ebury Street

District/Circle Line Air Vent
Area covered by canopy
Covered passenger access
Main Entrance and Concourse

at Victoria Coach Station had been greatly eased and there remained only the matter of completing the purchase of the Grosvenor Club site.

ɔઠ 𝒆𝒐

On resumption of services after the war it had been decided to retain the system of issuing all agents and booking clerks with a set of loose-leaf timetables in a spring binder, but the timetables were to be renumbered to ensure that all printed schedules of any one company would appear together. In the 1930s a straightforward numbers-only system had been used but, chiefly because of the introduction of new services after the numbering system had been set-up, anomalies had arisen; for instance, the Midland Red London/Birmingham timetable was numbered 39, while its London/Llandudno service was numbered 50, with all the intermediate numbers having been allocated to other companies' routes. Likewise the United Counties London/Nottingham service was numbered 41, but its London/Oxford service (which it had taken over from Varsity Coaches) was numbered 49. The revised system allocated a number to each company, and the individual route timetables were allocated a letter. Thus, for example, United Counties was allocated the number 16 so its London/Oxford service became 16A, and London/Nottingham service 16B.

The fact that each operating company also had its own system of route numbers could easily have created untold confusion. Maidstone & District prefixed its route numbers with the letter E (E1, E2 etc.); East Kent used L as a prefix; Midland Red, North Western, Thames Valley and Eastern Counties did not use numbers but gave each route a letter, Crosville used route numbers in the 100s, United Automobile in the 200s; and so on. The Coastal scheme, which basically numbered the timetable rather than the route, was straightforward and easier to use, particularly for agents and booking clerks concerned with all the routes of all the companies, as opposed to staff in the provincial offices of the operating companies who mostly only needed to know about their own services, and were more familiar with the route numbering system peculiar to that company.

ɔઠ 𝒆𝒐

Turning our attention to the coach network, we have seen how, by the end of the 1930s, there had been a good deal of consolidation in the coaching industry. In particular long distance coach services to London had become over-ridingly controlled by the bigger operators, and were for the most part operating into Victoria Coach Station. By comparing the route patterns and scheduling of 1949 with 1939 we can see how the coach operating companies had not only recovered from the setbacks of the war, but had either returned to or further developed the immediate prewar services.

Then by looking at schedules for the next ten-year period to 1959 we can see that an almost stable operating pattern existed which was still based to a large extent on the late 1930s services and routes, with very few modifications except for the

COMPANY NUMBERS ALLOCATED BY COASTAL CHIEFLY FOR TIMETABLE PURPOSES	
Maidstone & District	2
East Kent	3
Southdown	4
Aldershot & District	5
Thames Valley	6
Royal Blue	7
Greyhound	8
Westcliff	9
Eastern National	10
Eastern Counties	11
Lincolnshire	12
Midland Red	13
North Western	14
South Midland	15
United Counties	16
Yorkshire Services	17
Standerwick/Scout/Ribble	18
Crosville	19
Associated Motorways	20
United Automobile	21
S.M.T.	22
Western S.M.T.	23
Timpsons	24

loss of a small handful of late journeys on some of the shorter routes such as to Maidstone, Gillingham, Farnham and Reading. Obviously, the pioneering work and learning curves of the 1930s had been sufficiently steadfast to provide sound foundations on which to move forward, and that despite a major World War.

The Maidstone & District route structure changed little between the late 1930s and late 1950s. There were a couple of minor reductions; the once-a-day extensions of the London/Tenterden service to Woodchurch, and the London/Rye service to Iden and Wittersham were withdrawn after the war. On the service from Leyton to Gillingham and Sheerness, the restriction on some of the prewar journeys to Naval Ratings Only was withdrawn. This route had originally been operated from Stratford to Chatham by Fleet Transport Service whose headquarters were in Tramway Avenue, Stratford, but had been taken over by London Transport in 1934 when most of its routes came under the Green Line umbrella; however, as Chatham was outside the London Transport area, the route was transferred to Maidstone & District. This is one of the few Coastal-controlled services that did not operate from Victoria. The routing of the late evening Victoria/Gillingham and Victoria/Maidstone services via Horse Guards Avenue for the benefit of theatregoers was withdrawn early in the 1950s.

The prewar arrangement for the London/Rye and London/Hastings routes continued after the war. This involved drivers of the morning services in each direction changing vehicles at a point between Tonbridge and Sevenoaks, thus

Three pictures showing the London Underground (District Line) air vent. The first, above, and taken during the 1930s, and the second, right, in the first half of the 1950s, show how the vent effectively created a barrier at the far end of the yard. In both, parked coaches were backed up against the side of the vent. In the picture above the vent is located behind the wall at the very top of the illustration and in the second picture the *Thames Valley* double-decker 'bus is parked against the wall separating Victoria Coach Station from the bakery building, which Coastal eventually bought. *(LCCc)*

The Underground lines beneath Victoria Coach Station which formed part of the District and Circle Lines were some of the earliest on the system to be built. The first underground lines which were just below street level were, of course, steam operated and therefore required adequate ventilation. The concept was continued and a large vent occupied the Coach Station yard, as seen as seen in these pictures.

The third picture taken in the second half of the 1950s shows the rebuilt, and much smaller air vent. Coaches now faced in the opposite direction and could exit beyond the air vent and into Semley Place. The bakery building became a waiting room, and a Skyways Terminal, with a new staff canteen on the first floor. *(LCCc)*

Traffic coming into the Coach Station had to queue at busy times, and here we see two lines meeting in August 1962 at the junction of Buckingham Palace Road with Ebury Bridge (which crosses the lines into Victoria railway station), over which the facing line of vehicles is standing, headed by an East Kent half cab Dennis Lancet. *(Chris Nash)*

returning whence they had just come. This arrangement applied only to the morning services; the drivers of the afternoon departures in each direction operated the full route and also the evening return journeys, and so were saved from an overnight stay away from home. Obviously, keeping to schedule was essential for the change of drivers to work; the actual journey time between Tonbridge and Sevenoaks is shown as 15 minutes in the 1937 timetables, and 18 minutes in 1960 so there was very little leeway for early or late running.

At first one wonders why this driver/vehicle change did not take place at the Camden Hotel, Pembury, just a short distance south of Tonbridge, and the refreshment break for the service, but it must have been better for the northbound and southbound services to arrive separately at the refreshment venue, thereby preventing too much pressure on the available facilities during the ten-minute halt. Experience had obviously taught that it was easier to ensure that the two vehicles met between Tonbridge and Sevenoaks than to expect the two coachloads of passengers to be back on board within their allotted time. (The refreshment-break location changed in the late 1950s to the Blue Boys Inn at Kippings Cross, four minutes from Pembury).

East Kent routes from Victoria Coach Station changed very little except that by the late 1940s, on summer Saturdays the London/Dover service called additionally at the Romney, Hythe & Dymchurch Light Railway station in Hythe, no doubt for passengers using the railway to complete their journeys to holiday camps along the coast in the Dymchurch area. This became unnecessary when East Kent introduced a new summer Saturday service from Victoria Coach Station direct to Dymchurch and New Romney. A suggestion in the late 1930s timetables of the London/Deal and London/Dover routes that services operated from King's Cross Coach Station as well as Victoria Coach Station is not backed up with actual timings from King's Cross.

> "I remember an occasion when a Southdown coach arrived in the coach station; the driver slid open the centre passenger door and then proceeded to unload luggage from the boot leaving passengers to help themselves off the vehicle. He then reboarded and began manoeuvring his vehicle on to the departure bay. While reversing, he managed to run over a passenger's suitcase left standing in the yard. When a member of the coach station staff asked a Southdown inspector where the passenger stood legally, the answer came 'They have no case'!".
> Chris Nash – ex Victoria Coach Station employee, and transport historian.

> "One Sunday during a rail strike we had so many pre-booked and pre-ticketed passengers for the London/Farnham service, I had to organise twenty-two crew operated double-deck 'buses as duplicates to Victoria Coach Station".
> Ray Le Mesurier-Foster – ex Aldershot & District Inspector.

Services by Southdown to Brighton at weekends and bank holidays in the late 1930s operated both from Horse Guards Avenue and Victoria Coach Station, (a haunting reminder that it was still only a little over thirty years since those original and ill-fated Vanguard excursions to Brighton had operated from just around the corner in Northumberland Avenue). Even the timings on the Southdown routes remained hardly changed at all from those of the late 1930s through to the late 1950s, and for much of the time the Victoria/Brighton service had a frequency almost the same as Southern Railway; with departures every hour, on the hour; the only difference being that Southern Railway completed the journey in sixty minutes as opposed to Southdown's two and a half hours.

Thames Valley services, transferred post war to Victoria Coach Station hardly altered, with a route to Reading via Maidenhead, and another via Wokingham, although the 1930s route to Henley was discontinued after the war. Aldershot & District until the mid-1950s continued its half-hourly service from Victoria Coach Station to Farnham including a once-daily extension to Bordon and Whitehill, although the once-daily service to Fleet and Crookham was discontinued postwar. The service from London to Hindhead and Haslemere was transferred from Aldershot & District to Southdown in 1937 with Hindhead being incorporated into the Victoria Coach Station/Portsmouth service, and Haslemere into the Victoria Coach Station/Bognor service.

An anomaly on the Victoria Coach Station/Farnham route was that Aldershot & District was permitted to carry passengers from London to Egham, Virginia Water and Sunningdale; destinations within the London area and served by Green Line. For most companies the first permitted setting down point out of London was beyond the Green Line operating area, although the Southdown/Beacon once-daily service from London to Crowborough was permitted to carry passengers from Victoria to East Grinstead.

Those wishing to travel to Oxford from London had the choice of the South Midland service via Maidenhead or that of United Counties via High Wycombe. United Counties had taken over the London/Oxford service of Varsity during the mid 1930s.

Routes and frequencies were the same in the late 1940s as they had been in the late 1930s, including the twice-daily South Midland extension beyond Oxford to Worcester. At the end of the 1940s South Midland was also offering sightseeing tours of Oxford at add-on prices to their London/Oxford fares with the opportunity to view the City of Dreaming Spires on foot with a guide-lecturer for 5/- (25p) above the London/Oxford day return fare, or by coach for 7/6d (37½p). Services altered in 1950 when the British Transport Commission acquired South Midland and transferred to them the United Counties route via High Wycombe. The timetables were then revised to a regular hourly service, on the hour from Victoria Coach Station, with alternate journeys via Maidenhead or High Wycombe.

The United Counties route from Victoria Coach Station to Nottingham remained unaltered from the late 1930s through to the late 1950s and beyond, except that in the 1930s the early evening service from London continued beyond Northampton and terminated at Leicester. This is one of the few northbound services that did not at any time call additionally at King's

Cross Coach Station, although from the resumption of service after the war an additional picking-up point was included opposite Marylebone Town Hall.

The pattern of Associated Motorways services from London to Cheltenham remained virtually the same from 1934 through to the late 1950s and beyond, although in the 1930s services terminated at the Terminal Coach Station in Clapham Road, and were routed to and from there via Victoria Coach Station. One service a day, usually operated by Red & White, travelled by the slightly longer route via Reading and Cirencester and the remainder, usually operated by Black & White, took routes via Oxford and Witney. Connections in Cheltenham of interest to passengers from London were chiefly to South and Mid Wales and to Herefordshire, Worcestershire and parts of the West Midlands. Use of Associated Motorways for journeys from central London to Wolverhampton involved a travelling time of nine hours compared with two hours less by Midland Red/North Western.

In the late 1930s the London/North Devon service of Royal Blue, and one each of its London/Bournemouth and London/Bristol services, operated both from King's Cross and Victoria Coach Station, but this arrangement did not resume after the war. Apart from this, the route patterns and, to an enormous extent, the actual timetables on Royal Blue and Royal Blue/Greyhound (Greyhound was owned by the Bristol Tramways and Carriage Company Limited) routes remained the same from the late 1930s through to the late 1950s and beyond, although during the 1930s Cornwall was poorly served during winter months. Noticeable though, and understandable when considering the ever increasing popularity of the British seaside holiday at that time, was the effect of seasonal demand on Royal Blue schedules to places such as Newquay, Weymouth, Swanage, Torquay and Bournemouth where passenger numbers were such not only to justify non-stop services from Victoria Coach Station, but also extraordinary numbers of duplications, often using vehicles from the fleets of a wide mix of independent operators as well as from associated companies. It is told by one hapless chartroom clerk that on one August Saturday in the 1950s he went in search of a passenger on the nine o'clock non-stop service to Newquay in order to put right a booking error, to be faced not only by the service coach, but no fewer than twenty-one duplicates.

One has to admire the fortitude of passengers who set-off on these long expeditions, with the journey from London to Plymouth taking 9½ hours, Ilfracombe 11 hours, and Penzance 14 hours. But then with the cost of a Royal Blue high season Saturday return ticket to Penzance in 1949 costing just £2.16s.3d (£2.81) one can appreciate the attraction of coach travel.

The majority of companies using Victoria Coach Station operated most of their services on a year-round basis, but Westcliff and Eastern National were exceptions. Their routes to Southend and Clacton were purely seasonal. (This changed in later years, but here we are simply comparing the late 1930s with the late 1940s, and then with the late 1950s).

By the late 1930s Coastal was controlling two Westcliff routes from London to Southend; one from Victoria Coach Station and Walthamstow, and the other from Holloway (where the terminal was, amusingly, the Orange Coach Station

in Parkhurst Road   Orange Luxury Coaches being a PSV Operators member), Islington and Dalston; but from the late 1940s the route, still operating from Victoria Coach Station, skipped Holloway, and went via Islington, Dalston and Walthamstow. Westcliff has always been involved in a miscellany of routes from various parts of London to Southend, notably the service started in the 1930s by New Empress Saloons who were subsequently bought out by the City Coach Company of Peckham and ran from Kentish Town and Wood Green. Initially Westcliff ran in competition but later operated a joint service. Immediately after the war, again jointly with City Coach Company, Westcliff planned a new coach terminal in Lordship Lane, Wood Green, although as early as February 1933 it had been reported in the trade press that Westcliff Motor Services in conjunction with Orange Luxury Coaches had bought property in Lordship Lane for the "erection of a motor coach station", and that a separate company was to be formed to manage and exploit the new station. Eastern National eventually operated the service and the Wood Green terminus became an Eastern National depot. At no time since its inception was the service ever pre-bookable.

The Eastern National service from Victoria Coach Station to Clacton was operated basically only on summer Saturdays, but with a daily service at the very peak of the season. This rather poor service is not too surprising when one considers that Suttons Crossley had been operating to Clacton since the 1930s on a three times daily basis throughout the year from Charing Cross Embankment (transferring to King's Cross Coach Station after the war); Empire's Best also operated three times daily throughout the year from the late 1920s from both London Terminal Coach Station in Clapham and Central Coach Station (transferring, postwar, to Bayliss Road, Waterloo and Pancras Road, King's Cross); and Grey-Green was also operating from King's Cross Coach Station on a thrice-daily, all-year-round basis. There really was very little London/Clacton business left for Eastern National.

Eastern National's main routes into London were from Braintree and Halstead to King's Cross Coach Station, and for many years timetables continued to show the name Hicks Brothers (the company eventually being acquired by Eastern National in 1950). These were originally services of Horn of Braintree, Quest of Maldon, and Hicks Brothers, but although having the Quest operating rights from London to Maldon, the service was never operated by Eastern National   passengers travelled to Chelmsford and then by local bus service. The services operated daily through the year and made connections in Braintree to several towns and villages in Essex and Suffolk. In 1954 Eastern National transferred this service from Judd Street to Coastal's newly opened terminal in Euston Square, but then in 1963 it transferred from Euston Square to the Tilling Coach Station in Northdown Street, which was taken over by Eastern National.

Above, an early morning scene on a Saturday in August 1962. Empty coaches from Wilts & Dorset, Southdown and Maidstone & District fleets queueing along Sutherland Street northwestwards towards the Ebury railway bridge junction with Buckingham Palace Road.

In the view opposite, in Buckingham Palace Road, coaches are even three deep in places. Sutherland Street coaches will turn right at the traffic lights at the top of the picture. Across the road from the Coach Station prominent on the left is the BOAC Airways Terminal whilst on the other side of the road is the site of the former Russian Church.

Below, another 1962 shot; this time an aerial view from the roof of Victoria Coach Station showing the heavily duplicated Standerwick coaches assembling for the morning departure. Apart from six Gay Hostess Leyland Atlantean double-deck vehicles with MCW bodywork, also visible are Leyland-bodied Royal Tigers of Standerwick and Maidstone & District and Burlingham Seagulls from the Standerwick or Ribble fleets. *(Chris Nash all)*

101

Although our concern is chiefly with Victoria Coach Station, we sometimes need to look closely at the independent sector if we are to have an accurate idea of prevailing situations affecting services to Victoria. This applies particularly to the services that ran on routes from London to East Anglia and particularly to north Essex, north Hertfordshire, Suffolk, and parts of Norfolk and Cambridgeshire.

Whilst Eastern Counties, operating from Victoria Coach Station, had a near monopoly on the trunk routes from London to Cambridge, Norwich, Bury St Edmunds and north Norfolk, it had considerable competition on routes to Ipswich, and, even with its whole series of diverse seasonal routes to Great Yarmouth, was not ever the principal operator to points along the coastal fringe from Yarmouth and Lowestoft southwards to which Grey-Green and, for a time, Norfolk Motor Services were operating at least twice daily on a year-round basis from King's Cross Coach Station.

But it is the smaller, independent operators who present us with the most interesting collection of East Anglian routes, and always from whichever of the various King's Cross Coach Stations was current at the time. Morley's Grey to Lakenheath; Primrose to Chelmsford; Grey Pullman to Haverhill; Jennings to Thaxted and Clare; Corona to Stowmarket; Whippet to Huntingdon; and in particular Premier Travel (who acquired Grey Pullman) to Saffron Walden and, according to their 1950s press advertisement, 32 other destinations. Somehow or other these operators and their routes were able to resist being swallowed up by the bigger companies, and one admires their fortitude.

In the late 1930s and 1940s most northbound services, including Eastern Counties, Lincolnshire, North Western, Standerwick, United Automobile Services and Yorkshire Services, operated from both Victoria and King's Cross Coach Stations. By the end of the 1950s most used only Victoria Coach Station.

It took Lincolnshire Road Car slightly longer to become re-established after the war with its express services to London. It was not until 1950 that the service resumed, but it returned to its prewar schedule of a daily service from Victoria Coach Station to Cleethorpes via Peterborough and Lincoln, and a seasonal service via Skegness.

Services between London, Birmingham and Manchester were, for the most part, the preserve of joint operations between Midland Red, North Western and Majestic although by the 1950s the name Majestic no longer appeared. The route pattern and times remained virtually unaltered until the late 1950s. Midland Red also operated a through service from London to Llandudno. It is interesting that in the 1930s, Ribble connections between Manchester and the Lake District & Scotland were included in the London/Manchester timetable, but these ceased to be shown after the war when Ribble became associated with the Standerwick/Scout services to Lancashire, and the Ribble Lake District connections were shown via Preston instead.

The 1930s Standerwick services were shown in the Coastal timetable index as incorporating Bracewell's and John Bull, but by the 1940s there was no mention of these two companies, although by then the service had become a joint Standerwick/Scout operation. The routes and times remained virtually the same both prewar and postwar.

Apart from East Anglia, it was only on routes to Manchester, Blackpool and intermediate towns that any year-round competition from a PSV Operators member existed, that being from Yelloway Motor Services who had been operating between London and Lancashire from soon after the company's formation in 1932, and who during the 1930s had its own London office at 116 Euston Road. Operating at first from Central Coach Station and later from the various King's Cross Coach Stations, Yelloway scored an advantage over Coastal by serving Derby, Ashbourne and Leek, destinations not available on services from Victoria Coach Station. Their London/Lancashire services operated until the end of 1976 when an exchange of services was agreed between Yelloway and National Travel (North West), which took them off routes to the capital. Yelloway Motor Services had always been a major member of PSV Operators, and there was a Yelloway director on PSV's Board from 1936 until 1977.

Possibly it could be argued that the Northern Roadways services of the 1950s from King's Cross Coach Station to Scotland were in direct competition with the Scottish Omnibuses services from Victoria Coach Station, but they were short lived and do not warrant too much attention in the present context.

London to Liverpool remained a purely Crosville route both in the late 1930s and into the 1940s and 1950s although some 1930s advertisements quote "previously operated by Pearsons Happy Days Motor Ways". Two routes were always operated: all-year-round via Cannock and Chester and summer only via Crewe; the summer season extension from Liverpool to Southport of the year-round service was discontinued when the services were resumed in 1947. An unusual feature in the Crosville timetables of the late 1940s and 1950s was the inclusion of the local agent's details beside the name of each place on the route, within the body of the timetable itself rather than as a separate list.

In 1949 the London to Newcastle timetable still showed the operating companies as United Automobile and Orange Brothers but the Orange had disappeared by the 1950s; there had been some slight changes to schedules and the route structure remained more or less unaltered, although services to Edinburgh and Glasgow that appeared in much of the companies' advertising during the 1930s were not featured after the war.

Services between London and Yorkshire had always been operated by the pool of companies known as Yorkshire Services, with the Yorkshire Pool having been one of the first such arrangements to be established, earlier even than Associated Motorways. The two main routes, the Midland Road via Northampton and Leicester, and the Great North Road via Stamford, remained almost unaltered from the early 1930s, but during the later part of that decade two additional seasonal routes were operating, one via Bedford and Kettering, the other through Royston and Huntingdon. The additional seasonal routes were not immediately resumed after the war, but from the 1950s services were introduced via Cambridge and Huntingdon.

The services of Scottish Omnibuses, SMT and Western remained virtually unaltered from the late 1930s through to the late 1950s and beyond, and usually carried two drivers. They continued to offer connections and through bookings on

W Alexander services to points beyond Edinburgh and Glasgow (Oban and Aberdeen via Glasgow, and Inverness and Aberdeen via Edinburgh and, from the late 1940s, additional connections and through bookings were available on the Highland Omnibuses service from Inverness to Wick, Thurso and Scrabster). Even the rather luxurious two-day services from London to Edinburgh, which had been operating in the late 1930s, had already been resumed by the end of the 1940s; one route with an overnight stay in York, and the other in Chester, and soon after, a three-day service operated with overnight stops in Stratford-Upon-Avon and Windermere.

It was the postwar popularity of the holiday camps that were springing up and flourishing throughout Britain that brought the majority of new or improved coach services to Victoria Coach Station (although it should be added that Butlins had opened their first holiday camp in Clacton in June 1938). Summer Saturday Southdown departures to Hayling Island, or the beach areas of Bracklesham Bay, Selsey, Wittering, Earnley and Pagham were always heavily duplicated; Maidstone & District operated services to Leysdown and Minster; Rockley Sands became a new destination to be served by Royal Blue direct from Victoria Coach Station, and it was already serving Osmington in Dorset, and Minehead in Somerset where Butlin's had a particularly popular camp. The holiday camps in the Great Yarmouth/Lowestoft areas created an increased demand for Eastern Counties services, and the Lincolnshire services via Skegness, another Butlins location, were always fully booked long in advance. Passengers to the Butlins camp in Pwllheli travelled by the Friday overnight Crosville service to Chester, and made a Saturday morning Crosville connection across North Wales, with return connections from the holiday camp on Saturday to link once again with the overnight service between Chester and London. Passengers for Scarborough or Butlins Camp at Filey had only a Yorkshire Services Friday overnight coach with a Saturday overnight return, but there were severe restrictions on the number of passengers the carrier was permitted to carry. Scarborough was not, however, a very coach-friendly resort at that time as the following report from Coaching Journal in July 1950 shows: "In spite of the boasted increase in rail excursion traffic as the result of Scarborough's determination to keep unsightly coaches away from the front, traders are still bemoaning the loss of coach passengers. A number of operators have either cancelled or reduced their excursion to the one-time popular resort because their patrons object to being set down and picked up in the Weaponness Valley Road, a good half-hour's walk from the sea front".

Fortunately for Yorkshire Services passengers, they used the main bus station in the town.

The only hitch to upset what had become a steady and satisfactory state of affairs was the Suez War, which brought back fuel rationing in the autumn of 1956. It was fortunate that this disruption happened during the winter months, and although coach operators in no way welcomed it, it did enable them to cut out a lot of unprofitable journeys. Off-peak services were most affected; many once-a-day schedules lost their mid-week departures; three times daily services forfeited their middle journey; and some routes were curtailed. Possibly worst affected were those departures which normally needed duplication, and which had to be restricted to one vehicle.

Aldershot & District reduced its London/Farnham service from a half-hourly to an hourly frequency, and the Maidstone & District London/Hastings and London/Rye services were amalgamated so that the Rye section operated only between Pembury and Rye, with passengers to and from London travelling by the Hastings coach and changing vehicles at the Camden Hotel, Pembury, the long-established refreshment break on both routes.

The immediate anxiety was how to prepare for the following summer months, and how could advance bookings be planned, for it was certain that if the cut backs were to continue, availability could not possibly match demand.

A decision was made to produce booking application forms that were available from agents, Victoria Coach Station booking hall, and by post. Needless to say completed application forms were received back in their tens of thousands, and in order to ensure absolute first-come-first-served fairness each one was numerically referenced, with absolute control being maintained by the post bookings department; specifically by Cuthbert Embleton who was head of that department at the time, and who ensured that direct applications from the public should not be treated with any greater favour than those received from agents.

In any normal year, summer bookings on most routes would begin by March at the latest, but it was quite impossible to know what would happen for the summer of 1957 so schedules were guessed at, and applications tentatively entered onto charts. A big problem was that many people had placed applications with more than one agent, and often made a direct application to Coastal as well, so close attention had to be paid to determining duplicate applications, with the one bearing the earliest reference number being accepted.

It came as a great relief to everyone when fuel rationing was withdrawn at very short notice in the spring of 1957, and most services were soon back to normal, with another very busy summer season indeed to follow, although the Aldershot & District service did not return to a half-hourly frequency but remained an hourly service thereafter, and the Maidstone & District arrangements for the Hastings and Rye service were reintroduced for the following winter's operations.

A busy Summer Saturday, again in 1962. Departure bays 1-12 are shown with Southdown and Maidstone & District coaches supplemented by hired-in vehicles. Bodywork by Beadle, Duple, Eastern Coach Works and a Weymann's Fanfare, amongst others can be seen. *(Chris Nash)*

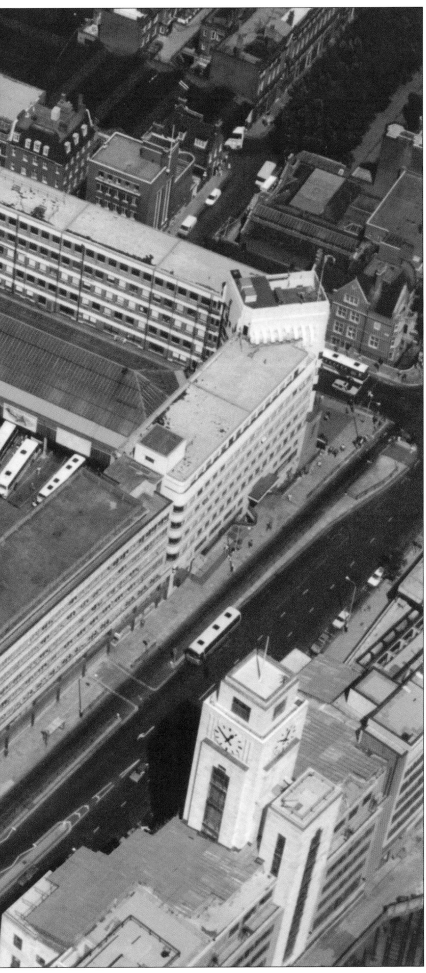

An aerial view of Victoria Coach Station from a later period showing how well the new extension matched the original building (more then 30 years its senior) and the new canopies over bays 15-22. BOAC Airways Terminal is seen in the bottom right hand corner in front of the (hidden) railway tracks from Victoria. *(Peter Scammell collection)*

From the roof of Victoria Station in 1962, looking along the length of the yard. Lots of colour, lots of hustle-and-bustle, lots of different coaches and companies and lots of passengers wandering around. East Kent Beadles seem to have dominated at this particular moment. *(Chris Nash)*

A few well-loved liveries of yesteryear (STA)

A – Y of Regular well-known Visitors to the Coach Station – Part One

A – Y of Regular well-known Visitors to the Coach Station – Part Two

Independent Operators from East Anglia who served Kings Cross Coach Station at its various locations

Left from top to bottom:

Blackwells
Blackwells
Hicks
Hicks

Right from top to bottom:

Jennings
Premier
Suttons
Whippet

Control

Transferring our attention now from the services operated, to the methods of their control, it was not only the diverse route numbering schemes of the operating companies that Coastal needed to amalgamate; they each had their own charting and ticketing techniques as well. If Coastal was to act as the London charting office for twenty or more different companies, it needed either to devise a comprehensive arrangement that could accommodate the system variations of all the companies or to train its reservations staff to handle more than twenty different methods of record keeping; it chose the former. Building on the experience gained in the 1930s, the Coastal reservations system and documentation of the 1940s encompassed virtually every need and was to hold good well into the 1960s.

Fortunately, during the period late 1940s to 1960s only five of the companies with services from Victoria Coach Station allocated specific seats at the time of booking: SMT, Western, Timpsons, London Transport and Samuelsons. The booking charts for the two Scottish companies were held at the Scottish Omnibuses office in Regent Street so were of no concern to Coastal, and the Timpsons charts were held at its office in Catford, so again presented no problems for Coastal. London Transport provided Coastal's chartroom with its own seating plans/booking charts for its sightseeing tours, and the charts for Samuelson day and half-day tours were hand-drawn and duplicated (by Gestetner machine – there were no photocopiers in those days). But what to do about all the others?

To add to the mix of possibilities, some coach companies insisted that passengers reserve places for both outward and return journey at the same time; some would only book the outward journey, and leave the passenger to book the return journey upon arrival at the destination; and others left it to the passengers to decide whether or not to book the homeward journey when booking their outward reservation. And, of course, different operating companies were using different vehicles, with different seating capacities.

Coastal generally held the charts for all outward departures from Victoria Coach Station, and charts for inward journeys to Victoria were held at the operating company's distant terminal. This way only one chart was held for any particular departure, usually at the starting point of the journey, and it told the whole story – most importantly, how many passengers, where from and where to.

But if inward journey booking charts were held at operating companies' distant terminals, what should be done about recording passengers' return journey details if it was being booked at the same time as the outward journey? The system decided upon was to include the passenger's return travel details on the outward journey chart, and then pass the information to the operating company's charting office handling the journey in question. Each of the operating companies for whom this system applied provided pads of preprinted forms on which to note the inward to London reservations, and in Coastal's chartroom the outward journey charts would be trawled constantly, and inward journey details listed on the forms provided, which were then sent as 'On Company Service' (OCS) mail by the next coach setting off to wherever the inward journey charts were held.

This system worked well for those services (the majority) where operators were not restricted in the number of passengers they were permitted to carry. It was the carrier and not the operating licence that dictated when to say 'sorry, fully booked'.

❧ ❧

"The up and down coaches did not meet at Pembury, where there was a refreshment halt, but passed each other a short distance north of Tonbridge. Along this stretch of road each driver was on the look out for the other coach. The two vehicles then stopped a short distance from each other; each driver got out, crossed the road and took the coach going in the opposite direction. Traffic congestion was relatively uncommon in those days and the change over happened more or less at the same spot. What would have been interesting would have been if the down coach had been running late and they had met on the winding and quite steep (1 in 9) River Hill".
Alex Fairley

"I recall a journey I made by Midland Red from Victoria Coach Station to Llandudno. At one point the coach was slowly climbing a hill when it was overtaken by a car, which flagged it down. The car driver told the coach driver that his boot doors had come open, and he was slowly depositing suitcases on the road, one by one!".
Chris Nash

"On an overnight journey by North Western to Manchester, having endured the horrors of crying babies, changing nappies, and a tin can that rolled under the seats every time the coach pulled up a traffic lights or rounded a corner, I can remember longing for the dawn to break and our arrival at Lower Moseley Street coach station".
Chris Nash

"During a very busy period in the ticket office, a ticket clerk began losing patience with a passenger, and asked, 'are you an RTG?' [RTG was a term used for a passenger with an open return ticket wishing to book their return journey]. The passenger thinking it was a term for a mental disability was not amused."
Chris Nash

Four pictures showing how the destination boards at Victoria Coach Station changed over the years. The first two pictures, taken during the early 1950s, show the boards positioned at right angles to the departure bays with additional numerical signs over the bays themselves, with the second picture showing how Bays 1 & 2 did not quite conform. As the third picture shows, later in the 1950s the boards were repositioned above the departure bays below the numerical signs. The fourth picture taken at Easter 1970 shows the updated, and more design conscious signs, with the bay numbers displayed more clearly. The traditional term 'departure bay' remained for many years to come, but was eventually changed to 'departure gate' during the 1990s. *(LCCc)*

Administration

Most of the coach companies had their own inspectors at Victoria Coach Station, and it was they who kept a weather eye on how the booking situation on any particular journey was developing. In most cases it was a general rule of thumb that about 40 people could fit into one coach so when the number of passengers booked on any service was nearing that figure, particularly if the departure was reasonably imminent, a decision needed to be made whether to operate a duplicate vehicle, or whether to refuse any more bookings. Obviously, it is better to turn away two or three passengers (or persuade them to travel at another time) rather than run a duplicate coach with just a handful of people on it. If the operating company decided that a second coach was to operate, a second chart page would be started, and likewise the third, and the fourth, and the fifth, and so on. On the other hand, some companies preferred bookings to be taken until the cows came home regardless of the 40-passenger rule-of-thumb, so chart clerks just added extra chart pages ad infinitum. The

operating company's inspectors would not usually look at the situation until a day or two ahead, and they would then plan for the provision of sufficient vehicles accordingly, and cut off departures as appropriate. Obviously, the inspectors worked in close liaison with the traffic departments of their own companies, and although these arrangements might at first seem somewhat casual and rather risky, the sixth-sense which most of them developed usually ensured the maximum efficiency in vehicle utilisation, and the highest possible number of passengers carried. It was just another of the intuitive attributes that helped to make a professional coachman.

The difference between the two systems was just a matter of fitting people to coaches in the first instance, and coaches to people in the second. But whichever of these two arrangements applied, a heavy line drawn across a chart with the word STOP written below it meant just that.

In other cases, usually when the operating licence put strict limitations on permitted passenger numbers and where, therefore, overbooking had to be carefully avoided, the operator would allocate a set number of seats for each departure in each direction to Coastal and hold a second chart at its own office for the remainder of the accommodation; the two charts were amalgamated nearer the time of departure. In these instances where Coastal held allocations of seats, and therefore separate charts as well, for inward journeys to Victoria Coach Station, care had to be taken when reservations were being made to ensure that seats were available (and charted) for each direction. This system of double charting applied only to the services of United Automobile, Yorkshire Services, Lincolnshire Road Car and Crosville, although it was also used for the Midland Red motorway services between London and Birmingham when they were first introduced.

It can be seen therefore that there were different sets of circumstances for which to plan but the Coastal system, simple as it was, covered them all and involved just one design of booking chart usable for all situations — basically a sheet of paper ruled with lines to indicate the number of seats available, and headings to show where the coach was going to and when.

As the 24-hour clock was little used at that time, charts for AM departures were printed in black and for PM departures in red. Each chart was printed, one side only, on very heavy grade paper, 8 inches x 13 inches. Individual charts were then collated between thick board covers in loose leaf books and held together with two adjustable canvas-webbing straps about ¾ inch thick. Spaces were provided at the top of each chart to show details of destination and route, day of departure, date of departure and time of departure. A box in the top right hand corner was available for numbering the chart on those occasions when more than one vehicle was required, and additional pages added. Despite the colour differentiation, and so that there could be absolutely no confusion, the letters AM and PM were also included in a very large font.

Initially (when coaches were smaller) the pages were ruled off into 32 lines numbered from 40 to 71, but this was later increased to 40 lines, numbered from 51 to 90, with columns headed; agency number, pick-up point, ticket type (S Single, D Day return, P Period return, RTG return half of an open-dated ticket), ticket number, return date, return time and destination. The lines were numbered from 40 (and later 51) rather than from 1 so that it could never be thought that they might refer to seat numbers on the coaches. All chart entries were made in pencil using one line per passenger and in cases where the number of seats available was limited the chart would be marked off at the appropriate point and the word STOP written below it. The system was simple and could be used universally for all the services from Victoria Coach Station; it gave instant information about the state of any departure, and there were rarely any errors.

The details for the chart heading (destination, date, time, etc.) were entered using a very large John Bull printing set or by rubber stamps specially made to show specific destinations and routes; large-print adjustable rubber stamps were used for the day, date and time details. The charts were prepared and made up by the chartroom clerks themselves; it was a time-consuming and very messy job.

So far, so good: there was a chart for every departure, and the charts were ready to collate and insert in the loose leaf binders. Here again differing types of service needed to be accommodated in ways most convenient to and easily useable by the chart clerks, the inspectors or anyone else needing access to them; the binders could be very heavy and unmanageable if they contained too many charts. However, the adjustability of the loose-leaf system covered any arrangement decided upon.

Dividing up the charts into binders was a case of practice makes perfect and finding the most easy-to-use plan. Charts for high-frequency routes were usually collated strictly in date and time order and placed in separate binders for each month (the Maidstone & District charts for the high-frequency Maidstone and Gillingham routes were further divided into AM and PM departures); South Midland charts were also divided on a month by month basis, but were sub-divided according to route (i.e. via Maidenhead or via High Wycombe); on the other hand charts for a once-a-day service might need only one binder for a complete season. The system was totally flexible, extra charts could be added in the correct chronological order in seconds, and it probably could have not been improved upon at that time.

Even in the case of the truly odd-man-out London Transport Sunday Bus Excursions it was possible to use the "one size fits all" Coastal chart. These excursions were very inexpensive, operated with ordinary London Transport double-deck buses and ran on Sundays during the summer months from local areas throughout London and the suburbs to such places as Chessington Zoo, Hampton Court and Kew Gardens. Advanced bookings were made with Coastal agents and charted at Victoria Coach Station. It proved unworkable to hold separate charts for each of the local picking-up points, but, in any case, as London Transport would operate as many vehicles as were needed and from wherever they were needed, it was easier to use one chart per destination regardless of from where the passengers were travelling, and sort the whole thing out at the end. Thus, for example, a chart headed Chessington Zoo could well show passenger picking up at Golders Green, Plumstead, Putney, Barnet or any one of dozens of other bus stops in London Transport's Central Area, with the only common feature being the destination. At 6.00pm each Saturday, when most agents had closed, the total bookings would be summarised and details of passenger numbers from each picking-up point passed to London Transport, whose

representative came in person to the chartroom at 7.00pm sharp for the final details. Timing was crucial as London Transport had then to advise each of its garages how many of their buses and crews would be needed the next day. It was impossible even to try assimilating the passenger totals at any earlier time because the situation was constantly fluctuating, particularly if the sun was shining on Saturday afternoon and half the population of London made the last minute decision to have a Sunday trip out. Car ownership was minimal and these bus excursions were very popular; with so many picking-up points available throughout London the total passenger numbers handled by the chartroom at Victoria Coach Station could go into many hundreds each weekend.

But regardless of whatever arrangement was decided upon for each route, or operator, or departure time, or simply for convenience, there would always be at any one time, summer or winter, come rain or shine, tens of thousands of reservations, written on thousands of charts, held in hundreds of binders.

☙ ❧

As soon as coach services had resumed after the war, and the fire service had relinquished the accommodation it had borrowed from Coastal, the chartroom was urgently re-established, and was quickly up and running again. The room, which covered the width of part of the first floor in the Buckingham Palace Road wing of Victoria Coach Station, was divided into sections, each one handling reservations for one or more companies; each section was connected, usually with three lines, to the main Victoria Coach Station switchboard and there were two extensions from a separate internal telephone system which connected each section of the chartroom with the booking hall and the public enquiry office. These sections handled reservations from agents and the coach station booking hall only and were not available to the general public; an additional section within the chartroom was used specifically to handle public telephone enquiries.

The charts in their binders were stored in racks above the telephones, and above the racks there were intricately drawn diagrammatic maps showing every town and village served on the routes being handled by that particular section. Often, greatly enlarged copies of the timetables for the inward journeys to London were also placed above the racks so that chart clerks could check inward journey details with maximum ease while at the same time and with great dexterity holding the chart open with one hand, entering the details with a pencil held in the other hand, clutching the telephone under the chin and continuing to speak to the agent on the line. Headsets had not been introduced in the chartroom at that point.

Agents were instructed how to give telephone reservation requests, and the order in which to pass information, thus an efficient agent and speedy chart clerk could complete a booking in seconds rather than minutes. Although on the face of it this might seem a little militaristic, there were few who did not appreciate the need for speed and efficiency in such busy circumstances. In fact a great camaraderie built up between the agents and the chart clerks and more often than not it was unnecessary to ask an agent for his identity because the voice was familiar. By now Coastal had well over 1,000 agents and they were encouraged to visit the chartroom by appointment

The rail strike, which began at Whit weekend at the end of May 1955, put immense pressure on Victoria Coach Station. This picture shows the queue on May 31st stretching out of the booking hall and into Elizabeth Street....... (LCCc)

...... and round the corner into Buckingham Palace Road. (LCCc)

No chance of a day trip while the train strike was on. (LCCc)

This 1950s picture was originally captioned 'First Strike' but, sadly, is undated. It is obviously posed, and one is uncertain who is on strike – maybe the lady sitting on the cases! (LCCc)

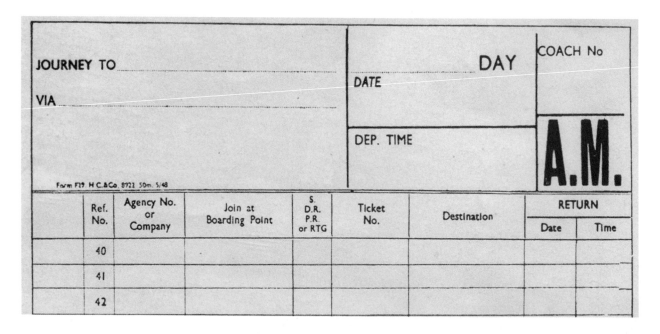

	Ref. No.	Agency No. or Company	Join at Boarding Point	S. D.R. P.R. or RTG	Ticket No.	Destination	RETURN	
							Date	Time
	40							
	41							
	42							

JOURNEY TO ....

VIA ....

DATE

DAY

DEP. TIME

COACH No

A.M.

Form F29. H C.&Co. 8922 50m. 5/48

to see how things worked at the other end of the line.

By today's standards, the booking arrangements of a half-century ago for all transportation companies — road, rail, sea and air — seem inefficient, labour intensive, and slow. Apart from carrier pigeons, the only means of communication were OCS mail, letter post, telephone or telegram.

Telephone costs were based on a charge-per-call basis for local calls, and on a time basis for toll or trunk calls, so for London area agents it was expedient to telephone the chartroom for every booking, but for agents outside the London local call area a postal system was preferable for all but very urgent requests. Incoming calls to Victoria Coach Station grew in number phenomenally. After the war, agents were given an ex-directory telephone number to the switchboard at Victoria Coach Station, and the original SLOane 0202 number was kept for the public, but for provincial agents (whose calls were time-critical) a direct line to the chartroom was provided which was not answered until a clerk was available and ready to handle the booking with the greatest possible speed.

Agents based outside the London local call area were supplied with reservation request forms, which were sent in duplicate by post to Coastal (or by coach as OCS mail if they were on a handy route). The requested reservation was charted using the reservation form number as a temporary ticket number, one part of the form was filed in the chartroom and the other part returned post-haste to the agent, who then issued a ticket from a ticket-book that included yellow confirmation copies. The confirmation copies, nicknamed yellow perils, would be sent to Coastal who would substitute the reservation form number on the chart with the ticket number. It all seems such a lot of time and paper, but time and paper was all that was then available — and the system worked.

Eventually the substitution of reservations form numbers by ticket numbers on the charts was done away with. Inspectors and drivers were not collecting tickets until passengers had boarded, by which time it was too late if the service was overbooked to check each ticket and in any case tickets were rarely checked against charted details.

Within a year of coach services being resumed after the

Top of a Coastal booking chart before the 1950s. Reservations numbering started at 40.

Typical Coastal booking chart of the 1950s/early 1960s with reservations numbering from 51.

It was intended only to show pictures of working coaches, at work, but we felt we might make an exception and include this image of an RFW vehicle. Seen here, *London Transport* **LUC 389** is a preserved vehicle on display at Victoria Coach Station on July 27th 1992. *(Chris Nash)*

Below is a contemporary scene when these vehicles were in regular service. *(GHF Atkins © John Banks collection)*

Samuelson New Transport was based at 3 Eccleston Place, Victoria (opposite the Elizabeth Street wing of Victoria Coach Station). *Samuelsons* coaches were used on day and half-day tours and for private hire work. **445 BXD**, an AEC Reliance with Duple Britannia bodywork, was delivered in the contract livery for British United Airways that was subsequently adopted as the *Samuelsons* fleet livery. This picture shows the vehicle about to make an airport transfer to Gatwick for Lyons Tours on July 18th 1969. *(Chris Nash)*
Based at Catford in southeast London, *Timpsons* coaches were seen at Victoria Coach Station either on private hire work, day or half-day tours, or feeder services. **PXO 972**, seen her in the summer of 1963, is an AEC Reliance built in 1955 and has Park Royal Royalist bodywork. *(Chris Nash)*

The *East Kent* section of the chartroom in early summer 1955. This was one of the first of four sections to have separate direct lines for agents, but was also connected by three additional lines through the main Coastal telephone exchange, and by two internal telephones to the booking hall and the traffic office (public enquiry office). Telephone headsets had not been introduced to the chartroom - the chart clerk on the right, being left-handed, needs to be very versatile in order to hold open the loose-leaf binder of charts with her left elbow, write with the left hand, and hold the telephone in her right hand. For right-handed chart clerks it was easier, although the left elbow still played an important part, as did the trick of clutching the telephone between the shoulder and the chin. *(LCCc)*

With the 1955 rail strike, 'officialdom' seemed to become more aware of the true status of that 'coach station just round the corner from Westminster', as witnessed by this visit to Victoria Coach Station by Mr Hugh Molson, joint Parliamentary Secretary, Ministry of Transport. Seen here on June 13th 1955 at the *Royal Blue* section in the chartroom. (*l to r*) Jim Russell (Assistant to Traffic Manager), Jack Ashmore (Chartroom Supervisor), Hugh Molson, Len Corbett (Traffic Manager), Rene Corbett (chart clerk, and Traffic Manager's wife), Norrie Murphy (chart clerk). This was another section to have direct telephone lines for agents. In the picture Rene Corbett is answering one call, but at the same time lifting off another receiver, which, although remaining unanswered for a short while, at least enabled the agent to hear that, he was connected to the right place. Calls were not charged on a time basis at that time. *(Fox Photos/LCCc)*

May 31st 1955, at the height of the rail strike, Miss Marjorie Robbins, Booking Hall Supervisor, and with ticket books in hand, meets the Minister of Transport, *(Fox Photos/LCCc)*

After the alterations to the chartroom in winter 1957/8 **every** section had direct telephone lines for agents, as well as the three lines via Coastal's telephone exchange, and two internal lines to the booking hall and the traffic office. This picture shows the *Southdown* section in the winter of 1958. To the left of the picture is June Warne, a particularly experienced chart clerk, and on the board above her head can be seen the diagrammatic route maps which showed every request stop on every route. *(Fox Photos/LCCc)*

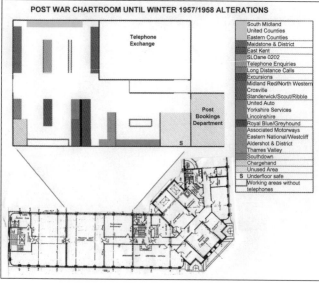

POST WAR CHARTROOM UNTIL WINTER 1957/1958 ALTERATIONS

Telephone Exchange

Post Bookings Department

S

	South Midland
	United Counties
	Eastern Counties
	Maidstone & District
	East Kent
	SLOane 0202
	Telephone Enquiries
	Long Distance Calls
	Excursions
	Midland Red/North Western
	Crosville
	Standerwick/Scout/Ribble
	United Auto
	Yorkshire Services
	Lincolnshire
	Royal Blue/Greyhound
	Associated Motorways
	Eastern National/Westcliff
	Aldershot & District
	Thames Valley
	Southdown
	Chargehand
	Unused Area
S	Underfloor safe
	Working areas without telephones

This page

Victoria Coach Station Booking Hall during the 1950s *(Dexter Studios/ LCCc)*

This diagrammatic plan of the chartroom before the winter 1957/58 alterations shows how impractical the layout was. Most positions were beyond the direct view of the chargehand, so it was difficult to assess easily where additional help might be needed. Similarly at quieter periods (evenings and Sundays) when one chart clerk might be looking after two or even three sections, a continuity of working was more difficult.

By relating the diagram to the architects plan one sees clearly the location of the chartroom on the first floor of the Buckingham Palace Road wing

A typical coach booking agency in 1957. Wakefield's in High Wycombe was a very productive Coastal agent indeed, particularly as it was directly on the busy *South Midland* service from London to Oxford (originally a *United Counties* route, and before that *Varsity*). *(C. Roberts)*

Opposite
Victoria Coach Station Telephone Exchange in 1950 *(LCCc)*

The chartroom at Victoria Coach Station in January 1948. *(Topical Press Agency/LCCc)*

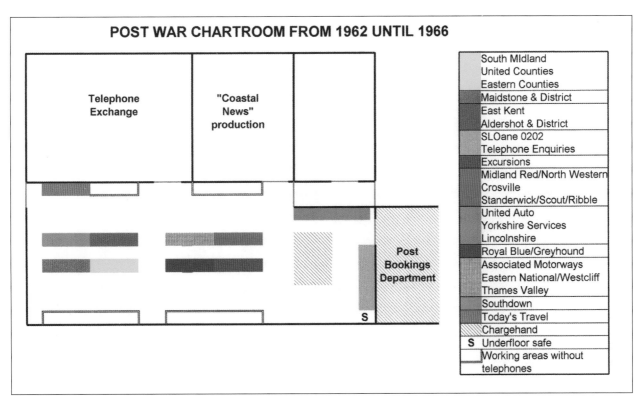

POST WAR CHARTROOM FROM 1962 UNTIL 1966

Telephone Exchange	"Coastal News" production

Post Bookings Department

S

	South MIdland
	United Counties
	Eastern Counties
	Maidstone & District
	East Kent
	Aldershot & District
	SLOane 0202
	Telephone Enquiries
	Excursions
	Midland Red/North Western
	Crosville
	Standerwick/Scout/Ribble
	United Auto
	Yorkshire Services
	Lincolnshire
	Royal Blue/Greyhound
	Associated Motorways
	Eastern National/Westcliff
	Thames Valley
	Southdown
	Today's Travel
	Chargehand
S	Underfloor safe
	Working areas without telephones

As this diagrammatic plan of the chartroom after the winter 1957/58 alterations shows, all the sections of the chartroom, including telephone enquiries, were within the view of the chargehand. The long distance telephones (more often than not answered by the chargehand) remained close to the chargehands' desk. It was quite usual during winter months for there to be some combining of sections – *East Kent* with *Southdown* for example.

Further re-arrangements to the chart room were made in 1962 with the establishing of a separate 'todays' travel' section, and separation once again of *United Auto, Yorkshire Services* and *Lincolnshire* charts from *Midland Red/ Standerwick/Crosville* cluster. Obviously, though, other alterations took place from time to time as shown by the next photograph that has clearly combined *Aldershot & District* and *Eastern Counties* and put them in the place normally occupied by *Midland Red!*

A separate 'Today's Travel' section was set-up in the chartroom to control reservations for all same-day departures regardless of operating company. Seen here are long serving chart clerk, Anne Harman, and John Marsh who eventually set-up the Ramsgate Telephone Enquiry Centre. *(LCCc)*

war, the demand on the switchroom became unmanageable; the four switchboards were increased to six, and a team of ten operators worked in shifts from 8.00am to 10.00pm. Nevertheless the telephone lines were often jammed, so in 1948 Coastal experimented with direct telephone lines to some sections of the chartroom. Individual ex-directory telephone numbers enabled agents to by-pass the main Victoria Coach Station switchboard, and each of the numbers had three or four parallel lines. Initially, the sections equipped with direct numbers were those handling bookings for Southdown, East Kent, Maidstone & District and Royal Blue routes, and with these direct lines, plus the three lines through the main switchboard and the internal lines from the coach station booking hall, it was not unusual for there to be as many as ten incoming calls to a section at any one time. The pressure was often great; agents frequently had long waits before they were answered and an unofficial practice arose whereby the handset would be lifted off as the telephone rang and laid unanswered on the desk. The agent could thus hear the other calls being taken, know he was connected to the right section and feel confident that calls were being handled quickly. To employ additional staff would not have eased the situation because only one clerk could use a chart at any one time.

A system in place in the late 1940s but abandoned from about 1950 was to divide telephone bookings into two categories: "immediate" when the date of travel was within 14 days, and "advance" for others. The chart room accepted immediates from 8.00am to 10.00pm daily (but not from agents on Sundays), but advances were accepted only from 10.00am to 6.00pm Mondays to Saturdays. in the summer of 1950 it took twelve men and 48 women to staff the chartroom.

The situation on the day that summer bookings opened was particularly chaotic; frequently an opening "day" would be spread across several days and opened not just on a company by company basis but also route by route. Patience, speed and efficiency were paramount as the following words from Coastal's General Manager, Fred Robinson in April 1949 reflect: "Our greatest concern at this period of opening summer bookings has been to avoid the enormous queues and the consequent telephone congestion we suffered last year. We have, therefore, deliberately kept our opening dates top secret until a few days beforehand. There has been no panic booking, and communications, although severely tried for a few days, stood up to the strain. Some agents have had refusals on the West Country Saturday and Sunday bookings, but there have been more alternatives to offer this year, and in any case there are not enough Saturday seats to go round.

Other factors which have eased these opening periods have been an enlarged chartroom, additional direct chart lines, more trained and efficient staff, and improved methods such

A quieter period in the chartroom – probably a winter Sunday – in the foreground *United Auto* inspector Charlie Patterson. Just two part time staff are manning all four sections on this side. *(Ron Fairhead)*

SLOane 0202 telephone enquiries after the 1956/57 chartroom alterations. Either side of the map, sturdy folders hold the timetables of all the B.E.T and B.T.C. local 'bus services throughout Great Britain. *(LCCc)*

Peter Scammell *(Peter Scammell collection.)*

as splitting the charts for departures and dividing routes etc. On the agents' side there is generally a recognition of the value of sticking to the booking drill and thus saving 'phone time".

But demand continued to grow and the need to find ways of easing the pressures on the telephone system became vital.

It was clear that apart from those services on which passenger number restriction applied because of their licence, and for some peak-date departures, very few passengers were ever turned away or bookings refused. More often than not it was not until a day or two before departure that the number of passengers booked on a service became relevant; until then reservations were being taken by telephone without restriction.

Department Heads and Executives 1955. Standing *(l to r)*: Frank Garman (agents), Briah Andrews (publicity & public relations), Mrs Buckingham (catering), Bill Adams (tours), Jock Bell (accountant), Teddy Rutland (cashier). Seated *(l to r)*: Frank Hodges (Samuelsons), George Newman (Secretary), Fred Robinson (General Manager), Len Corbett (Traffic Manager). *(LCCc)*

> *"Johnny Batho told me one day that he had decided to ask for a pay rise. On entering the Traffic Manager's Office, Mr Corbett asked John if he could lend him a fiver! John left without asking for a pay rise."*
> Chris Nash.

> *Once, when working a late duty in the traffic office I recall telling the people in the queue that I would be closing the office in five minutes time. As I turned out the light and went out of the side door, a young lady, whom I had not noticed in the queue, came up to me and asked if I could get her a seat for the overnight coach to the Northeast as it was fully booked. I politely told her that I was now off-duty and in any case she would have to see the* United Auto *inspector just prior to the coach leaving at 10.30pm in case a passenger had failed to turn up, and a seat had thereby become available. The young lady then said, somewhat provocatively, that she would 'do anything' if I helped her to get on that coach. Of course, being a true Coastal employee, I refused the offer and walked away smiling. I wonder if she did get on that coach?*
> John Marsh, ex Senior Traffic Clerk, Victoria Coach Station.

It was obvious that for the majority of journeys it would be perfectly safe for agents to issue tickets without first checking if space was available, so long as a copy of the ticket arrived in the chartroom in good time for the booking to be charted before passenger numbers became relevant. In 1954 Coastal introduced the experimental "ad lib" system, and supplied selected agents with a second ticket book that included a pink confirmation copy. Agents were now able to issue tickets without prior reference to the chartroom for the majority of services from Victoria Coach Station. Addressed envelopes were supplied to agents, together with, very importantly, a list of operators and services that were not included in the scheme. The system worked extremely well from the outset, very few errors occurred, and soon it was extended to all agents. The ad lib system was sometimes called the confirm system and in due course (as in other areas of the travel industry) sell and record.

Until now London area agents had been issued with tickets whose numbers were prefixed with the letter MA (Municipal Agent), and out-of-London agents had tickets with numbers prefixed PA (Provincial Agent), which had in addition a yellow confirmation copy. The booking hall at Victoria Coach Station had ticket books with numbers prefixed VS and VC, the VS series were single-journey-only tickets, and this was the only Coastal outlet to hold single-ticket stock. Other offices and agents booking single trips would use a return ticket and issue only the outward journey portion. The new ad lib ticket numbers were prefixed AL and were used by London and provincial agents as well as the coach station booking hall.

The introduction of ad lib bookings saved the Coastal telephone communication system from total collapse, but the strain on the switchboard was at times still very acute.

When the chartroom was re-established after the war, it was done very hurriedly and the layout was perhaps not as convenient as it might have been had more planning time been available, and space was not being used to best advantage. The telephone exchange had become rather dated so during the winter of 1957/8 a new switchboard was installed and the chartroom was redesigned with eight sections, each with its own ex-directory telephone line with a bank of five or six telephones, as well as three lines to the main switchboard and two lines on the internal system to the booking hall and public enquiry office. As every section now had direct lines, agents could by-pass the switchboard completely and it was only the three or four very busy agents with direct telephone connection from their offices to the Coastal switchboard that now needed to use that route to the chartroom.

The SLOane 0202 public enquiry number was transferred from the main coach station switchboard and became a direct line to the telephone enquiry section in the chartroom, which thereby also had a bank of telephones. These were huge improvements, which not only eased the strain on the main switchboard, but eased telephone access for agents.

In 1962 further improvements were made, notably by the setting-up of a Today's Travel section in the chartroom. At midnight every night, seats available on each service for the following 24 hours were listed on special monitor charts and transferred to the Today's Travel Control section, where they were mounted on a board, enabling the booking situation on any service to be seen at a glance.

CB   BD

In 1952 another of Coastal's original directors died. Charlie Holmes had joined the original board in 1925 and his company, West London Charabanc & Motor Company (later West London Coaches), was one of the few independent companies to have come within the Coastal fold. West London Coaches operated from Lupus Street Coach Station and later Victoria Coach Station to Aylesbury until the route was taken over by LPTB in 1934 and operated as a Green Line service.

Two years later Coastal's original Chairman, Bert Smith, resigned and was succeeded by Raymond Beddow, a director of the BET Group and Chairman of several BET companies. Raymond Beddow remained as Coastal's Chairman for just two years and his place was then taken by A F R (Michael) Carling, another BET Group executive.

The total Coastal operation was very labour intensive: for much of the period from the late 1940s to the late 1960s, apart from the company executives, staffing fell into seven categories. All catering activities came under the control firstly of Mrs S Price, then Mrs Buckingham and later Mrs Glascock with Mrs Harris as linen keeper. Ticket auditing and accounting functions, including refunds and issue of ticket books, were the province of Charlie Howard with a very able supervisor in Miss Dot Sawyer. Jack Wheeler, the Station Master, had control not just of the vehicle operations within Victoria Coach Station but other essential aspects of passenger provision including the public toilets, lost property and the left-luggage office. The Tours Department was headed at first by Bill Adams and later by Cuthbert Embleton. Bill Adams joined Coastal in 1940. Virtually his entire career was involved with coach touring, and in 1972 he became Tours Planning Manager. He retired from the National Bus Company in 1977. Publicity was the responsibility of Mr BriaH Andrews (BriaH not Brian but known as Andy). Everything to do with the agency network was the responsibility of Frank Garman as agency superintendent and his two agency representatives Bert Snoad and Roy Walker; and everything involved with reservations, service information, and communications was the responsibility of the Traffic Manager, Len Corbett.

Much of the maintenance of Victoria Coach Station was under the day-to-day control of chief maintenance engineer Reg Garman (brother of Frank Garman agency superintendent). The left-luggage office was, for much of this period, under the supervision of Howard Barker, aided by Colin Probert and Leslie Tomlinson. Len Corbett's Traffic Department was the most heavily staffed and was divided naturally into separate but interlinking operations. The booking hall was headed throughout by Marjorie (Robbie) Robbins and was an almost totally female preserve; the Post Bookings Department (which included the Post Room and Reception Office) was headed in the 1950s by Cuthbert Embleton who eventually became Tours Manager (his place in Post Bookings taken by Jack Ashmore); the chartroom was under the control of Jim Russell and a series of chartroom supervisors; the switchboard, upon reorganisation in 1957, was supervised by Irene Thorpe, who had until then been a chart clerk; and the Public Enquiry Office (for some reason referred to as the Traffic Office) was, for staffing purposes, an adjunct to the chartroom and staffed by so called traffic clerks who would sometimes work in the enquiry office and at other times as

chargehand in the chartroom. And tucked away along the corridor between the chartroom and the restaurant was the office of Jock Bell, the chief cashier. Jock Bell joined Coastal in 1948 and was still working at Victoria Coach Station in 1973 when he received his 25 years service award

Peter Scammell joined Coastal in 1954s as a chartroom clerk and remained with the company until his retirement in 1995 at which time he held a post most easily described as Victoria Coach Station Manager or "Mr Coach Station", he had headed the Post Bookings Department, been Chartroom Supervisor, Traffic Assistant Reservations, and Reservations Manager. Then, under the National Bus Company, he became Terminals Manager responsible for Victoria Coach Station, King's Cross Coach Station (the Eastern National one), Catford Coach Station and a travel agency in Slough; his title eventually changed to Assistant Commercial Manager (National Travel SE).

With 41 years at Victoria Coach Station, Peter Scammell was the longest-serving employee apart from Len Corbett who beat him to the record by just one year. It is probably no exaggeration to equate Peter Scammell's influence on the day-to-day operation of Victoria Coach Station during his more-than-four-decades there with those of his predecessors, the original 'Coastal' pioneers. His forward thinking ideas together with his actual hands-on experience were instrumental to a enormous extent in the development of the ever-improving reservations and information systems that were to make London Coastal Coaches Limited and Victoria Coach Station so vital to the coaching industry as a whole, even though some people probably found his exhilarating enthusiasm quite daunting.

And there is a wry twist to the chronicle of Peter Scammell's involvement with Victoria Coach Station, but it is being saved until the end of our story.

Raising glasses to wish bon voyage to three lady tourists who were the first to buy 'Coachmaster' tickets. Pictured here (l to r): Mr F.W.J. (Fred) Robinson, Director and General Manager of Victoria Coach Station; Peter Scammell, at this point Reservations Manager, Victoria Coach Station; Mrs Marjery Francis from Ottawa; Mrs Mary Thomson from Albany, Western Australia; Mrs Pauline McCutchion from Florence, Ontario; and Mr C.A. (Frank) Hodges, Operating Manager, Victoria Coach Station. *(Fox Photos/LCCc)*

A moment or two's reflection...

. . . as the author indulges in some relived memories. It's the late 1950s, quarter to eight on a summer Saturday morning. I left home about quarter past six and the Green Line, which has brought me from Potters Bar, is turning onto Elizabeth Bridge. The cloudless sky is bright blue over the coach station, the sun is already shining brightly and one can sense that a warm day lies ahead. I'm the early shift chartroom chargehand today. I love these hectically busy days and, even now, the adrenaline is pumping madly through my veins in anticipation.

In through the main entrance; there is already a queue forming in the booking hall. The two Today's Travel windows are already open with Edie Daniels and Marjorie Ballard busy issuing tickets. I call to them and wave as I pass. (Other booking hall stalwarts at the time included Jo Sedgwick, Pat Tapp, Mary Lambourne, Connie Guest, Kath White and others whose names, regrettably, I have forgotten.) Through the adjacent doors and up the stairs two at a time to the first floor.

"Nothing much to report," says Harry Sedgewick, who has been on night duty and from whom I am taking over, "but phone enquiries have been going mad as usual."

Ernie Price has arrived early and has already settled into answering telephone enquiries from the public we're a bit pushed for staff, he'll be on his own for a while but there should be some part-timers in very soon. (The chartroom relied very heavily on part-time staff, particularly in the evenings and at weekends. All the part time staff was male, and included postmen, night workers on newspapers, telephone engineers, schoolteachers and others needing to find a supplementary source of income. Many worked for several years at the coach station and amongst them were Phil Boucherat, Ron Fairhead, Des Waughman, Phil Burns, Lance Robinson, Reggie Barnes, Bob Bacon, Eric Walker and many more.)

Elsa is the first to arrive in the switchroom and the nightlines are no longer connected to the chartroom; she'll be joined by two or three more operators as the morning progresses. (The switchboard was unmanned at night from 9.00pm to 8.00am and the main SLOane 3466 lines were transferred to the chartroom. Elsa Hatcher worked for many years on Coastal's switchboard, latterly as supervisor. Her silky, golden-toned voice on the coach station public address system was familiar to all. She retired in 1978, but in 1994, at the age of 83, she was persuaded to come out of retirement in Paignton for a few days to record a series of new public announcements for use at Victoria Coach Station, but the recording was not considered good enough to use.)

Johnny Batho is on early shift in the traffic office (public enquiry office) and, having joyfully and graphically told us of his big win last night at Walthamstow dog-track, has just picked up the traffic office keys. (Johnny Batho was just one of the traffic clerks who staffed the public enquiry office. He was a very colourful East Londoner with a notable sense of humour, and great skills as a cartoonist. Other traffic clerks included John Walker, Roy MacDonald, Wally Boyes, Teddy Hill, David Dubber, Ben Braham, Bob Wallace, Roy Mansfield, John Marsh, Chris Nash and numerous others.)

Not quite eight o'clock; most of the dozen-or-so early-shift staff have arrived and all the sections have at least one person on duty. (The chartroom was divided into sections, each one handling reservations for one, or a small group of, operating companies.)

The telephones will be a bit quiet for the first hour until the agents open for business. Apart, that is, from the booking hall, which now has four or five advance booking windows open as well as the Today's Travel positions, and as the day progresses more will be opened. The harsh buzz of the internal telephones is now heard every few seconds the booking hall is obviously becoming busy.

The postman has brought several big red bags of mail these get left for the post bookings staff, except for the four or five hundred special envelopes kept separate by the local Royal Mail sorting office, which bring the thousands of confirmation copies of tickets issued on the ad lib system. Let's get these envelopes opened quickly, and the confirms distributed to the appropriate sections of the chartroom. With luck a lot of them will have been charted before the telephones get too busy.

It really is going to be a hot day; already we've opened all the windows overlooking Buckingham Palace Road and the sun is pouring in.

A couple of part-timers have arrived early knowing that on a busy day they are guaranteed several extra hours; one joins Ernie on telephone enquiries and the other joins Johnny B. downstairs in the traffic office.

A quick look at the large two-pages-to-a-day diary; we've got about a dozen or so yard queries. (In cases when it had been impossible to contact passengers in advance in the event of booking or ticketing errors by agents or coach station staff, every attempt was made to contact them on the coach just before departure. Sometimes the operating companies' own inspectors would take on these tasks, but more often chartroom or traffic clerks handled them.) I hate doing yard queries but Bob Bacon, one of our best part-timers, has offered to come in early to look after them all; he's really good at this job cool, calm, confident, determined and a perfect gentleman. I have peace of mind knowing that all the queries will be sorted out properly. (An early lesson learned by all Coastal staff was never to be seen in the yard carrying a clipboard, unless one wanted to be harangued by every passenger in sight who would have presumed one to be in charge.)

The overnight services are arriving now within a few minutes of their arrivals all the paperwork from the offices at other terminals or places en route will arrive in the chartroom. Standerwick from Lancashire, and North Western from Manchester; Mr Hughes (the only inspector whose first name we never get to use) is probably looking after both services so will have a lot for us reservation forms, sheets of return journey reservations to be charted, and bundles of horrible North Western and Midland Red confirmation copies with heavy carbon backings that make everything filthy especially in hot weather when the carbon seems to become almost viscous. (Operating companies' offices and agents outside of London issued their own tickets. Most were like Coastal tickets and involved using loose carbon paper placed between each part of the ticket, but some, notably North Western and some Midland Red and Royal Blue, were heavily precoated with carbon on the reverse. NCR paper was unknown in those days.) Dennis, the Crosville inspector, will soon have seen in the overnight service from Liverpool; Jack, the SMT inspector, will have seen off the day services to Edinburgh and Glasgow, and seen in the overnight services from Scotland — he'll be here soon with reservations from across the border, before he goes on to the Scottish Omnibuses office in Regent Street. Then Charlie Patterson, the United Automobile Services inspector, will bring the paperwork from Newcastle. If we can get the reservation forms from Manchester dealt with quickly we can send the replies back on the 9.00am service.

Nine o'clock, and more staff has arrived. The agents' offices are open and the telephones are beginning to demand attention. Within ten minutes or so all the lines will be busy; within half an hour it will seem like chaos.

At ten o'clock another wave of staff arrives; we are now at full strength. We have three on telephone enquiries and three in the traffic office so I don't need to worry too much about them. Each section has a total of ten or more phone lines of one sort or another; there are eight sections, plus a special bank of phones for incoming long-distance calls, plus the public telephone enquiry section: a total of about 100 phones — and it sometimes seems as if they are all buzzing at once.

I have now at least three people on each section, and in some cases a fourth just to look after the paperwork, which seems endless as each arriving coach brings more — and coaches from all over will arrive at frequent intervals all day.

I keep an eye open as I walk round; Southdown's getting a bashing — everyone wants to go to the seaside tomorrow — can I afford to move someone over from Associated Motorways? And its just as bad on East Kent and M&D — it seems as if every man woman and child in the London area has flocked into a local agent wanting to buy a ticket to coast or countryside.

From within the hustle and bustle I catch snatches of telephone conversations: "Oxford tomorrow at nine am OK — how many?"; "Liverpool, Sunday August 8th, 10.30pm, how many?"; "Yes, you can book to Abbot's Ann Turn, it's a request stop, I'll check what timings apply"; "Ystrad Rhondda, Tuesday August 10th, 10.45am — OK…."; "2.15 Eastbourne today, picking up Ding-Dong, how many?" (Ding-Dong — the Chimes Garage, a picking up point in South London and one of several places to become familiarly known); "L for London, S for Sugar, two, fifty-six to fifty-eight" (booking references were given for all reservations, which comprised the chart clerk's initials, in this case Lesley Silcox, the chart number, in this case two, suggesting that there were already two vehicles allocated and the row numbers on the chart, in this 56 to 58 — three passengers, hence three rows on the chart. The strict 'alpha, bravo, etc.' phonetic alphabet regime familiar in the police, the forces and the airline industry was unknown at Victoria Coach Station; the staff invented some strange and unusual combinations); "King Charlie, one, seventy-five and six"; "2.30 Loughborough — how many?"; "Keswick, tomorrow, 8am — OK — how many?"; "Apple Harry three, sixty to sixty-four." Dozens of voices, hundreds of conversations, thousands of reservations.

There is such vibrancy in the air and, as we become busier, so it is becoming even more pulsating, even more exciting. Welshman Charlie Gough, an energetic part-timer who arrives at about 10 o'clock each morning from his full-time work as a

night shift operator in a nearby telephone exchange, is the self-appointed organiser of tea and toast — some say it's a skive, but everyone is pleased when he arrives with the mammoth pot of tea and huge tray of cups from the restaurant kitchens along the corridor, plus a pile of toast for which he has been round the chartroom taking orders. This morning is no exception. (Eventually a staff tea-trolley service was introduced. Ethel the tea-lady, a long serving member of the catering staff, served tea, coffee and biscuits — her arrival and her good service were always very welcome.)

And all the time the long-distance phones have been busy. At the moment I am the only person free to look after them, and I am also looking after the not-quite-so-busy excursions section. The young lady from Grace Travel in Dorking is on for two seats on tomorrow's 8.30am service to Bognor, picking up Dorking. With this perfect weather, she's likely to be on a dozen or more times with similar requests; I make a quick decision; she's sensible and reliable so, against all the rules, I pencil-in a further 20 seats for her, and tell her to call me later in the day with the ticket numbers. That'll save a few phone calls and it gives me a terrific sense of satisfaction to be able to work in such a sensibly cooperative fashion.

Never a dull moment — the next long distance phone is already ringing, its Hansell's Booking Office in St Albans; they've got a couple of passengers wanting to travel on the 10.43am from St Albans to Manchester. Must hurry, it's already gone half past ten; the coach left Victoria Coach Station at nine o'clock, and the chart has already been filed away. Kay Tatters retrieves the chart, there were five seats available when the coach left Victoria. Kay, one of the full-time chartroom clerks is chiefly involved with Midland Red, North Western, Standerwick, Scout, Ribble and Crosville reservations but, like most of the full-time chartroom clerks, can work on most sections. (Other full-time chartroom clerks at that time included Anne Harman, Leslie Silcox, Frank Doughty, Betty Morris, June Warne, Pam Lloyd, Norrie Murphy, Joan Rees, Irene Thorpe [Thorpie — who took over at Switchroom Supervisor for a while], Kath Coles, Dave Kimber, and the Traffic Manager's wife Rene Corbett and many more). "OK," I say to Hansell's, "issue a 'risk' ticket"(Often, when a passenger wished to join a coach along the route, but after it had left Victoria Coach Station, and it was reasonably certain that seats would be available, agents would be allowed to issue risk tickets endorsed "subject to space"); no, it's OK, the Manchester coach is just pulling up outside Hansell's office (the official boarding point for most services through St Albans) and, yes, there are seats available; the driver puts the passengers' cases into the back of the coach while the ticket is being hastily written out and the coach, with its two last-minute passengers, departs only a couple of minutes behind time. This is what I like best, the cut and thrust, and the co-operation; this is coaching — and Coastal at their very best.

It's hotter than ever. All the windows are open, and the hum of the traffic is not too much of a problem; until, that is, men from the Brigade of Guards, as they do every morning, pass by on their way to Buckingham Palace, playing their instruments in full Sousa style. No matter if you can't hear what's being said on the phone for a minute or two; nobody can do anything but feel proud and patriotic. The Guards passing Victoria Coach Station each morning is as much part of tradition as it is, a few minutes later, when the Guard is changed at Buckingham Palace.

It's a quarter to twelve. Billy Bloomfield, the late shift chargehand, has come in early. My shift is eight to four and his is two to ten, but an extra pair of hands on a busy day is more than welcome — as is the overtime. Between twelve and three all the staff need to have an hour's lunch break so Billy goes on Southdown for an hour so that Anne can have early lunch. Then he'll take over from me, so that I can lunch from one to two, and I'll return so that he can eat from two to three. There's usually a bit of a lull between 12.30 and 1.30, and in any case we have enough people to ensure at least two per section right across the lunch period.

One o'clock, and off for something to eat. Cross the yard to the canteen and listen to the din, the hubbub, the noise of coaches revving up, the excited voices of so many excited passengers, and breathe the air heavily laden with fumes.

The tannoy announcements, which were heard only in a distant, muffled way in the chartroom, are now clear: "the one-fifteen Southdown service to Eastbourne…", "would Mr or Mrs Jones meeting…please call at the Station Master's office", "long-distance telephone call for the Royal Blue inspector…"

Coaches are gently edging their way through the crowds of people milling around the departure bays; there's the feeling of general confusion characteristic of all busy transport terminals; the prevailing feeling is one of adventure — the sheer magic of setting off on a journey — it can be felt everywhere — even the luggage being loaded into the coaches seems to be in holiday mood.

It seems as if there are a thousand coaches in the yard; so much colour: Black & White, Royal Blue, the reds of Midland Red and Thames Valley, the emerald of Southdown, the darker hues of East Kent, the creams, the browns, the yellows and the golds — a rainbow whose colours cascade to every corner of Britain. And here am I, helping to keep the cogs turning.

Bill Cobb, the Eastern Counties inspector, grabs my arm and gives me the paperwork just arrived from Cambridge. Southdown's Inspector Jack Card is explaining to the distraught father of a family with several noisy excited children that the Hayling Island coaches are leaving from Samuelson's garage today when, apparently telepathically, the tannoy announces "Southdown services to Hayling Island, etc., etc…" Toby, another Southdown inspector, is trying to help a very deaf lady who has arrived from Worthing and wants to know where to catch the 24 bus to Pimlico.

Probably the most famous image of Victoria Coach Station. This early 1950s picture showing the guardsmen marching past *en route* to Buckingham Palace has been used for posters and postcards, and as the inspiration for paintings and drawings. There must be countless millions of identical views taken through the camera lenses of the crowds who thronged the pavements both sides of Buckingham Palace Road each morning, to witness these exciting moments, and to enjoy the stirring brass band music which filled the streets all around. *(LCCc)*

Top: A view from 1956, looking across the yard to the old bakery at the far end, already a first-floor staff canteen, and soon also to be a Continental Terminal and waiting room. But how long must the photographer have waited in order to get a shot without any passengers in it? *(LCCc)*

Above: "Earth hath not anything to show more fair. Dull would he be of soul who could pass by a sight so…… *totally exciting as a row of coaches!*" With apologies to William Wordsworth. *(LCCc)*

Across the yard now, and up the stairs into the canteen. It's busy today with so many drivers relaxing before the long journeys ahead of them. A couple of Midland Red conductresses in their rather austere uniform hats sit together, a bit out of place I expect they'll be returning to Brum on the 2.30. (On busy days, particularly summer Saturdays, conductresses often accompanied the Midland Red J service between Birmingham and London.)

It's very much a pie, chips and beans sort of menu, with steamed pudding and custard to follow, all washed down with a cup of tea; but for a couple of bob, who's complaining. There's a spare seat over there with some of the booking hall girls and Bill Chandler, the South Mid inspector, I'll park myself with them.

The tannoy messages are also broadcast in here, although at slightly lower volume. "Would the driver of the Horseshoe Coaches relief Royal Blue service to Bournemouth please return to his vehicle."

I have finished my meal with bags of time left; it's such a hot day and very sticky in here so I think I'll make a move. In any case I'm itching to get back and get stuck in again. I'll go back the long way and get a breath of fresh air. There's a lift, intended for tenants in the upper floor, at the end of the Elizabeth Street wing of the coach station. I take it to the top, then up the short flight of stairs onto the flat roof. Gosh, it's stifling up here. A couple of the staff have brought sandwiches and a Thermos of tea, and are sitting up here having a picnic lunch and enjoying the sunshine. It really is quite odd being up here, looking across the rooftops, everything below so tiny like ants and Dinky Toys; so high up, so utterly isolated and yet so close to all that activity below. I walk along the roof to the centre block, in one door and out the other onto the roof of the Buckingham Palace Road wing. Walk the length of that roof, gaze down on the buses and taxis below, and the line of coach upon coach waiting to get into the coach station; down the lift

at the other end; past the tours department on the mezzanine floor, and back into the chartroom, back to the telephones, back to the buzz and back to the busy rough-and-tumble.

Billy B. takes his lunch break. I put a part-timer on the excursions section now; it's getting a bit busy with bookings for tomorrow's Stratfords, Woburns, Windsors and the London Transport Bus Excursions. I give Sammy's a call, (Samuelson's New Transport operated a programme of day and half-day tours from Victoria Coach Station): "tomorrow's full-day Stratford's almost chocker, the afternoon Woburn's down to about fifteen, and Chiltern Hills down to ten." "OK, I'll call you back."

Grace Travel calls from Dorking with the ticket numbers for tomorrow's 8.30am Bognor, can she have some more please? It getting a bit tight and the Southdown inspector will soon be wanting to sort out how many vehicles he's going to need to cover all tomorrow's journeys. "OK, have ten more, but call me as soon as they've been sold."

And the paperwork continues to arrive reservations to be charted, forms to be checked and replies to be sent back as soon as possible to their offices of origin.

Sammy's on the phone, "Can't do another whole day Stratford, but we've got a spare vehicle for the afternoon. Put it on Woburn or Chiltern Hills, whichever one fills up first, I leave it to you." "OK, thanks."

Billy B. is back from lunch.

It's 1956, with the new staff canteen on the first floor of the old bakery. ('Bus & Coach'/LCCc)

Another 1962 photograph taken from the roof of Victoria Coach Station with more than 20 coaches queuing in Buckingham Palace Road with, at the fore, a Dennis Lancet of *East Kent* followed by *Maidstone & District* and *Southdown* vehicles, and the usual plethora of hired-in vehicles to cope with a typical summer Saturday demand. We have, of course, seen a similar view in glorious colour earlier in the book. *(Chris Nash)*

On Royal Blue, Norrie has worked through the lunch break so she's finishing at three o'clock. Highly experienced part-timer Ron Fairhead takes Norrie's place with Rene Corbett, but she too is due to go at four.

There's no let-up, the phones keep ringing, and ringing, and ringing, but funnily enough an almost carnival atmosphere pervades the whole place. It's as if we are all enjoying a wonderfully fulfilling battle.

Four o'clock is approaching. I should be finished but I'm staying on till six. Most of the early-shift people are getting ready to leave. Billy B. is now chargehand and does a quick reshuffle of the staff to make sure all the sections are adequately covered when the four o'clock people go home. It's a fine day, and several of the part-timers haven't shown up so we might be a bit thin on the ground — might be? We are!

Ron Fairhead takes M&D on his own, I take over Royal Blue on my own and between us Billy B. and I look after excursions (which, conveniently, is the section next to Royal Blue). The hustle and bustle continues, but it's less noisy now with fewer staff about.

Coming up to five o'clock and things are quietening down a bit on the telephones. Chance to catch up a bit with the paperwork. Half-past five, most agents are closed now so the phones have quietened down almost completely; just the booking hall, and they're down to four windows. The SLOane 0202 public enquiry number remains as busy as ever and still needs three staff. A couple of "sorry I'm late" part-timers arrive, so there's enough cover now for the evening.

Nearly six o'clock, those people who started at ten this morning will be going home. I too will finish as planned at six o'clock.

Sometimes I cadge a strictly unofficial but inspector-approved lift on the half-past six United Counties Northampton service and the driver drops me off at South Mimms, a couple of miles from my home, but even with a service car and two duplicates it's a bit tight this evening so I won't embarrass the inspector by asking. Anyway he needs to cover himself for any chance "risk" passengers at Golders Green or Barnet. (Coaches were often referred to as cars — no doubt a throw back to 'road car', as in East Kent Road Car Company for example.)

I cross the road to Elizabeth Bridge and wait for the Green Line; it's a delightfully balmy summer evening and I'm still keyed up. The 717 Green Line arrives; it's Taffy and George, the same crew that brought me in this morning. "Cor, it's all right when we bring them to work and take them home again," jibes George. "Yes," I reply, "but you've been on a spread-over, and I've been working non-stop all day." The camaraderie of the coaching industry is, as always, to the fore.

I'm home by a quarter to eight. Tomorrow I'm early shift chargehand again, but there's no early Green Line on Sundays so at twenty past six in the morning I shall be waiting outside Potters Bar bus garage, in the early morning peace and quiet of a summer Sunday, waiting for the first 134 to creep out of the dim, dark, depths of the depot to start its first trip of the day to Pimlico. Every minute of that long and lovely journey, as the bus meanders through Muswell Hill, Highgate and Camden Town, and then on past Trafalgar Square and the Houses of Parliament, will have my every nerve-end reeling with excitement and anticipation of the busy, hurly-burly day

Global/Overland tour departures on Bay 7a with coaches to the new, longer, dimensions in the majority. *(LCCc)*

Below: After the old bakery at the top end of the yard had been acquired in 1956, it soon became possible to set-up a separate terminal for *Skyways* departures. This early picture shows *Skyways* passengers boarding the *East Kent* coach which was to take them to Lympne Airport. The archway, at the right of the picture, which led from the yard into Elizabeth Street, was enclosed shortly after in order to further increase the size of the Skyways Air Terminal. *(LCCc)*

Bottom: An early *East Kent/Skyways* departure at Lympne Airport in Kent. *(Jim Russell collection)*

Opposite page from top

Coastal's Social Club goes to Woburn Abbey. Frank Hodges (Manager of *Samuelsons*) meets the Duke of Bedford, and with him *(l to r)*: George Newman (Secretary), a Woburn Abbey guide, Fred Robinson (General Manager), and Len Corbett (Traffic Manager). *(Dexter Studios/LCCc)*

Coastal Social Club members - flying off for the day. Elsa Hatcher, a very long serving staff member from Coastal's telephone exchange is in the middle. *(Ron Fairhead)*

Seen working an airport transfer for *Skyways Coach/Air* to Paris, this *East Kent* coach is of semi-chassisless structure with pre-war Leyland TD5 components and a Beadle body built in 1951/2. *(Chris Nash)*

Early 1960s, *Blue Cars* tour in Switzerland with writer and broadcaster Godfrey Winn. *(Blue Cars Continental Coach Cruises Ltd)*

ahead. And next week I'm on late shift. I love absolutely every second of it.

> *I recall one summer Saturday in the early 1960s, looking through the chartroom window and seeing dozens of coaches along Buckingham Palace Road waiting their turn to come into Victoria Coach Station. Apart from a few taxis and number 11 'buses, it was a sea of East Kent, Maidstone & District, Southdown and Royal Blue and many others 'on hire' to these well-known companies.*
> *John Marsh*

☙ ❧

Back to our story. After the war, the social side of the coaching industry in London did not quite return to 1930s' standards, and though for quite a few years the annual PSV Dance was held at the Porchester Hall, and Coastal held the annual 'Coastal Ball' in Hammersmith Town Hall for agents and staff, these events were soon to become memories of times past. For some time, too, several of the larger independent operators continued to hold their own celebrations for staff, agents and guests, including Grey-Green whose 1949 annual dinner and dance was held at St Pancras Town Hall, and at which, it was somewhat whimsically reported, "the orchestra tunefully inspired the merry throng on the dance floor in waltzes, jigs and modern trippings".

> *The Coastal football team used to play on a pitch somewhere on the edge of Croydon Aerodrome. Those of us not in the team were press-ganged into being supporters, and I seem to remember several occasions when senior management would examine the duty roster and admonish any off-duty staff that had not supported the footballers. They told me once they'd changed my duty so that I could support the team; but unfortunately they'd forgotten to alter the duty-roster so when I turned up for late-shift after the match I got a ticking off from the chartroom supervisor for not being on duty during the day. It seemed I was damned by someone, whatever I did! But it was fun.*
> *Roy Mansfield, Traffic Clerk at Victoria Coach Station from 1949 to 1953, and afterwards at the P.S.V.Operators' Kings Cross Coach Station in Pentonville Road.*

At Victoria Coach Station, however, for a number of years from the mid 1950s, Coastal had a small but active staff social club organised for the most part by Peter Pearson of Samuelson's, Mrs Strickland (secretary at that time to Coastal executives and directors) and members of staff from different departments. The social club was open to staff of Coastal and associated companies, and numerous dances and social evenings were held in the Victoria Coach Station restaurant. In true busman's holiday tradition, excursions (using Samuelson's vehicles) were made to Eastbourne, the New Forest, by boat along the Thames, and in 1960, just a few days after its re-opening, to the Bluebell Railway at Sheffield Park and even on one adventurous occasion to the risqué Collin's Music Hall in Islington. In the early summer of 1955, the year in which the Duke of Bedford and his family opened Woburn Abbey to the public, Coastal executives and staff were some of the first visitors, and the Duke was on hand personally to shake hands with them all and to provide afternoon tea for everyone.

The Coastal Social Club even entered the world of aircraft chartering on one occasion and chartered an aeroplane from Manston to Rotterdam for the day, with coaches waiting at Rotterdam Airport to take Coastal staff to Keukenhof Gardens. For several of the staff this was not only their first time in an aeroplane, but also their first time abroad.

And to show that all's fair in love and war, Coastal's social club reserved two entire carriages one Sunday in 1959 for a train excursion from Waterloo to Portsmouth with a trip across the Solent for a day on the Isle of Wight. It was no doubt with wry amusement that British Railway staff produced the window notices for those reserved railway coaches emblazoned RESERVED FOR VICTORIA COACH STATION SOCIAL CLUB, with the words 'Victoria Coach Station' in particularly large and bold lettering.

☙ ❧

By now more and more of the travelling public were venturing abroad. The coach station alterations which had taken place in 1956 had included the introduction of a Continental departure area, with a Skyways Office at the far end of the yard, and the departure bays at that end were soon to become very busy with coaches setting off for the continent or to be more exact setting off more often than not for Dover where, in most cases, passengers would transfer to the cross channel ferries, and join continental coaches on the other side.

The drive on-drive off facilities which were in due course to become usual for cars did not, at first, witness too many coaches, not just because of cost, but because very few of the coach tour operators had applied for licences to operate through to the continent. On the other hand, East Kent had made sure that its London to Dover licences were amended to include through journeys to Dover Harbour, and this smart move ensured that it would carry a huge majority of the passengers to Dover on behalf of the continental tour operators.

In the mid 1950s Global Overland began using Victoria Coach Station as the London departure point for their continental tours, with East Kent taking their passengers on the first stage of their holiday; Lyons Tours used East Kent to Dover and the West Belgium Coach Company from Ostend, and at around the same time BET had acquired Blue Cars who also used Victoria Coach Station and East Kent for the first stages of their tours. In addition to the regular tour departures, Blue Cars also had an ultra-luxury programme of coach tours operated under the Red Line name.

Despite continental travel being such a busy and rapidly growing aspect of coaching, the area of Victoria Coach Station that included continental departures (departure bays bays 14-22) remained open to the elements and was not provided with a canopy until the early summer of 1973, sixteen years after its opening.

There was also an increasing demand from audacious independent passengers looking for low-cost travel to Europe. There grew up quite swiftly a series of coach/air and coach/boat services, some using existing regular coach and air or shipping services, and others being designed purely and specifically as through services.

Skyways Coach Air was introduced in the early 1950s and enabled passengers to travel by East Kent from Victoria Coach Station to Lympne airport, near Ashford, and to fly in HS748 jetprop airliners for the short journey to Beauvais from where coach connections were provided to the centre of Paris. Compared with the scheduled services of Air France and British European Airways from Heathrow the fares were remarkably low, with fares from London to Paris at around £5. Even as late as 1970, Skyways fares from London to Paris started at £7.14s.0d (£7.70p), and you could get there and back for just over £11.

Before the opening of the Continental Terminal, Skyways check-in desks were in Coastal's rather insalubrious Traffic Office (public enquiry office), so for them the opening of the Continental Terminal was a huge advantage. Eventually Skyways increased their network and operated deeper into France with coach/air services to Lyons, Clermont-Ferrand and Montpellier, and in 1965 Skyways Coach/Air services were also available to Paris from East Midlands Airport. Although not a coach/air service, in 1961 the airline, operating as Skyways of London, was also flying from Heathrow to Tunis and Malta.

Coach/Air services were to become more widely available as the 1960s wore on, with Eastern National services linking with Channel Airways flights from Southend to Ostend, Paris and Rotterdam; Jersey Airways continuing their prewar services from Southampton to the Channel Islands, with Royal Blue carrying passengers to the gates of Eastleigh Airport; and, for a while, Southdown providing an alternative service to the Channel Isles with Channel Airways via Portsmouth Airport. Jersey Airways was to become British United (C.I.) Airways, and with Standerwick/Scout provided coach/air services from Victoria Coach Station to the Isle of Man via Squires Gate Airport in Blackpool. At the end of the 1960s there was an alternative coach/air service to the Isle of Man via Liverpool involving Crosville and Cambrian Airways. Although nothing to do with Coastal, there was a proposal to operate to Dublin via — then named — Derby Airport using Yelloway from King's Cross Coach Station; this didn't materialise but the concept generally was a huge success.

The Europabus coach network was introduced in 1953 and originally centred chiefly on Brussels whence routes operated throughout much of Western Europe. An oddity was that it was the various European railway companies that had set up this network, although one cannot clearly see why as, for the most part, it only served principal cities, and could be thought of as in competition with the railways. In order to embrace London in its network, Europabus included East Kent into its system, with passengers, having already interchanged in Brussels and travelled by coach to Ostend, then joining the cross channel ferry to Dover, from where East Kent (in a vehicle in Europabus blue livery) carried them to Victoria Coach Station. Probably because of the need for so many **en route** changes, the Europabus service from London, at least at the outset, never really took off. Reports in the trade press during 1973 record through National Travel services from London to Frankfurt being a great success, and the heavy traffic being carried by Europabus from Frankfurt onwards. Other reports, however, tell us that the service finished on 9th September of that year, despite the imminent Frankfurt Show that took place between 13th and 25th September, so we must assume it was successful only on a seasonal basis. Nevertheless several more continental through routes were introduced during ensuing years.

An added hindrance to the wider use of continental coach services at that time was the need for V forms. For most of those early days, British people travelling abroad, outside the sterling area, were restricted to a £50 per year travel allowance to cover not just spending money but the cost of accommodation and food as well. In cases where accommodation and meals were part of the fare (as quite frequently happened in the case of Europabus) or a proportion of the cost of a coach tour or package holiday, a deduction was made from the passenger's travel allowance to cover the perceived cost of the bed and board — this deduction was known as the V form content and details were entered into passengers' passports.

Other coach/boat services included routes to Belfast and Dublin via Liverpool, using Crosville from Victoria Coach Station and crossing by Belfast Steamship Company or B&I Line. These became available from the mid 1950s and were negotiated on Coastal's behalf with the shipping agents Coast Lines Limited by Cuthbert Embleton, who at the time was heading the Post Bookings department. Initially, ferry tickets and berth reservation tickets were held by Post Bookings, who handled reservations for Coastal agents as well as bookings received direct from passengers by post. Also for a time Eastern National linked with Eagle Steamers from Southend to provide services to Paris, Ostend and Calais.

On the domestic front, connections with Royal Blue were available to the Isle of Wight via Royal Pier Southampton and Cowes, using Red Funnel Steamers, with separate Coastal tickets being issued for the coach and boat journeys. Coastal tickets could also be issued for Southern Vectis bus journeys from Cowes to points around the Island. Similar arrangements were available to the Scilly Isles via Royal Blue services to Penzance, and the sea crossings by Isles of Scilly Steamship Company to St. Mary's, when again separate Coastal tickets were issued for the boat journey.

CB   EO

Very quickly after the war, coach touring within Britain took its place once more as the sophisticated face of the coaching industry, and it was not long before the names that had been important in prewar days were again offering quality touring holidays. The Coastal associated companies' programmes of Southdown, South Midland, SMT, Eastern National/Westcliff and Black & White soon reappeared, and PSV Operators agents again had access to Wallace Arnold and Glenton. The centred holiday became as popular as it had been in prewar days, but most of the cheap-jack operators had fallen by the wayside, and little was heard of "fantail" tours.

Nevertheless, there remained the differences between coach touring in the true meaning of the word, and coach holidays

Above left: A Coastal trade advertisement from April 1949. *(Jim Russell collection)*

Above right: A *Southdown* publicity vehicle. *(LCCc)*

Right: A *Southdown* tours advertisement of 1949 that appeared in the United States of America quoting prices in dollars, and directing potential passengers to USA Travel Agencies. *(Jim Russell collection)*

based in one centre. The term coach tour was applied to both styles of holiday and there was a need to make the meaning clear to the travelling public. Praise must go to Coaching Journal who in a Coach Tour Supplement in April 1949 defined 'Coach Cruises' as: "The full coaching holiday, with the tour extending over a wide area, pausing each evening at some different town or holiday resort usually outstanding for its beauty or historic interest. Of great scenic interest this is a jolly, communal holiday of the restful type".

The same journal defined centred holidays as 'Inclusive Holidays' and further explained that: "With these holidays there is one centre normally a first-class hotel at a holiday resort or at some beauty spot with half or full day coach tours to surrounding areas".

The problem still arose with inclusive holidays in separating those which used separate touring coaches for the journey to the resort, such as the South Midland holidays to the Wye Valley and Porthcawl, and those that used regular express services such as the Easy-Way holidays offered by Standerwick/ Scout and Ribble.

To avert the risk that the inclusive holiday might be seen in any way as a poor relation to the coach cruise, many operators made a point of describing the luxurious quality of the hotels they used and the wide extent of their touring programme. In the early 1950s, a promotional article for South Midland claimed that the Seabank hotel, which it used for its Porthcawl inclusive holiday, was the most modern in Wales with 177 rooms (many with private bathrooms and telephones), spacious lounges; reading, writing, and games rooms; a fine sun lounge; a ballroom and a Spanish bar and sherry lounge. The hotel stood in its own grounds, had hard tennis courts, lawns, rockery and its own kitchen garden. The eight-day holiday included no fewer than four coach tours including one whose route was described as "through the glorious mountain scenery in the midst of which are many of Britain's nationalised coal mines". Coalmines, rockeries and a sherry lounge: who could possibly resist?

A clever if rather sly explanation came from Orange Luxury Coaches, carefully explaining that theirs were not extended tours in the accepted sense, but were "…designed to transport the holiday-maker from his own environment to a specific and attractive destination, and then convey them at leisure to various beauty spots. The big attraction being that the same hotel is utilised for the eight day stay, thus avoiding the trouble often incurred in travelling from place to place".

1950s and early 60s - Victoria Coach Station Tours Department on the Mezzanine floor at the far end of the Buckingham Palace Road wing. *(Dexter Studios/LCCc)*

It seems strange for a company whose sole purpose involved the transportation of passengers, to highlight the trouble in travelling from place to place, and Grey-Green advertised a variation, which, albeit not promoted as a coach tour, offered a package price of £1.11s.3d (£1.58p) for four excursions over four days to four different seaside resorts, with the same driver and the same seats on the same '1949 luxury coach' returning back to "Home Comforts" every night.

Some seaside resorts were also taking the initiative, creating their own all-in holidays with accommodation, admission to local amenities and theatres and rides in pleasure parks. These were available to coach operators to add to their regular express services in order to provide inclusive holidays. One of the first resorts to do this was Southend-on-Sea.

Southdown deserves particular praise where coach touring is concerned, for the introduction of their Harrington Cavalier touring coach which had only 29 seats, three to a row (two on one side and one on the other of the central aisle). Always very forward-thinking and innovative, Southdown was exhibiting at the Ideal Homes Exhibition by 1949 and in the same year, realising the importance of the rapidly expanding market from overseas visitors, was widely advertising its British coach-cruising programme in the United States. Particular attention was drawn to its 18-day Grand Tour of Britain, which had weekly departures at a cost of 215 dollars and was bookable in advance in America. With an exchange rate at that time of 4.04 dollars to the pound, this luxury tour of Britain at less than £3 per day all-inclusive would always be appealing to the visitor from overseas. Blue Cars also had their eyes on the overseas market and opened their own office in Lexington Avenue, New York.

Soon after its introduction in 1955, Southdown also took advantage of the new commercial television, and were featured in a consumer programme entitled Jim's Inn, which featured a group of elegant people standing around the fictitious but sophisticated bar of Jim's (Jimmy Hanley's) pub. Conversation among these fashionable people revolved around the latest luxury items they had bought; on the occasion that Southdown was featured a telephone number was given to viewers to call for a copy of the coach cruise brochure. Being early in the season and before all the sections of the Victoria Coach Station chartroom were in use, the number given was one of the temporarily unused ex-directory agents' numbers. The programme was broadcast during the middle of the evening, and so the chartroom saw an unusual flurry of activity from around 8.30pm that evening and all day long during the following few days.

Coach touring was to remain a vibrant and important part of the coach industry throughout the fifties and sixties with the big names offering even bigger programmes. In 1967 South Midland were operating eleven different tours from Victoria Coach Station, each with weekly departures from May to September; the SMT programme with similar frequencies, was operating as Eastern Scottish; and Southdown were advertising over 900 departures from London and the South.

The tours department at Victoria Coach Station was located for many years on a mezzanine floor at the end of the Buckingham Palace Road wing, and whilst the space it occupied for its sales office and adjoining administrative office was adequate in its earlier days, the rapid growth and the consequent increased importance to Coastal and its associated companies of coach touring, coach/air and coach/boat services were

One of the new *Midland Red* CM5T motorway coaches; specially developed to operate the first motorway service on Britain's first full-length motorway. *(B.M.M.O/R.E.S. Richards collection)*

soon to put strain on the department's facilities. Furthermore the huge influx of overseas visitors added immensely to the demand for more and more tours with a greater variety of durations and itineraries; not surprisingly this was particularly apparent in London.

Without doubt the eventual alterations that provided a smart, modern ground-floor sales office specifically for the tours department was an important and long-overdue improvement at Victoria Coach Station, but that was not to happen until 1966.

ভ ৶

The year 1958 was witness to the start of a development that has probably brought about more change to the face of coaching in this country than anything else before or since, for that was the year in which the Preston by-pass was opened the first stretch of motorway road in Britain. Eventually it was to become the section of the M6 Rugby-Carlisle Motorway between junctions 29 32.

In October of that year, the Birmingham & Midland Motor Omnibus Co. Ltd (BMMO), better known as Midland Red,

Midland Red CM5 motorway coach on a test circuit. *(R.E.S. Richards/Midland Red Coaches collection)*

Tyres needed to be thoroughly examined after each test drive of the *Midland Red* CM5 *(R.E.S. Richards/Midland Red Coaches collection)*

applied to the authorities for a Road Service Licence to operate a non-stop express service from London to Birmingham via the M1 Motorway   and this more than a year before the motorway was scheduled to open.

Then on Monday 2nd November 1959 the M1 opened for a length of 72 miles from Berrygrove (St Albans) to Crick (Rugby). This is now the section between junctions 5 and 18 of the 200 mile M1 London to Leeds Motorway; originally constructed to cope with 13,000 to 14,000 vehicles per day (usage reached on the day it opened), it today carries 130,000 to 140,000.

At 8.30 on that memorable morning a brand new, in-house designed and built specially for the task, Midland Red CM5T coach left Birmingham's Digbeth Coach Station for London's Victoria Coach Station, to mark not just the historic moment of the opening of Britain's first full-length motorway, but the start of the first regular motorway coach service, which fittingly linked Britain's first and second cities.

However, after the initial impetus brought about by the events of that November day in 1959, motorway development was rather slow, and although the M10 and M45 spur roads

807 HHA, shot on January 15th 1960. The original caption used for this photograph was 'Midland Red arrives on time in bad weather'. One can only assume the driver skidded into Victoria Coach Station backwards, as this *Midland Red* CM5 is the wrong way round on the stand. *(LCCc)*

Interior of the *Midland* Red CM5T motorway coach. Passenger comforts included adjustable headrests and forced air ventilation. *(Wheels Heritage/Midland Red Coaches collection)*

were opened at either end of the M1, most progress was simply in the form of by-passes built to motorway standards. In 1959 the Chiswick flyover was built, which eventually became junction 1 of the M4 South Wales Motorway; in 1960 the Lancaster by-pass opened (to become the junctions 33-35 section of the M6) and the Maidstone by-pass (east) opened as the A20(M) later to be part of the M20 London-Folkestone Motorway. In 1961 the Maidstone by-pass (west) opened, the Doncaster by-pass opened as the A1(M), and the Maidenhead by-pass opened as part of the M4. In 1962 the Stafford by-pass (junctions 13-14 of the M6) opened, as did part of the M5 Birmingham to Exeter Motorway. In 1963 the Slough by-pass added junctions 5-7 to the M4, and the Medway Towns by-pass was the start of the M2.

There were no extensions to the M1 for six years after it opened; between late 1965 and 1968 all the sections from junctions 2 to 42 Page Street (Mill Hill) to East Ardsley were completed.

Between 1965 and 1967 much of the M4 opened in stages, with the Severn Bridge being opened by Her Majesty Queen Elizabeth II in 1966; in 1971 the two ends of the motorway were joined with the section covering junctions 9-18.

The M6 opened in stages during the late 1960s but even in 1970 the most southerly point was junction 9 and there was no connection between the M1 and the M6.

The M3 London-Southampton Motorway opened in the early 1970s, and in the same period the Ditton by-pass was added to the M20. In 1974 the M23 London-Crawley Motorway was started; 1975 saw the beginnings of the M11 London-Cambridge Motorway and the M25 London Orbital Motorway (which eventually took eleven years to complete). Between 1977 and 1991 the M20 was completed, and the London to Oxford section of the M40 London-Birmingham Motorway was started late in the 1980s.

From this, it can be seen that it was not until many years after the opening of the M1 that coach operators had much scope to improve their journey times unless substantial parts of the 72 miles of M1 could be suitably fitted into their schedules (which ran the risk forfeiting too many intermediate off-motorway points). Nevertheless, the opening of the first stage of the M1 was a straw in the wind – there were immense changes to come. The Midland Red/North Western joint service to Manchester and the Standerwick/Scout/Ribble services to the northwest were obvious beneficiaries, as were Yorkshire Services and to a certain extent United Counties. On the independent scene, Yelloway was soon operating via the M1, and even Birch Brothers managed to fit a tiny stretch of the M1 into the London to Bedford service.

Because our story revolves chiefly around London Coastal Coaches Limited, and as the company never owned a coach, it is not the aim of this book to look in any great technical depth at the vehicles used. However, in considering motorways and their governing influence on the coaching industry, it is impossible not to pay some attention to Midland Red's initiative in designing and building its own motorway coaches.

Midland Red had since 1923 designed and built most of its own vehicles at its Carlyle Works at Edgbaston, Birmingham. Midland Red was an extensive operator of both buses and coaches and it is not surprising that there should be some continuity or overlap of design between the two. During the 1950s the latest model single-deck buses being designed by the company were called the S14 and S15, and as evidence of design flexibility, the S15 was planned to be suitable for use both on long-distance bus routes and for coaching. Midland Red categorised its vehicles with the letter S for single deck buses; D for double deck buses and C for coaches. The M and T in the classification of the CM5T indicated that it was a C5 coach built to motorway operating specification and had on-board toilet facilities.

The last of the S14s was constructed as a prototype for the new C5 coach and advantage was taken of glassfibre and light alloy to ensure a truly modern, streamlined design; there is no doubt that this was a fine, ground-breaking vehicle with lots of potential, but with its 48mph maximum speed it was not a practical proposition for use in high-speed motorway operations, which at that time were not restricted by speed limits.

Experimentation with turbocharger technology led to speeds of 85mph. It is easy to make a vehicle go fast but not so easy to stop it without comparable improvements to braking systems, and hydraulically operated disc brakes (on all wheels – unusual at that time) with continuous flow servo-assistance were added to the specification. Apart from their size, tyres were redesigned along the lines of those specified for racing cars. Soundproofing for such high-speed operation had to be considered carefully and was achieved as an added advantage

The coaches might have got faster, but the passengers, seen here at Coventry Pool Meadow, stayed much the same. *(R.E.S. Richards collection)*

The 45ft *Midland Red* coach produced by *BMMO* to support the crusade for the licensing of longer vehicles. The coach travelled from Birmingham to London with only one manoeuvring difficulty; that being the Sheldon roundabout on the outskirts of Birmingham. *(R.E.S. Richards/Midland Red Coaches collection)*

of the heat insulation provided by glassfibre sheeting between the inner and outer roof skins. The toilet compartment was fitted on the nearside at the back of the vehicle. The 34 seats were covered with leopardskin moquette and the interior colour scheme was officially described as peony and white. The exterior of the coach was red with a black roof, and aluminium trim.

The new service and its new coaches were extremely successful from day one, and it is estimated that in the first year over 100,000 passenger journeys had been made on the route; and that was despite the initial scheduling, which proved to be somewhat adrift with the first timetables showing a journey time between London and Birmingham of 3 hours 25 minutes. In the event, services were consistently arriving 45 minutes early, and the advertised journey time was soon reduced to 2hours and 55 minutes, and eventually further reduced to 2 hours and 15 minutes.

Initially, and (bearing in mind the government's motorway expansion plans) perversely, the licence granted to Midland Red by the Commissioners for this new service imposed draconian limits on the number of vehicles to be operated; in most cases only one vehicle per journey — just 34 seats — was permitted which, with the inevitability of motorway expansion, was a somewhat King Canute-like attitude.

The arrangement between Coastal and Midland Red was for an allocation of seats on all journeys (northbound and southbound) to be held both at Digbeth Coach Station, Birmingham, and at Victoria Coach Station. At first, the allocation to Victoria Coach Station was ten seats per journey, with additional seats being allocated on telephone request. Needless to say, the railways were anxious about the potential threat of unbridled motorway coach services, and they had eyes everywhere to ensure that the licence, and in particular its restrictions, was strictly observed. Immense care, therefore, had to be taken to ensure that not a single overbooking occurred. Eventually the situation eased slightly, but there were strict allocations for some years.

Encouraged by the success of the service from Birmingham to London, Midland Red soon successfully applied to the authorities for a licence to operate a similar service from Coventry to London, and this started barely ten months after the start of the Birmingham service. Similar coaches were used, but they did not have the on-board toilet facility and were thus classified C5M; and within 18 months the service was extended to and from Bedworth and Nuneaton.

The story of these specially designed and built motorway coaches does not end there. It was obvious that a 34-seat coach was operationally inefficient on such a high-demand prestige route. The law at that time dictated that single-deck vehicles were to be restricted to dimensions of 30ft length and 8ft width, but Midland Red wanted a bigger vehicle with greater seating capacity for its motorway services. No doubt the designs for the next generation motorway coach had long since been drawn up at Midland Red's Carlyle Works, and were simply sitting on the drawing board waiting for the law to catch up with progress. The company did, however (undoubtedly with tongue in cheek), produce a sample coach 50% longer than the maximum permitted length and they put this 45ft vehicle before the Ministry of Transport in 1960.

On 1st August 1961, the Ministry increased the maximum permitted dimensions to a length of 36 feet and a width of 8 feet 2½ inches, and it comes as no surprise that by the end of the same year Midland Red had unveiled its prototype vehicles S16 and S17 to the new dimensions. The new 44-seat motorway coach (CM6T) was based on the S17; it replaced the CM5T on the motorway services.

It was over two decades before the motorway network as we know it today began to take shape from those early beginnings in 1958, but the pioneering spirit that we witnessed with the 1904 Vanguard service to Brighton, the 1919 services of Len Turnham and Shirley James and the plethora of services of the 1930s had once again emerged with the far-sighted attitude of Midland Red's management.

Late 1950s Coastal display unit (LCCc)

Coastal posters – always bright, and always readily available to Coastal agents.   Coastal's publicity department, under the direction of Briah Andrews, not only designed and produced publicity materials; it also had its own window display team who would regularly dress agents' windows. *(LCCc)*

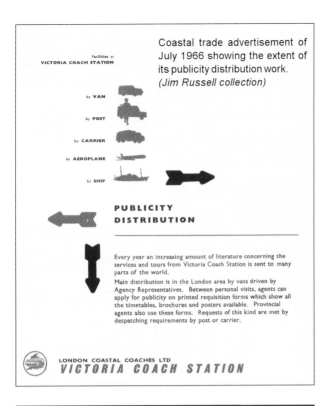

Coastal trade advertisement of July 1966 showing the extent of its publicity distribution work. *(Jim Russell collection)*

'Travellers' Guide' was produced as part of the massive 1967 'Coach Wise in Britain' campaign. *(Chris Nash collection)*

'Coach Wise in Britain' – this leaflet was distributed throughout the country and by all the Coastal associated companies. Its colourful and attractive design reflects the promotional 'style' of the period, and one suspects there was more than a slight touch of input by Briah Andrews and his team at Victoria Coach Station. *(Chris Nash collection)*

London Transport publicity, traditionally always up-to-date as shown by these two Conducted Coach Tours programmes. Ten years separates these publications and though they are quite different, they are both supreme examples of good publicity literature. *(Transport for London/London's Transport Museum)*

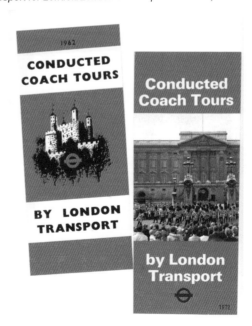

Publicity

Publicity and Public Relations were as important in the postwar period when coaching in general, and Coastal in particular, were already well established, as they had been in the groundbreaking days of the 1930s.

Briah Andrews joined Coastal in 1935 in a role then described as Agency Publicity Representative and was to remain as Coastal's Publicity Superintendent and Public Relations Officer until his retirement from the position of Public Relations Officer for National Travel (NBC) Ltd in 1974. Another of those transport-in-the-blood coaching men, he began his career at Central London Coach Station in 1929, but went north in 1932 to take charge of Orange Bros until they were bought-out by United Automobile Services Ltd, when he returned to London and joined Coastal to set up what was to become a strong and progressive publicity department.

The publicity department was a warehouse and distribution centre for operating companies' timetables and publicity materials and also designed and produced printed publicity items, posters and other items specifically for Coastal. For many years its work included the production of window displays in its workshop at Victoria Coach Station, which it provided and installed for agents throughout the London area. In no small way, Coastal's publicity department, particularly in formative years, was instrumental in the professional development and image building of coaching and the coach industry.

A large storage and despatch area in part of the basement under the Buckingham Palace Road wing of Victoria Coach Station was used for holding stocks of operating companies' timetables and posters. From here supplies would be drawn as needed by the agency representatives who carried publicity stocks with them, and by the coach station's public and postal enquiry offices, but another crucially important distribution function was the speedy and up-to-date supply of publicity to agents, of which there were soon to number almost 1,500. Constant accurate stock control was vital to ensure that printed items should always be available; for much of the time until his retirement in the late 1950s this was under the control of Mr C Poole and from 1961 became the responsibility of Dick Humphreys. Dick was another dyed-in-the-wool coachman who had spent the previous 32 years working for Southdown, much of that time as uniformed staff at Victoria Coach Station. He retired in 1972.

In 1967 a huge combined publicity campaign for express coach services in Britain was mounted by more than 60 operating companies throughout the country. Whether this was motivated by rapidly increasing competition from the private car is uncertain although likely. Coastal's publicity department joined in with their counterparts in the Tilling and Scottish groups and with planning and execution by the British Omnibus Companies Public Relations Committee promoted the "Coachwise is Travelwise" campaign, which was advertised with a double-spread advertisement in the

Southdown Touring Coach available for public inspection during a quiet period at Victoria Coach Station. *(Ron Fairhead)*

British Travel Association's publication Holidays in Britain 1967.

Members of the public were invited to ask for three free booklets of which one, Carefree Holidays by Coach, gave information about holidays and coach touring; another, Express Coaches Everywhere, gave specific information about the coach network through the country; and the third, Traveller's Guide, gave information about bus and coach services in England, Scotland and Wales and included a detailed route map.

This campaign and these booklets comprised probably the most far-reaching and sophisticated publicity effort ever launched until then for express coach services in this country, and in it is evident the work and style of Coastal's Briah Andrews, particularly the introduction to the Travellers Guide which, having painted a broad picture of Britain's principal coach and bus networks, continued by sportingly mentioning also the many independent companies that were operating throughout the country. It closed with the challenging statement that "no other country in the world is so generously served as Britain by such a formidable link up of bus and coach routes".

The launch of this campaign was followed with heavy advertising in the national press, which itself was supported with a good deal of editorial. The booklets were distributed widely, and agents everywhere were encouraged to hold ample stocks, with bulk supplies being available from Coastal's publicity department and from provincial bus and coach companies.

Nor was it unknown in the noble cause of publicity for Coastal to get out and about and mix business with pleasure. The Coastal exhibit at the Biggin Hill Air Fair in May 1972 was staffed for much of the time by Frank Garman, Coastal's Agency Superintendent, and Peter Scammell, the Reservations Manager, both reportedly aviation enthusiasts as well as coachmen.

By 1961 Victoria Coach Station was coming to the end of its third decade and, understandably, was beginning to look a bit jaded in places, not least the booking hall, and even more so the traffic office (public enquiry office), which was still occupying an area that had, in prewar days, been two of the sublet shops in Buckingham Palace Road (made one by the removal of a dividing wall), which during the war had become the vital information centre for bus services throughout Britain.

The somewhat unappealing character of the traffic office was not helped by the fact that for much of the time only half of the original two-shop area was used; the other half remained empty and unused but not disguised from public view. The two doors of the original shop being used were for public use; these, at either side of the building, opened directly onto Buckingham Palace Road on one side, and into the coach station departure area on the other. One long open counter stretched for most of the distance between the two doors and staff entered the area behind the counter through the yard-facing door of what had been the second shop. The second shop's other door (opening onto Buckingham Palace Road) was not used. Very little had ever been done to make this public enquiry office attractive and upgrading was overdue.

Until that time the left luggage office had been situated within the booking hall at the Buckingham Palace Road wing end. It occupied the full width of the building and was by then hopelessly small for the demand. Possibly to the casual observer, the need for a left luggage office might seem rather unimportant: what demand could there be? After all, surely people took their baggage with them on the coach? Maybe the original planners had thought the same and had thus allowed only a limited space. As it turned out, a great many passengers noticeably family groups, and conspicuously at Bank Holidays or on summer Fridays would bring most of their cases and bags to the coach station the day before departure, and thereby make the journey from home the next day, when public transport would be particularly crowded, a good deal easier.

The ensuing 1961 alterations brought modernisation to the booking hall, and saw a move of the traffic office, now more accurately referred to as the enquiry office, into the booking hall to take part of the area which had until then used by the left luggage office. The left luggage office was relocated and given more space and the new enquiry office had a more attractive and professional appearance, with its counter having a glass screen between the staff and the enquirers.

These improvements were essential from practical and aesthetical points of view, but the very need for them was further proof of the more substantial part that coaching and the coaching industry was by then playing in the travel industry as a whole. It was sad in some ways, though, to see that, as with all modernisation, some of the original homespun personality of Victoria Coach Station was giving way to a somewhat impersonal slickness.

CB BD

Despite these changes, there were still ongoing problems at Victoria Coach Station. The SLOane 0202 passenger enquiries line continued to be one of the most difficult London telephone numbers to get through to and remained, as it had always been, a tricky service to cope with. From early morning until late evening the calls were incessant, and it was impossible to see how to improve the situation in the prevailing circumstances; the scope of the service was far greater than was originally intended for it back in 1932 and to do the job properly would need more space and more staff.

Just as in the war years (albeit then in emergency circumstances), Coastal's public and telephone enquiry service gave information for all local BET and BTC bus services

The public enquiry office (known then as the traffic office) in 1956 – overdue for more than just a facelift, although it was several years before any changes were made. Traffic clerks on duty *(l to r)* Peter Scammell, John Walker, and Reggie Barnes. *(A.C.V. Sales/LCCc)*

Christmas eve 1962 and heading north for the holiday. Always an anxious moment though, until they know their tickets are correct. And it's going to be a wet journey north for the clutch of Western SMT Leyland Leopard coaches with their Scottish-built Alexander coachwork. Two lines of these impressive vehicles stand side-by-side awaiting their passengers before the long run begins. In the night sky behind, the BOAC sign is a portent of things to come when air travel between London and Glasgow would become quite commonplace. (STA)

throughout the United Kingdom in addition to details of coach services from Victoria Coach Station. The service had expanded as a matter of course to include express coach information for the whole country and not just services to and from London, so what had begun as a purely Victoria Coach Station enquiry line had over the years become a country-wide service.

Jumping ahead in our story, a point came in late 1973 when an exasperated GPO, no doubt encouraged by an even more exasperated public, monitored the telephone lines and were able to report that they were recording 32,000 engaged tones per week on SLOane 0202, which meant that Coastal could be losing an average of about 4,500 calls every day. Obviously something had to be done, but the situation was made particularly difficult because suitable staff were just not available in London.

Soon after, and quite by chance, Peter Scammell was talking about the problem to the chairman of National Bus Company (Mr Brooke), and as a result, it was arranged that

> *"I spent a short time working in the enquiry office and on one occasion heard a colleague tell a passenger that the Aldershot & District service to Farnham departed at ten minutes to, and fifty minutes past each hour. The passenger, thinking there were two departures an hour had just missed the ten minute to and would therefore catch the next one at fifty minutes past!"*
> Chris Nash

> *"The new enquiry office in the booking hall had glass sliding windows which were kept spotlessly clean. It was usual to have two opening serving position available, but sometimes enquiry clerks would stand between the two open positions. Passengers would walk confidently down the booking hall to where the clerk was standing and not see the glass. Having banged their head on the glass they would be less confident when directed to the available serving position to ask a question!"*
> Chris Nash

Left Luggage Office – March 1962 *(Fox Photos/LCCc)*

Coastal should take over the East Kent uniform store at Westwood Bus Garage Ramsgate and set up one of the first of a new breed of service – a call-centre. The GPO advised that the SLOane 0202 number could remain, and calls could be transferred automatically from anywhere in the country, so the Ramsgate location was a positive solution to a long-standing problem.

A plan was devised to employ a manager, ten full time staff, and 16 part-timers; the latter had to be flexible, covering short shifts between the hours of 8.00am and 10.00pm, and were to be responsible themselves for arranging cover if they were unable to work any shift: a situation ideal for the "working mum". The first advertisement resulted in 250 applications.

The call centre opened on 2nd July 1974 and had one of the first telephone answering control systems. Staff sat at key-and-lamp consoles and simply switched on; calls were presented in strict order and as a call was cleared the next one waiting was connected immediately. A supervisor could see from a control panel if any console had been switched off, and a display indicated to all the staff how many calls were awaiting reply, and how long the caller had been hanging on.

John Marsh, an out-and-out transport enthusiast, was appointed manager and was instrumental in setting up the service and training its staff. John Marsh had joined Coastal's Post Bookings department at Victoria Coach Station as a teenager in January 1958 to help in the handling of passenger enquiries received in the mail. From Post Bookings he had moved to the chartroom, spending several years therein before moving on to spend more than nine years in the traffic and publicity departments of East Kent, where he worked almost entirely on local bus and express coach timetables; he put the final touches to his travel industry expertise by managing travel agencies in Sevenoaks and Birchington for a time. He was the perfect person with the knowledge, skills and enthusiasm to set-up a central enquiry service.

At last there was an efficient service, properly staffed and equipped with the latest equipment, including telex to receive up-to-the-minute information from all NBC bus and coach companies. From the day the service began, calls answered never fell below 2,000 daily and more often than not exceeded that number considerably; soon after, it was extended to include the despatch of timetables, information and booking forms by post.

The transfer of the telephone information centre to Ramsgate was an important development and is relevant to the Coastal story. An appendix, which tells of the Ramsgate centre, and based on John Marsh's recollections, has been included at the end of our story.

There was, and still is, an unsolvable problem. Ever since the day of its opening, there has always been a stream of passengers transferring between Victoria Coach Station and the main line and underground stations at Victoria. This irritating journey is too short to justify taking a bus (it is only two stops), but is a long way if time is precious, baggage heavy, or the weather inclement. Nor would it have been practical to consider opening a new underground station on the District Line between Victoria and Sloane Square because the distances

"*A common question from passenger at the enquiry office was, 'What time is the next coach to..'. When told the departure time they would say, 'isn't there one before then?' The clerk would then say politely, but loud enough for everyone else to hear, 'no there isn't one before the next one'!*"
Chris Nash

Above right: Ramsgate Telephone Enquiry Centre *(John Marsh collection)*

Right: Ramsgate Telephone Enquiry Centre. John Marsh with two of his team. The wall map had been transferred from the telephone enquires section at Victoria Coach Station seen in an earlier picture. *(John Marsh collection)*

Below: August 12th 1961. Taxis and cars along Buckingham Palace Road for as far as one can see, bringing passengers to Victoria Coach Station. Over the wall are the railway tracks from Victoria Station, to be spanned four decades later by The Colonnade shopping centre. *(LCCc)*

Bottom: August 12th 1961 – 9 o'clock in the morning. Foot passengers! *(LCCc)*

A *Standerwick* 'Gay Hostess' Leyland Atlantean recently arrived from the Lake District leaves Victoria Coach Station for overnight garaging. *(LCCc)*

Standerwick caused quite a stir with the introduction of double deck 'coaches' in the 1959/61 period. The Leyland Atlantean coaches had Weymann bodywork, and were equipped with refreshment facilities, extra luggage space at the rear, and onboard toilet facilities. A hostess was employed to serve refreshments during the journey. **NRN 608** is seen here on the morning of August 12th 1967. *(Chris Nash)*

between stations would have been little more than half a mile in either direction. At busy times, and particularly on summer Saturdays, there were always plenty of young, and not-so-young, unofficial porters touting for business at either end of the haul; their business was usually very brisk.

Several attempts have been made to operate shuttle bus services between the two points, but these were never successful and, despite quite heavy promotion, rarely lasted long. On 1st July 1972, London Transport introduced another experimental, but unsuccessful, service route 511 between Victoria Railway Station forecourt (by then, to the confusion of many, called Victoria Bus Station) and a stop in Buckingham Palace Road near "The Coachman" bar at Victoria Coach Station. With a one-way fare of five pence the service operated on Saturdays and Sundays only at 15-minute intervals from 6.30am to 11.00pm.

ℭ𝔰 𝔰𝔬

It is difficult to decide which of the events of the early and mid 1960s most marked the changing face of long distance coaching from Victoria Coach Station.

May 1960 saw the introduction of the "Gay Hostess" double-deck Leyland Atlanteans on Standerwick/Scout services between Victoria Coach Station and Blackpool. Many purists considered that a coach could, perforce, only be a single-deck vehicle, but this new type of service, on which a refreshments service and toilet facilities saved the need for many *en route* stops, was popular.

The last of the original Coastal directors, Shirley James retired in 1963 from the board of Coastal. Had it not been for the decision he made in 1920, during his early days with Pickfords, to contact Len Turnham, London Coastal Coaches Ltd might never have happened, and his influence over the events of the ensuing 43-year period was enormous. It was not only in the coaching world that Shirley James had been successful; as the founder of Shirley James Travel, which he ran from prestigious offices in Belgravia, he was well respected throughout the whole of the travel industry.

From the standpoint of impending industry changes it is probably the formation by the government of the Transport Holding Company (THC) that must take precedence among the events of the 1960s. In 1963, the THC took over the bus and coach operating interests of the BTC, together with the shareholdings in BET companies which the BTC had itself acquired 15 years earlier from the railways, including, of course, a substantial holding in London Coastal Coaches. This significant event in itself made little immediate difference to the operation of Victoria Coach Station.

A particularly significant year was 1966. As owners of the valuable property in Buckingham Palace Road previously occupied by the Russian Church and the Grosvenor Club, Coastal was obviously keen to develop the potential of these assets. At the same time, on the other side of the road, British Overseas Airways Corporation (BOAC) was rapidly expanding with the introduction of new routes and new aircraft, and had its eyes set on even greater increases in the foreseeable future with the introduction of larger or faster aircraft such as the Boeing 747 and Concorde. Eventually, negotiations between Coastal and BOAC led to plans being drawn up for a joint development of the site and, in 1966, the opening of the West Block extension to Victoria Coach Station. (As the result of

Ribble Motor Services, based in Preston, had used double-deck vehicles for its long-distance express services since 1948, but it was the first operator to introduce such vehicles specifically designed for motorway services, when, in 1959 on the day the M1 opened, it introduced the first Leyland Atlantean coach with MCW body on its Lancashire – London services. It was fitted with a toilet and galley, with the services of a hostess, the shell of the body being constructed in Birmingham and the fitting out being carried out at Addlestone. Subsequent batches were introduced into the main fleet and that of the subsidiary company WC Standerwick the following year. Besides being geared for motorway operation, they had air suspension on the front axle and were way ahead of their time. These lower photographs show the view many motorists' had of these vehicles, as their top speed was in excess of that achievable by many family cars of the period. *(STA)*

The impressive 1966 extension to the Buckingham Palace Road wing. Thereafter the coach entrance was from Semley Place beneath the single-storey extension *(Fox Photos/LCCc)*

Coastal advertisement from 1964 detailing the facilities at Victoria Coach Station following the alterations that had been introduced, and which had mainly affected the booking hall, enquiry office and left luggage. *(Jim Russell collection)*

Opposite page upper: Another 1966 photograph, showing the extension and new main coach entrance from within Victoria Coach Station *(LCCc)*

Opposite page lower: An aerial view of Victoria Coach Station from a later period showing how well the new extension matched the original building (more than 30 years its senior) and the new canopies over Bay 15-22. BOAC Airways Terminal is seen in the bottom right corner. *(Peter Scammell collection)*

✱ FACILITIES *at* VICTORIA COACH STATION

BOOKING HALL

Booking Hall windows are open at 7.0 a.m. for *travel the same day* and at 8.0 a.m. for *advance* bookings (Sundays 8.0 a.m. for all bookings). Advance bookings close at 9.0 p.m.

SERVICE ENQUIRIES

The Enquiry Office for coach services and day tours is in the Main Hall of the Station and is open from 8 a.m. to 9 p.m. daily. Time-tables are also displayed outside the Station in Buckingham Palace Road and can be seen at *any* time.

TOUR ENQUIRIES

Information and reservations for British and Continental tours, Coach/Air services, Coach/Boat services and Continental coach services can be obtained from the TOURS OFFICE in the Buckingham Palace Road wing of the station
Hours: 9 a.m. to 5.30 p.m. Monday to Friday;
9 a.m. to 12.30 p.m. Saturdays.

POST BOOKINGS

Information and tickets for coach services and tours can be obtained by POST. Write to: Post Booking Dept., Victoria Coach Station, S.W.1.

LEFT LUGGAGE

This office is situated by Bay No. 1 in the Coach Station. Hours: *Summer:* from 7 a.m. (6 a.m. certain days) to 11.30 p.m. daily. *Winter:* from 7.30 a.m. to 11 p.m. Monday to Thursday and 7.30 a.m. to 11.30 p.m., Friday, Saturday and Sunday. (The night duty inspector will deal with emergency cases when the office is closed.)

DEPARTURE BAYS

On most pillars on the concourse in the station there is a poster showing the numbers of the departure bays of coach services.

REFRESHMENTS

Cafeteria is open from 6 a.m. to 11 p.m. (midnight on Sundays) in the summer; 7 a.m. to 11 p.m. (midnight on Sundays) in the winter. A fully licensed restaurant is open from 12 noon to 2.30 p.m. daily (except Sundays in the winter). Lounge bar open during normal licensed hours. Hot tea, coffee and chocolate available from machines in the waiting rooms at all hours of the night and day.

London Coastal Coaches, Ltd.

VICTORIA COACH STATION

BUCKINGHAM PALACE ROAD · VICTORIA · LONDON S.W.1

> *"In the seventies the public area was blessed with a chip machine amongst others. On one occasion a passenger put in the appropriate money and waited the three minutes it took to cook them. They were then greeted with a whoosh! as the chips passed straight through to the waste compartment at the bottom – the cardboard funnel had got stuck and had not fallen into place."*
> Chris Nash

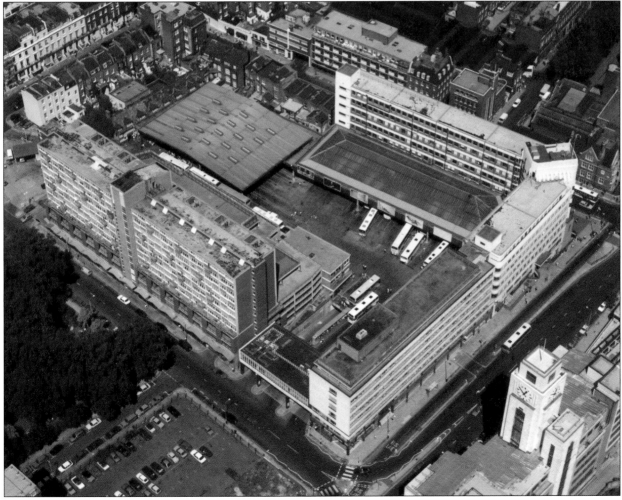

legislation, BOAC became British Airways when it was combined with British European Airways – BEA – on 1st April 1974. The Boeing Company first rolled-out the 747 Jumbo Jet in September 1968, and the British production Concorde flew for the first time in December 1973).

The new extension, which had taken two years to develop, almost doubled the Victoria Coach Station frontage in Buckingham Palace Road, and moved the coach entrance to its present position in Semley Place. This seven-storey office block, with a one-storey return in Semley Place enabled new amenities to be introduced in the public areas, and the updating of much of Coastal's administrative organisation.

Designed by architects T P Bennett & Son in close cooperation with consulting engineers R T James & Partners this extension to the original parts of the coach station was built by McLaughlin & Harvey Ltd. The efforts of the architects to ensure a building that blended harmoniously with the original one are clear to see, but their task was a difficult one. The original Thomas Wallis designs for the coach station were aesthetically a perfect balance of shape and dimension, and like any work of art complete in themselves. It would have been impossible to create a truly compatible addition to Wallis's designs, and if only for this reason, the work of T P Bennett & Son is to be much commended.

It was agreed that Coastal should occupy the ground floor and parts of the first and second floors of the extension and that BOAC, as tenants, would occupy the rest for its administrative offices, with its staff club – The Speedbird Club – located on the top floor. BOAC's Terminal on the other side of the road remained for the airline passenger check-in procedure and pick-up/set-down coach transfer to and from Heathrow.

With the added space it became possible for 36ft-long coaches to use the departure bays in the main yard, but unfortunately, and rather surprisingly considering the importance of the improvements and the forethought which must have gone into them, the entrance to an underground parking area which had been part of the new development was fractionally too shallow for many of the 36ft vehicles. The original agreement was for BOAC to use the basement garage for parking almost a hundred staff cars and Coastal was to have space for 25 coaches at night and at weekends.

Even with these alterations, coach arrivals and departures were still sharing the same areas, and it was not until the summer of 1981 that a separate arrivals areas was opened in what was until then Samuelson's garage. This new arrivals arrangement became essential because of the increase in trade brought about by the 1980 Transport Bill and the lifting of licence restrictions on express services of over 30 miles. But we have jumped ahead of ourselves.

With the new 1966 extension, Coastal was now able to improve passenger facilities by introducing a ground floor passenger lounge, which included a licensed bar – The Coachman. The change in passenger attitudes and, in many ways, the type of passengers travelling, is reflected in the changes to Coastal's catering arrangements at Victoria Coach Station. There were now fewer passengers wishing to enjoy a relaxed meal in the restaurant (which thirty years earlier had been the pride and joy of Coastal) as a prelude to their journey and, more than ever, the demand was for fast, easily available

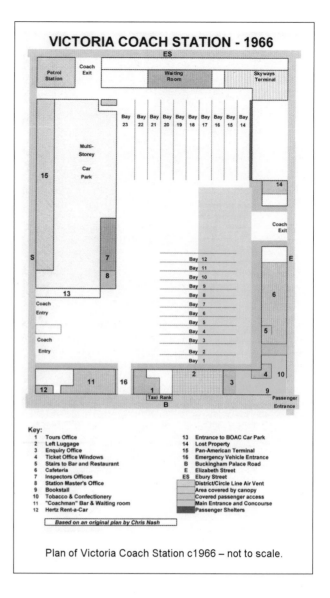

VICTORIA COACH STATION - 1966

Key:
1   Tours Office
2   Left Luggage
3   Enquiry Office
4   Ticket Office Windows
5   Stairs to Bar and Restaurant
6   Cafeteria
7   Inspectors Offices
8   Station Master's Office
9   Bookstall
10 Tobacco & Confectionery
11 "Coachman" Bar & Waiting room
12 Hertz Rent-a-Car
13 Entrance to BOAC Car Park
14 Lost Property
15 Pan-American Terminal
16 Emergency Vehicle Entrance
B   Buckingham Palace Road
E   Elizabeth Street
ES Ebury Street
    District/Circle Line Air Vent
    Area covered by canopy
    Covered passenger access
    Main Entrance and Concourse
    Passenger Shelters

Based on an original plan by Chris Nash

Plan of Victoria Coach Station c1966 – not to scale.

snacks obtainable at any time of day or night. Many passengers were happy enough with the freshly packed snack boxes available from the cafeteria at 3/6d, 4/6d and 5/6d (17½p, 22½p and 27½p). Thus it was that a 24-hour automatic vending section was included in the new lounge, and it is sad to reflect that ten years later the catering at Victoria Coach Station was to be described as scandalous by Egon Ronay writing in the 1976 issue of the Lucas Guide to hotels, restaurants and inns in Great Britain and Ireland. The restaurant closed in 1972 and together with the extensive kitchens was converted into office accommodation, with all the catering requirements being handed to an outside caterer, although the Elizabeth Room – a meeting and function room – remained available for hire until the mid 1990s. Eight years later the licensed bar was closed in order to provide space for a larger travel office.

Administratively too, Coastal was able to make some significant changes with the opening of the new extension. Three departments moved into new offices; the tours department had administration offices on the first floor but now for the first time also had a ground floor reception and sales office, with 11ft open-display windows letting onto Buckingham Palace Road. The ground floor sales office and the administrative office above were connected by an electric

In the new tours department computerised ticketing was eventually introduced, initially for day and half day tours. Seen here soon after it became operational (l to r): Peter Scammell, Jackie Ramsey, and Ian Milligan (National Bus Company, Overseas Marketing Manager). *(LCCc)*

"Because the old building had four floors and the West Block seven, it was not possible to continue with the tea-trolley service for the staff. There was a new state-of-the-art tea machine that used a threepenny piece. The first person to use the machine was Mr Len Corbett who put in his threepenny piece, pressed the appropriate button and, to his horror, got a cup of hot milky WATER!"
Chris Nash

When I introduced the new charting system I had, in particular, total support from Fred Robinson, the General Manager, although I think he was a little surprised at the plentiful amount of space each chart clerks had to work in.
Peter Scammell – Reservations Manager at the time.

It was only the Crosville *London/Liverpool service that could not be charted easily on the new simplified system. This service carried a lot of shorter intermediate journeys, so it was necessary to know the exact situation in order to maximise the seat usage, particularly on busy days. For example they might have a passenger booked London to Oxford, another from Oxford to Shipston on Stour, another from Shipston on Stour to Erdington, and another from Erdington to Liverpool. Four passengers, making four journeys, on just one seat.*
Peter Scammell

This column, top to bottom

Its move into the new extension, together with the new charting system, completely transformed the appearance of the chartroom. A team of clerks received telephone calls from agents, whilst another team entered the bookings onto the charts as well as handling all the paperwork received by post or arriving by coach. This picture shows telephone reservations being received. Rather different from the chartroom of 1948 pictured earlier – and yet less than 20 years had passed. *(Fox Photos/LCCc)*

Booking slips from the telephone reservations section together with other incoming reservations being sorted. Our picture shows very long serving chart clerk, Norrie Murphy. *(Fox Photos/LCCc)*

Reservations were then entered onto the simplified charts. The new system involved just two carousel files each holding 550 charts. *(LCCc)*

hoist to enable the speedy interchange of documents (a much-publicised feature though not, one might have thought, such a momentous innovation); the post bookings department also moved into new first floor accommodation; the chartroom not only moved to a new office but also introduced radical changes to the system of charting.

The charting system that had been more than adequate in previous years was, by now, seen as cumbersome and too time-consuming, and it was realised that much of the information that was being recorded for each booking was totally unnecessary. The new system separated the acceptance of booking by telephone from the actual writing of the bookings onto the charts. The ad lib or confirm system used by agents, introduced more than ten years before, which dispensed with the need to telephone for reservations, was the mainstay of advanced bookings with several thousand ticket confirmations being received in the chartroom each day to be charted as quickly as possible.

Nevertheless it was still vital to have an efficient telephone booking service for journeys where the confirm system was not applicable. Under the new system agents still used ex-directory numbers for individual companies, or groups of companies; the chart clerks taking these calls had before them full details of availability, including exact indications of services that had reached D (for danger) level: that is, the stage where a STOP point was imminent. Bookings received by telephone in this way were entered onto telephone booking forms and passed to the chart clerks responsible for the actual writing up of the reservations onto the charts.

To complete the arrangement, a controller (a far more suitable title than the previous chargehand) sitting in the middle of the chartroom, had a card index set of control charts which were brought up to date daily from the master set with urgent information being provided at any time throughout the day.

Instead of the old system of recording every detail of every booking onto a chart, the system used was simply to block off the numbers of seats needed for each reservation. This way the entire charting needs could be held in two revolving carousel files, and just four clerks were need to complete all the written entries. At a stroke the thousands of charts and the hundreds of binders of the old system had become redundant and the old telephone systems which had been so up-to-the-minute barely ten years before were replaced with key and lamp units, with chart clerks using headsets instead of balancing handsets under their chins.

The new system was similar in most ways to that which had been used by airlines for many years before the introduction of computerised systems, and Associated Motorways in its Cheltenham chartroom had, certainly since the 1950s, been operating a booking record system whereby reservations were entered simply as numbers of passengers joining a coach at any point and being set-down at another. Nevertheless the streamlining of the Coastal system, plus the addition of Telex communication, which had been introduced to the chartroom, was a major step forward. (In 2004 the National Express operations control centre in central Birmingham controlled the entire National Express network. With a fully computerised system, chart clerks – by then called controllers – handled operational matters as well as reservations. Up to a dozen controllers were on duty at any one time – a good deal fewer than in Coastal's chartroom during the 1950s and early 60s – and at night just one controller had the place to himself. Coastal had usually had two, but they also had responsibility for patrolling the entire building, including the corridors of the rented accommodation on the upper floors.)

෨   ෩

Coach services themselves, which had been little altered in the first half of the 1960s, were gradually being enhanced with the further opening of stretches of motorways, together with, in many cases, the reduction of the divisions between the BET/BTC (later THC) express service operators and the larger independent operators. The idea of pool services that had been seen first in the 1930s with Yorkshire Services and Associated Motorways, now appeared in East Anglia. In 1964 Eastern National, East Kent, Maidstone & District and Southdown began pooled through services via the newly opened Dartford Tunnel to Kent and the South Coast (thereby by-passing London, and Victoria Coach Station) – a trend that was to flourish with each passing year.

In 1967 Eastern National joined forces with Suttons and Grey-Green – two of the major independent operators on the London to Clacton route – to establish the Essex Coast Pool, and later that year Grey-Green joined Eastern Counties to form pool services along the London/Great Yarmouth and London/Ipswich/Felixstowe corridors. For the first time this brought Grey-Green, a major PSV Operators member, into Victoria Coach Station.

Motorways were changing the face of coaching and future benefits were becoming obvious, but those same roads were also encouraging private car usage: in 1965 there were four times more private cars registered in the London area than there had been fifteen years before, and this was bound to have an effect on public transport services of all sorts.

Dr Richard Beeching (1913-85) studied engineering and administration at Imperial College London and served as Chairman of the British Railways Board from 1963-5. He was created a life peer in 1965. During his Chairmanship, he devised the Beeching Plan for a substantial contraction of the rail network in the United Kingdom. This was to the advantage of local bus operations, which were increased or adjusted to provide replacements for discontinued rail services, but made little marked effect on express services. Passengers continued to travel by rail to the nearest of the remaining railheads, and took replacement buses (or cars) to their final destinations.

Changes were again taking place at King's Cross, where PSV Operators had closed its coach station in Pentonville Road (King's Cross Coach Station No. 3) and were to open yet another, smaller coach station in Caledonia Street (King's Cross Coach Station No. 4). Grey-Green and the other George Ewer companies, as well as Yelloway, had already transferred their services to the Britannia Airways terminal in Mabledon Place, so the 8,000 square feet of the new King's Cross Coach Station, which was more convenient for the railways and underground stations, and quite close to the location of an earlier King's Cross Coach Station (No. 1) in Belgrove Street, was adequate for the remaining PSV Operators' journeys starting from or terminating at King's Cross.

෨   ෩

An announcement by the BET in November 1967, although not entirely unexpected, was the precursor to events that many will think of as bringing to an end the halcyon days of London Coastal Coaches Ltd and Victoria Coach Station. The BET announced that it was to sell all its bus and coaching interests to the Transport Holding Company.

In one fell swoop Victoria Coach Station, Coastal and all the associated operating companies came under State ownership. Coastal would no longer be an equally balanced organisation under the controlling interests of two factions (public and private). The face of long-distance express coaching in Britain was to change irrevocably, and although there can be no denying that huge potential advantages lay ahead, this is still one of those defining moments in time which mark the changing of an old, notable and loved order.

The Transport Act 1968 (which took effect from 1st January 1969) was the official legislation that finally brought all the ex-BET, ex-Tilling and ex-BTC companies together as the National Bus Company and our story might well have ended here, but we need to continue for a further four years before we can draw events to a fitting conclusion.

Although it is easy and understandable to harbour feelings of nostalgic regret at the passing of the old establishment with its separate companies and individual characteristics, it has to be acknowledged that under the new regime a good deal more interavailability and interaction seemed likely. For example, it was at this time that the Coachmaster ticket was introduced for overseas visitors. With a Coachmaster costing just £8, visitors could enjoy eight days unlimited travel on virtually the whole of the network of express coach services in Britain; the tickets could be bought abroad or, upon presentation of a passport, from Victoria Coach Station. Eventually this scheme was to be sold under its new title of BritExpress Pass.

In 1969 changes to the Victoria Coach Station buildings at the rear of the yard provided a new Station Master's office with, for the first time, a specifically designated first-aid room; a much enhanced left-luggage office, and improved offices for the operating companies' inspectors, but apart from this the next couple of years saw few changes in the day-to-day operation. (Even these changes were insufficient to meet the ever increasing demand, and just ten years later, in the summer of 1979, John Millard, then general manager of Victoria Coach Station, announced a further major facelift which was to move the inspectors to superior first floor offices, with the area released being used for a new and yet bigger left luggage office). Chairmanship of Coastal fell at first to Tony Gailey and then in 1972 to Jim Skyrme both Chief Executives of the National Bus Company (NBC) and the Traffic Committee, which had been meeting regularly for 46 years, was disbanded in 1971. It was a settling-in period.

On the face of it, although later seen to be not so, passenger numbers were holding up quite well against increased car ownership and the adverse publicity that road transport was attracting with media reports of mammoth traffic hold-ups. These media reports were unfounded and the timekeeping of coaches, not just in normal times but also in adverse weather conditions and at peak periods, was very good. Using as a random but typical example, during the evening of Easter Monday 1971, in the six hours from 5.00pm, around 350 coaches arrived at Victoria Coach Station (almost one a minute), most of which were early or just a couple of minutes late. The worst delay was the isolated incident of a service from Manchester that arrived 30 minutes behind schedule.

By 1971 the M4 Motorway was fully open from London to South Wales, and Associated Motorways was now operating non-stop through services from Victoria Coach Station to Newport and Cardiff. On a cold January Sunday in 1972 the first Greyhound non-stop motorway service from Bristol arrived in Victoria Coach Station with no fewer than 200 passengers, including Susan Denning who had just been elected as the somewhat oddly named Miss Bristol Omnibus, and to meet the coaches were Coastal's General Manager, Fred Robinson, and Publicity Superintendent Briah Andrews.

Then, in the summer of 1972, Associated Motorways began operating through journeys from Birmingham to Bristol using the M5, and in the same year direct weekend operations were also introduced from Victoria Coach Station to Tenby; from Birmingham and Coventry to Tenby, and from Leicester and Coventry to Ilfracombe, so while the Cheltenham interchange continued to be the hub of the Associated Motorways network, it was becoming apparent that motorways were bringing with them huge changes to the pattern of long-distance coach operations, and several pioneer developments of the 1930s were at risk. Eventually, the Associated Motorways terminal in Cheltenham closed, and Cheltenham became just a picking up/setting down point, with National Express services transferred to Cheltenham's Royal Well bus station.

Also in May 1972, the Midland Motorways Link joined the M1 and the M6 resulting in the introduction of many new or improved services. Journey times on some Standerwick services from the Lake District to London were cut by a third with Kendal becoming a mere five hours twenty-four minutes from the Coach Station. New direct services to Victoria were introduced from Barrow-in-Furness and from Southport. Crosville reduced the journey time between London and Chester to 4½ hours, and Western SMT were completing the London to Glasgow journey in nine hours. The expression Express Coach Service was taking on a new meaning.

ᘓ ᘔ

In 1971 the NBC called in outside consultants to examine its entire coach operation throughout Britain. The conclusions drawn by the consultants indicated the need for a dramatic shake-up. It was suggested that the whole coaching network needed to be drawn closer together, and there should be a greater degree of centralised control and promotion. Rather than there being several companies albeit under one umbrella operating regionally through the country, just one name (as with Greyhound in America) should be used throughout the network that would, in the public's eye, be synonymous with long-distance coach travel throughout the land.

Furthermore, an official statistical survey showed that passenger journeys by public road transport in 1971 had declined more than 5.5% on 1970 carryings. Express service passenger journeys declined from 69 million in 1970 to 64 million in 1971, although passenger receipts had increased (*Passenger Transport in Great Britain 1971* – Her Majesty's Stationery Office*)*.

The NBC set up a new division called the Central Activities Group, which was to bring all NBC coaching activities and travel developments under the auspices of one central control. The executive director of this new division was David Glassborow, a Cambridge University-educated man with a mathematics and economics background, whose transport career went back to 1954 when he founded the Economics Division of the BTC. With the formation of the THC, which took over the responsibilities of the BTC, he became Head of Economic Research and then, in 1969, Chief Planning and Development Officer of the NBC.

It was clear that David Glassborow had the experience, determination and ability to pull the coaching industry up by its bootstraps. Commerce and industry were moving at a pace undreamed of in the 1920s and 30s and still barely conceivable in the 1940s and 50s, or even the early 60s. He made it clear that he saw the company as an international business operating on a national rather than local level and wanted to set higher standards of service in order to improve the status of the coaching industry. He suggested that the future for independent companies with old-fashioned ideas was not too bright, unless they too were prepared to adopt a similar concerted, competitive and thoroughly professional approach. He was reported in Coaching Journal in April 1972 as saying:

Although this chart shows an increase of receipts in 1971, it must be remembered that operating costs also increased considerably. Furthermore, the NBC's percentage increase was below the industry average. It is also clear from the chart that the percentage reduction in passengers carried for both express services and 'bus services was greater than for the industry as a whole. NBC's main interests (i.e. coaches and 'buses) suffered from a greater percentage loss of passengers, and a smaller percentage increase in revenue.

ANALYSIS OF PASSENGERS CARRIED, AND RECEIPTS 1970 & 1971

PASSENGERS CARRIED	1970	1971	% change
Passenger journeys on express services	69,000,000	64,000,000	-7.25
Passenger journeys on excursions & tours.	27,000,000	30,000,000	11.11
Passenger journeys on contract work	413,000,000	432,000,000	4.60
Passenger journeys by 'bus	8,645,000,000	8,113,000,000	-6.15
Total passenger journeys made by road public transport	9,154,000,000	8,639,000,000	-5.63

PASSENGER RECEIPTS	1970	1971	% change
- National Bus Company	£149,100,000	£169,800,000	13.88
- Scottish Bus Group	£28,300,000	£36,600,000	29.33
- London Transport	£63,200,000	£67,700,000	7.12
- Passenger Transport Authorities	£51,100,000	£59,200,000	15.85
- Local Authorities	£78,500,000	£89,600,000	14.14
- Other operators	£77,800,000	£88,100,000	13.24
Total passenger receipts for for the whole industry	£448,000,000	£511,000,000	14.06

"Before the 1992 refurbishments, the toilets were often described as awful. The charges were then 5p for ladies, and also the gents' cubicles, but free for the gents urinals. It was a fact that in those days the peak summer period meant every weekend toilets were blocked by newspapers, tin cans, clothing and anything else you can imagine. In the gents, cubicle doors were often kicked in – sometimes four or five in one weekend. The main basement public toilets suffered from the fact that they were below the sewer level and therefore had two ejectors to pump waste up into the sewerage system. As you can imagine, at times this was an extremely unpleasant job for the station engineers. The 1992 refurbishments brought both the ladies and gents toilets to a high standard although everybody would now have to pay 20p to pass through the modern turnstiles, but it did eliminate almost all vandalism. The old normal size toilet rolls and holders (which passengers used to pinch) were replaced by jumbo rolls in metal dispensers, washbasin taps are modern push down types that gradually rise to cut-off the water supply, and soap dispenser are of the stainless steel type. Hand towels were replaced by hot-air hand dryers. So you can see that things were greatly improved; although, of course, a toilet is only as clean as the last person to use it. At the peak of the season Victoria Coach Station toilets use up to 200 jumbo toilet rolls per week at a cost of several hundred pounds. A contracted cleaning company does hourly inspections to try and maintain standards".
Chris Nash

"The present coach station (year 2004) plays in the public areas soothing music intermingled with pre-recorded announcements like: 'Please do not lend money to beggars or students as you are unlikely to see your money again'. This can be interrupted at any time to make an announcement. On one occasion the message came over as 'would Mrs —— please go to the help point, you are unlikely to see your money again."!
Chris Nash

"...though it is no part of National's policy deliberately to establish a monopoly of all coach services, where there is business to be had we shall be there."

Then, later in 1972, following the independent consultation and the formation of the Central Activities Group, the new name National Travel was introduced as the organisation to operate the express services and tour operations of all the companies, and to complete the unified image all the vehicles were to be in the same all-over white livery.

How ironic, when science tells us that white light contains all the colours in the rainbow, that we were then about to see those rainbow colours, which for years had been the familiar

hallmark of such a huge chunk of the coaching industry, reduced into one white livery, and two new trading names: National Holidays and National Express. Far-sighted Mr H R Lapper, who had been a director and general manager of Black & White Motorways, and later chairman of the Committee of Management of Associated Motorways until his retirement in 1952, had already quite unofficially hinted at the name National Express Coachways and was prepared to see the demise of the title Associated Motorways.

Fortunately for National Travel several of the people who had been so important for so many years in keeping the whole Coastal machine in top working order were to continue under the new scheme of things. George Newman remained as secretary and administration manager; Briah Andrews was to remain public relations officer; Frank Garman, by then in his 39th year of service at Victoria Coach Station (he retired in 1978), remained as agency controller; W S Maisey, who had joined Coastal in 1948, was to be staff and training officer; Peter Scammell remained as reservations manager and later became Coach Station Manager and eventually Assistant Commercial Manager (National Travel SE); and Charles (Frank) Hodges, who had become involved with Coastal when he joined Samuelson's 46 years earlier, became terminals and air services manager. Charles Hodges joined Samuelson's at the age of 14; apparently he replaced a boy called Frank and nobody could get used to a different name and so he was called Frank throughout his 48-year career with the company. He became Samuelson's manager in 1950 and 20 years later was also appointed Operations Manager of London Coastal Coaches also with responsibility for Victoria Coach Station.

Several more of Coastal's coaching-in-the-blood stalwarts were also to become National Travel men including four who had all joined Victoria Coach Station in 1948: Frank Doughty a senior traffic clerk, chief inspector F H Nye, A G T Smith traffic superintendent with Samuelsons, and C G Tolley private hire superintendent with Samuelson.

There were also many members of operating companies' staff with long-service records at Victoria Coach Station who became National Travel men. One of the most familiar faces around the place, Bill Ashby, had started in 1938 with East Kent and spent 20 years as East Kent's Chief Inspector in London. With the advent of the National Bus Company, Bill Ashby took charge of a new London unit to include East Kent, Maidstone & District and Southdown. He retired at the end of 1976. In short: so many professional coachmen with such a wealth of industry knowledge, and so much experience in the many and diverse corners of the coaching business were to continue to serve under the new regime.

As part of the new arrangements, Fred Robinson, Director and General Manager of London Coastal Coaches Ltd, was to move on to become the managing director of the NBC's property development company. In a way Coastal was about to lose its pilot.

Fred Robinson had joined Coastal in 1946 as Company Secretary and had devoted himself to the company ever since; he was a very good figurehead and, in particular, had an honest understanding of what was important to agents and to staff. He was first to see what practical actions could be taken to make the jobs of staff and agents easier or more pleasant and he was approachable by all. Many of the innovations and new concepts of the 1950s and 1960s were either his ideas, or were the ideas of others for which he would quickly recognise the potential and to which he readily gave enthusiastic acknowledgement and support.

At times, when the coaching business was not taken too seriously by some in the travel industry at large, it was Fred Robinson who weighed in to represent coaching and the entire industry, notably with his attendances at the ABTA (Association of British Travel Agents) Convention each year.

It was the whole-hearted involvement of Fred Robinson in everyday coach station matters that ensured the continuing smooth passage of Coastal from how it had been in its formative days of the 1930s, through what had become seen as the more tranquil days of the fifties and early sixties, to the dynamic company that was stepping into an exciting future. Fred Robinson retired in 1976 and must surely stand equally with the three men who started it all — Len Turnham, Shirley James, and his namesake Colonel Robinson — in his efforts to create and recreate so much that contributed towards the mysteriously satisfying business of moving people from A to B.

And so it was that, in 1972, the company known for 47 years as London Coastal Coaches Ltd became National Travel (NBC) Ltd, and the title London Coastal Coaches Ltd was abandoned. (At the end of 1978 the ghost of Coastal was re-established as Victoria Coach Station Ltd and, in 1988 following the privatisation of the NBC companies, Victoria Coach Station Ltd was acquired by London Transport at the request of the Secretary of State for Transport.) Not without a good deal of nostalga, we now draw our story to its close.

The editorial column of Coaching Journal in August 1972 said: "What's in a name? The news that a famous old name has now disappeared will sadden those of us who have grown up with the coach industry since the late nineteen-twenties. London Coastal Coaches, founded in 1925 to set up a central booking organisation in London, has become synonymous with coach travel in Great Britain, and Victoria Coach Station, opened in 1932, has done yeoman service as the London terminal through which millions of passengers have passed over the years.

When anything is nationalised, major changes must follow. Moreover, when each succeeding chairman comes on to the scene another costly change around seems to be the order of the day.

Some years ago in a City of London hospital, the Sister apologised for the crockery that appeared on the meal tray. The hospital some years earlier had been given a set of first quality crockery by a Lord Mayor of London, but she said, following nationalisation, this was taken away, smashed and substituted by some cheap tableware bearing another name. The object of this story is to indicate one small example of the waste and difficulties that often arise in the wake of nationalisation.

Now, National Travel (NBC) Ltd might be a suitable name for a travel agent, but it is hard to see what it has to do with coach services. It is true that we had long suggested that the coach industry should play its full role as part of the world of travel and should lift its sights beyond the field of coaching pure and simple; nevertheless, since the main business of the NBC's Central Activities Group and the operation of Victoria Coach Station involved coaches to a major degree, National Travel seemed a strange title for such a coach-orientated organisation. At a time, too, when many people had had quite enough of nationalised industries, it seemed strange to try to make the word National more acceptable than names long accepted as a mark of reliable service.

There seemed some danger, too, that the NBC, on both bus and coach sides, was going to suffer in the same way as had the railways from a top-heavy administrative management. With so many bosses, the man on the job knows not where he is going or even what he is doing; railwayman can tell you a thing or two about that."

What else is there to say? Well, how about "Goodbye, Coastal…?"

SEVENTY GREAT NAMES FOR SALE

NATIONAL BUS COMPANY IS BEING PRIVATISED

The State-owned National Bus Company is being privatised – not as one company, not in regional groups, but as around 70 individual companies. Companies with well-known local names like Southdown, Crosville, Midland Red and Yorkshire Traction.

The companies for sale include bus and coach companies, engineering companies and the nationally-known names, National Express and National Travelworld, the travel agency chain.

And the sale is now on.

Many companies have a long tradition and are closely involved with their local communities.

The privatisation of National Bus provides opportunities for purchasers to become involved in progressive transport and leisure travel businesses.

Here are some of the options:

1. You can make an offer for a bus or coach company.

2. You could consider a joint venture with the local management team.

3. You could obtain a valuable advertising medium through involvement with a bus company.

If you would like further information, please contact the Chairman, National Bus Company, 172 Buckingham Palace Road, London SW1W 9TN.

NATIONAL BUS IS BEING PRIVATISED
Don't miss the Bus

This advertisement does not, and is not intended to, form the basis of any offer of the share capital of, or the undertaking or assets of, The National Bus Company or any of its subsidiary or associated companies.

This advertisement is issued on behalf of The National Bus Company by its financial advisers, Barclays de Zoete Wedd Limited.

In accordance with Part III of the 1985 Transport Act, on 7 April 1986 the Secretary of State for Transport issued a direction requiring the NBC to offer for sale each of its subsidiaries. The above poster was used in this connection. By April 1988 a total of 71 such subsidiaries had been sold, leaving only Victoria Coach Station Limited (formed in 1978 following a reorganisation of NBC's Central Activities Group), which was sold, by order of the Secretary of State, to London Regional Transport (LRT) on 31st October 1988. It was the wish of the Government of the day that VCS should remain in the public sector until an alternative location for a central London coach station could be found. *(STA)*

Appendix 1 – The wry twist promised earlier...

Eventually, the ownership of Victoria Coach Station passed from London Transport to Transport for London (TfL). However, before then, on 21st May 1986, Peter Scammell, who had by then worked for 41 years at Victoria Coach Station, together with J H Millard (Managing Director) and John Jackson (Company Secretary), set-up a company called London Coach Station Limited and made a sadly thwarted attempt to buy the coach station. It is particularly exciting to record though, that although currently dormant, the company still exists.

It was as if these entrepreneurs had stepped into the shoes of Toms and Boon, the owners of Blue Belle Coaches and London Terminal Coach Station Ltd, who nearly 60 years before had almost beaten Coastal in acquiring the site at the corner of Buckingham Palace Road and Elizabeth Street. Even the company name, apart from the word 'terminal' is the same.

Had these three gentlemen's plan succeeded one could imagine smiling down on them the amused if sardonic grins of triumph on the faces of Toms and Boon because Peter Scammell, before joining Coastal, had started his coaching career with Blue Belle Coaches. Full circle!

Appendix 2 – SLOane 0202 in Ramsgate

Ramsgate Telephone Enquiry Centre

Based on the recollections of John Marsh, the original manager of the centre, and the principal person instrumental in its successful set-up, its staff training and its highly efficient day-to-day operation. Unless shown otherwise, all the personal quotations are John's.

Prior to employing the people needed to staff the new centre, Peter Scammell and John Marsh interviewed over 150 applicants for the 26 vacancies, although in the later stages of this mammoth task it was left to John Marsh to undertake the interviews. Applicants were made aware that they would receive one of three letters: namely: 1. You have not been successful; 2. You have been successful so please report to this office on 24th June 1974 for training; or 3. You are considered as suitable, but owing to the very high number of suitable applicants your particulars will be kept on a waiting list for future vacancies. Many of those on the waiting list were not

On July 2nd 1974 I can remember I was in the middle of a staff training session when our G.P.O telephone engineer came into the room and told me that ONE line on SLOane 0202 was now coming through to Ramsgate T.E.C. directly. What he did not say was that the other nine lines would also be coming through soon after! This was the start of a 21-year association between Ramsgate T.E.C. and Victoria Coach Station.

employed at the centre until up to three years later, but they then continued to work at the Ramsgate TEC for many years.

Training started as planned on 24th June and the new centre, with its enthusiastic if nervous team, was up and running for its official opening day eight days later.

In the early days no supervisors were employed as, apart from John Marsh, only two other staff members, Betty Pocknall and Bill Hartly, who had both moved over from East Kent, had any travel experience. However, by the end of 1974 four more people (Gwen Light, Yvonne Richardson, Mandy Allen and Kim Headley) were promoted and a supervisor status established.

But it was not just the telephone information service that had moved from Victoria Coach Station to Ramsgate; the Coastal tradition of long and loyal service also moved with it. For many years telephone callers to Victoria Coach Station were to enjoy the outstanding service of John Marsh's team in Ramsgate, numerous members of which were to serve for many years. Indeed, in 1994, some 20 years after the Ramsgate project had opened, six of the original staff members were still employed there Marion Deverson, Gwen Light, Ann Altree, Pam Wratten, Kim Headley, and John Marsh himself.

In those early days everything relied on the telephone, as suitable computers had not then been invented, and in order to provide all the staff with maximum information, a giant whiteboard was erected on which up-to-the-minute records were written so that callers could be given the absolutely latest information particularly concerning fully booked services. This included not just the regular express services, but also Samuelson's day trips, Euroways, and Clipper (later under Eurolines) services, and the Scottish Omnibuses routes that were controlled separately by that company. The giant whiteboard even gave booking status information about the Sunday services to Hallesley Bay and Blundeston prisons. Very soon, one whiteboard was not enough and a second was installed.

At all times, the aim of the Ramsgate TEC was to give the maximum information to callers, even if their enquiry did not always specifically involve coach services; contact telephone numbers were listed and freely given for such as the London Tourist Board, the Passport Office, London Transport, British Rail enquiries, Student Travel and many more. Internally, and to ensure a consistency of accurate and up-to-date information being given, new data of all sorts was supplied to every member of the staff by means of internal distribution lists (for which each staff member had to sign to confirm receipt). Although very few, customer complaint letters were also distributed in this way to every staff member to ensure that any relevant mistakes did not recur. Complimentary letters were circulated in the same way.

After a few years it became clear that the Ramsgate TEC could often convert a telephone enquiry into a booking and a system was introduced so that staff could issue tickets against credit card payments. At a later date, when the Ramsgate centre had been updated with a computer system, the agents' reservations office was transferred from Catford (Timpson's old office at 175 Rushey Green) to Ramsgate.

It is clear that the Ramsgate operation was a highly efficient and very happy organisation. The loyalty and cooperative spirit, which had prevailed from the outset, was due to a huge extent to the first-rate management/staff relationship and the exceptional work attitudes of the staff themselves. This fostered the tradition of having a Thank You day-out each year, usually on the last Sunday of September, for staff and their families; among the most successful were visits to Windsor Castle, Hampton Court, Kew Gardens Chessington Zoo, the Isle of Wight, Le Touquet, and a Mississippi Riverboat (actually on the Norfolk Broads). Comparable in many ways to the Coastal social club of the 1950s, certainly in its spirit of friendship and bonhomie, the Ramsgate staff had the advantage of being subsidised by the company, so that staff went free and friends and families paid very little.

Ramsgate TEC later became part of National Express as the National Express Travel Sales Centre (NETS). It had a staff of 50 when, in 1993, John Marsh became Stops Manager (South), and Kim Headley took over as manager.

In 1995 the Ramsgate telephone enquiry centre closed, and National Express at Birmingham Digbeth took over all telephone enquiries. In 21 years of operation, Ramsgate TEC had dealt with over 30 million calls, with less than a hundred genuine complaints about the office. A proud record.

They said it could never happen! Such was the demand for coach travel information in the late 1970s that at peak times we would have two and sometimes three callers at the same time on ONE incoming line, trying to obtain information. Our G.P.O. engineer said that this could not happen so we let him monitor the incoming calls to prove the point. A few years later a brand new telephone system was installed, and this overcame the problem.

In the late 70s and early 80s, immediately we received a bomb scare call, the clerk receiving the call would signal to the supervisor who would pick-up the direct line to Victoria Coach Station and the entire coach station would be cleared. Fortunately they were all false alarms, but we could never take a chance in case it was for real. The clerks completed a form giving details of the call, and the information would be passed to Gerald Road Police Station who, in the early days, would send a police constable round to Victoria Coach Station to speak to the clerk! It took a while for them to accept that 730 0202 was answered down in Ramsgate.

One of my favourite jobs was my monthly visit to the Ramsgate Telephone Enquiry Centre. John's team was like one big happy family. It was like a well-oiled engine, the relationship between the T.E.C. and the East Kent staff was excellent, it was all so very very friendly and welcoming.
Peter Scammell

Our busiest day at Ramsgate T.E.C. every year was Maundy Thursday because in those days passengers always seemed to leave it to the last minute to finalize their travel arrangements, but in many cases coaches were already fully booked.

Appendix 3 —Miscellania

List of Tenants occupying Coastal Chambers at various times between 1932 & 1940

Airports Ltd – Gatwick & Gravesend Aerodromes
Batteries Ltd - Accumulator Manufacturers
A.E. Blakesley & Co. – Land & Estate Agents
Anglo-Continental Patentees Ltd
Automatic Amusements Ltd – Manufacturers & Vendors of Automatic Machines
Boabands Ltd – Case Strapping Specialists
E.R. Bolton – Analyst & Chemical Engineer
Bon Soldering Products Ltd – Specialists in solders & Fluxes
Bookstalls Ltd – Stationers & Newsagents
Bowser & Co. (London) Ltd – Manufacturers of Petrol Pumps
Mrs K.M. Bramall – Boys' Kit
Bright Brothers Ltd – Tobacconists & Confectioners
The British Legion
British News Theatres Ltd
W.H. Buck – Commission Agent
Capital & Provincial News Theatre Ltd
Gordon Cheshire – Commission Agent
Mrs C. Clarke
Coats Machine Tool Co. Ltd – Engineers & Machine Tool Merchants
Sir Alan J. Cobham – Guernsey Air Services
Council for Promotion of Occupational Industries among the Physically Handicapped
Continental & American Patents Ltd – Patent Agents
Cookson, Dale & Co. – Perfumery Manufacturers
Covington & Sons Ltd – Lightermen & Contractors
Crerar, Morgan & Co. Ltd – Merchants
Dunlop Rubber Co. Ltd – Rubber & Tyre Manufacturers
Electrical & Engineering Products Ltd – Meter & Power Equipment
Electrolux Ltd – Manufacturers of Hygienic Cleaning Systems
W. Ellis, Senior – Incorporated Accountant
Farm Ice Creamery Ltd – Ice Cream Manufacturers
W.R.V. Forbes – Consulting Engineer
Gearless Stokers Ltd – Automatic Stokers
Andrew Gibbs (Builders) Ltd – Builders
Grant Engineering Co. – Heating & Ventilating Engineers
G. Kay Green – Architect
W.H. Green & Co (London)Ltd – Furniture Manufacturers
H.M. Collector of Taxes
H.M. Customs & Excise

G.C. Harris – Designer & Craftsman in Metal
Harry & Co – Coal Contractors
Heat & Air Systems – Heating & Ventilating Engineers
Miss E.L. Herbert – Eye Consultant
Heseltine, Evelyn & Co. Ltd – Specialist in Lubrication
Heston Rubber Co. – India Rubber Manufacturers
N.B. Hill - Commissioning Agent
N.D. Howard – Advertising Art
A.N. Hutt – The 'Five Million' Club
Icematic Ltd
Miss Inman
A.C.M. Jackaman – Aeronautical Consultant
Jersey Airways Ltd
Herbert Kidd – Estate Agent
Percy A. Jones
Ministry of Labour Staff Association
Mollo & Egan – Architectural Decorators
National Training College of Domestic Subjects
O.D.E Construction Co. Ltd
Owen Brothers (Tobacconists) Limited
Captain E.H.B. Palmer – Transport Consultant
G.D. Pearce-Jones - Solicitor
Pearson's Antiseptic Co. Ltd – Manufacturing Chemists
Frederick Pollard & Co. Ltd – Machine Tool Manufactures
A.D. Rawlings, Rallie Health Appliances
Rebman Finance Service
Rowsell & Co. – Boiler Consultants
Miss Adeline Shield
Mrs A. Smith – Souvenirs & Brassware
W.A. Smith – Consulting Engineer
A.W. Speak – Amusement Caterer
R.A. Spottiswoode – Printing & Engraving
W. Stevens & Co. – Automotive Engineers
Stirling & Johnson Ltd – Slating & Tiling Contractors
L.J. Stordiau & Sons – Marble Merchants
Swan, Norman & Clay - Architects
H. Talbot Ltd - Confectioners
Talking Mirrors Ltd - Advertising Contractors
G.W. Thomas – Fruiterer & Florist
A.H. Thorne Ltd – Gentlemen's Outfitters
Leslie Turner – Civil Engineer
United Egg & Poultry Packers Ltd
Universal Automobile Insurance Co. Ltd
Wallis, Gilbert & Partners – Architects
E.E. Wells – Trade Protection Association
Wells Coates & Pleydell-Bouverie – Architects
H Weston - Architect
White & Greaney – Incorporated Accountants

Operational Developments during the 1930s

To	LATE 1920s &/or EARLY 1930s		MID/LATE 1930s	
	Company	Main departure points	Company	Main departure points
W. MIDLANDS AND THE NORTH WEST	Majestic	Terminal CS, Victoria & Kings X	Majestic	**VICTORIA CS**
	Standerwick	Woburn Place	Standerwick	**VICTORIA CS**
	John Bull	Kings Cross & Strand	Scout	**VICTORIA CS**
	Finglands	Kings Cross & Strand	Crosville	**VICTORIA CS**
	Bracewells (C.Smith)	Terminal C S	Ribble	**VICTORIA CS**
	Imperial	Southampton Row	Midland Red	**VICTORIA CS**
	Scout Motor Services	Southampton Row	North Western	**VICTORIA CS**
	Yelloway	Central CS	Yelloways	Central CS/Kings X
	Eniway	Central CS		
	Holt Bros	Central CS		
	Crosville	Central CS		
	National Coachways	Central CS		
	Albatros Roadways	Terminal CS & Russell Square		
	McShanes	Terminal CS & Russell Square		
	Samuelsons	Victoria		
	Palanquin	Terminal CS		
E. MIDLANDS YORKSHIRE AND THE NORTH EAST	Yorkshire Services	**VICTORIA CS**	Yorkshire Services	**VICTORIA CS**
	United Auto	**VICTORIA CS & Kings X**	United Auto	**VICTORIA CS**
	B&E Coach Services	Kings X	Orange Brothers	**VICTORIA CS**
	Orange Brothers	Kings X	Lincolnshire	**VICTORIA CS**
	South Yorkshire Motors	Terminal CS	United Counties	**VICTORIA CS**
	Blue Band	Central CS		
	Albatros Roadways	Terminal CS & Russell Square		
	Majestic Parlour Saloons	Terminal CS		
	Philipsons Stella	Terminal CS		
	Glenton Friars	Terminal CS		
	Fleetwyas	Kings X		
	Express Safety	Kings X		
EAST ANGLIA	Eastern Counties	**VICTORIA CS**	Eastern Counties	**VICTORIA CS**
	United Auto	**LUPUS STREET**	Eastern National	**VICTORIA CS & Kings X**
	Empires Best	Terminal CS & Kings X	Westcliff Motors	**VICTORIA CS**
	Corona	Embankment	Empires Best	Terminal CS & Kings X
	Suttons Crossley	Embankment	Corona	Kings X
	Quest	Kings X	Suttons Crossley	Kings X
	Grey Green	Kings X	Grey Green	Kings X & Mile End CS
	Bush & Twiddy	Terminal CS & Central CS	'W' Coach Line	Kings X
	Bird Motors	Central CS	Primrose	Kings X
	Eastern Motorways	Terminal CS		
	Westminster Coaches	Charing Cross		
	Varsity	Regent Street		
KENT	East Kent	**LUPUS STREET/VICTORIA CS**	East Kent	**VICTORIA CS**
	Maidstone & District	**LUPUS STREET/VICTORIA CS**	Maidstone & District	**VICTORIA CS**
	Russell of Folkestone	Central CS	MT Company	New Cross
	Weald of Kent	Central CS		
	Orange of Chatham	Charing Cross		
	Invicta	Terminal CS		
	Express Safety Coaches	Victoria		
	Thanet Express	Victoria		
SOUTH COAST	Southdown	**LUPUS STREET/VICTORIA CS**	Southdown	**VICTORIA CS**
	Underwood Express	Kings X, Regent Street & Victoria	Beacon	**VICTORIA CS**
	Perseverance	Terminal CS		
	Southern Glideway	Central CS		
	Solent Motors	Terminal CS		
	Alexandra Coaches	Victoria		
	Fairways Super Coaches	Terminal CS		
BOURNEMOUTH SOUTHAMPTON	Elliot Bros/Royal Blue	**VICTORIA CS**	Royal Blue	**VICTORIA CS**
	Orange	Kings X & Paddington	Orange	Kings x & Paddington
	Highways	Regent Street		
	Tourist Motor Services	Terminal CS		
WEST COUNTRY	Elliot Bros/Royal Blue	**VICTORIA CS**	Royal Blue	**VICTORIA CS**
	Highways	Regent Street		
	Red Bus	Central CS		
	Morning Star	Terminal CS		
	Silver Cars	Victoria		
	Superways	Terminal CS		
	Tourist Motor Services	Terminal CS		
BRISTOL SOUTH WALES	Greyhound	**VICTORIA CS**	Greyhound	**VICTORIA CS**
	Black & White	Hammersmith	Royal Blue	**VICTORIA CS**
	Red & White	Terminal CS	Black & White	**VICTORIA CS**
	Ensign Motor Coaches	Terminal CS	Red & White	**VICTORIA CS**
	South Wales Express	Victoria and Kings X		

List of Operators associated with London Coastal Coaches

1933	1934	1935	1936	1937	1938/1940
Aldershot & District	Aldershot & District	Aldershot & District	Aldershot & District	Aldershot & Dist	Aldershot & District
BMMO Midland Red	BMMO Midland Red	BMMO Midland Red	BMMO Midland Red	BMMO Midland Red	Associated Motorways
Black & White Motorways	Black & White Motorways	Black & White Motorways	Black & White Motorways	Black & White Motorways	BMMO Midland Red
C.Smith's Motors (Blackpool)	Crosville	Crosville	Bristol Tramways	Bristol Tramways	Black & White Motorways
Crosville	East Kent	East Kent	Crosville	Crosville	Bristol Tramways
East Kent	East Midlands	East Midlands	East Kent	East Kent	Crosville
East Midlands	East Yorkshire	East Yorkshire	East Midlands	East Midlands	East Kent
East Yorkshire	Eastern Counties	Eastern Counties	East Yorkshire	East Yorkshire	East Midlands
Eastern Counties	Eastern National	Eastern National	Eastern Counties	Eastern Counties	East Yorkshire
Eastern National	Greyhound	Greyhound	Eastern National	Eastern National	Eastern Counties
Glenton Friars	J. Bracewell	J. Bracewell	Ledbury Transport	Lincolnshire	Eastern National
Greyhound	Maidstone & District	Maidstone & District	Lincolnshire	Maidstone & District	Greyhound
London & South Coast	Majestic Express	Majestic Express	Maidstone & District	Majestic Express	Hants & Dorset
Maidstone & District	Majestic Saloon	Majestic Saloon	Majestic Express	Majestic Saloon	Ledbury Transport
Mayfair Transport	North Western	North Western	Majestic Saloon	North Western	Lincolnshire
Midland Bus	Orange Brothers	Orange Brothers	North Western	Orange Brothers	Maidstone & District
North Western	Pickfords	Phillipsons	Orange Brothers	Pickfords	Majestic Express
Orange Brothers	Redcar	Pickfords	Pearsons Happy Days	Red & White	M.T.Company
Pickfords	Red & White	Red & White	Phillipsons	Ribble	North Western
Redcar	Ribble	Ribble	Pickfords	Royal Blue	Orange Brothers
Ribble	Royal Blue	Royal Blue	Red & White	S.M.T.	Pickfords
Royal Blue	S.M.T.	S.M.T.	Ribble	Southdown	Potteries
S.M.T.	Southdown	Southdown	Royal Blue	Southern National	Red & White
Southdown	Southern National	Southern National	S.M.T.	South Midland	Ribble
Southern National	South Midland	South Midland	Southdown	Thames Valley	Royal Blue
Thames Valley	Thames Valley	Thames Valley	Southern National	United Automobile	S.M.T.
United Automobile	United Automobile	United Automobile	South Midland	United Counties	Southdown
W.Alexander & Sons	Varsity	United Counties	Thames Valley	W.Alexander & Sons	Southern National
W.C.Standerwick	W.Alexander & Sons	Varsity	United Automobile	W.C.Standerwick	South Midland
West London Coaches	W.C.Standerwick	W.Alexander & Sons	United Counties	West Yorkshire	South Wales
West Yorkshire	Weald of Kent	W.C.Standerwick	W.Alexander & Sons	Westcliff	Thames Valley
Westcliff	West Yorkshire	West Yorkshire	W.C.Standerwick	Western National	Tillings
Western National	Westcliff	Westcliff	West Yorkshire	Western S.M.T.	Trent
Western S.M.T.	Western National	Western National	Westcliff	Yorkshire Traction	United Automobile
Wood Brothers	Western S.M.T.	Western S.M.T.	Western National	Yorkshire Woollen District	United Counties
Yorkshire Traction	Wood Brothers	Wood Bros (John Bull)	Western S.M.T.		W.Alexander & Sons
Yorkshire Woollen District	Yorkshire Traction	Yorkshire Traction	Yorkshire Traction		W.C.Standerwick
	Yorkshire Woollen District	Yorkshire Woollen District	Yorkshire Woollen District		West Yorkshire
					Westcliff
					Western National
					Western S.M.T.
					Western Welsh
					Wilts & Dorset
					Yorkshire Traction
					Yorkshire Woollen District

SUMMARY OF SERVICES
Showing respective Leaflet Numbers.

	Leaflet No.
ALPHABETICAL INDEX TO ALL TOWNS SERVED, NOTICES, Etc.	1

MAIDSTONE & DISTRICT MOTOR SERVICES, LTD.

London—Milton—Sheerness	2
Leyton—Gillingham—Sheerness	2a
London—Chatham—Gillingham—Faversham	3
„ —West Malling—Maidstone—Charing	4
„ —Headcorn—Tenterden—Woodchurch	5
„ —Cranbrook—Benenden—Tenterden	5
„ —Goudhurst—Hawkhurst—Rye	5a
„ —St. Leonards-on-Sea—Hastings—Bexhill	6

EAST KENT ROAD CAR CO., LTD.

London—Canterbury—Margate—Ramsgate	7
„ —Ash—Sandwich—Deal—Dover	8
„ —Hythe—Folkestone—Dover	9
„ —Bridge—Lydden—Kearsney—Dover	9
Through-Bookings via London—Folkestone—Dover Service	9
London—Whitstable—Tankerton—Herne Bay	10
Through-Bookings to " East Kent " Area	10a

SOUTHDOWN MOTOR SERVICES, LTD

London—Uckfield—Hailsham—Eastbourne	11
„ —Crawley—Handcross—Brighton	12
„ —Lewes—Newhaven—Seaford (Direct Summer Service) ...	13
„ —Horsham—Worthing—Littlehampton (2 Routes)	14
„ —Haslemere—Chichester—Bognor	15
„ —Petworth—Arundel—Littlehampton—Bognor	15
„ —Hindhead—Petersfield—Portsmouth—Southsea	16
„ —Havant—Hayling Island & Holiday Camps (Summer Route)	16a
„ —West Meon—Fareham—Gosport	17
„ —Bishops Waltham—Titchfield—Warsash	17
Through-Bookings from London to the " Southdown " Area	18

THAMES VALLEY TRACTION CO., LTD

London—Wokingham—Reading, and the Thames Valley	19
„ —Slough—Maidenhead—Reading—Newbury	19a
„ —Slough—Maidenhead—Henley	19a

ALDERSHOT & DISTRICT TRACTION CO., LTD

London—Camberley—Aldershot—Farnham—Bordon—Whitehill	20
„ —Cove—Fleet—Crookham	20
„ —Hindhead—Haslemere—(SEE SPECIAL NOTICE)	21

" ROYAL BLUE " (WESTERN and SOUTHERN NATIONAL OMNIBUS CO.'s).

London—Andover—Tidworth—Amesbury—Salisbury—Taunton	22
„ —Basingstoke—Winchester—Southampton—Bournemouth	23
„ —Guildford—Winchester—Southampton—Bournemouth	23
„ —Honiton—Exeter—Torquay—Paignton—Plymouth (via Yeovil)	24
„ —Dorchester—Axminster—Exeter—Torquay—Paignton—Plymouth—(via Bournemouth)	24
„ —Wareham—Swanage—Weymouth	26
„ —Seaton—Sidmouth—Budleigh Salterton—Exmouth	26
„ —Taunton—Minehead—Ilfracombe—Lynton	27
„ —Taunton—Barnstaple—Bideford—Clovelly—Bude	28
„ —Exeter—Newquay—St. Ives—Falmouth—Penzance	29
„ —Exeter—Tavistock—St Austell—Mevagissey	29a

" GREYHOUND " AND " ROYAL BLUE " (Joint Services).

London—Chippenham—Bath—Bristol—Weston-super-Mare	25
„ —Devizes—Bradford-on-Avon—Frome—Wells	25
„ —Oxford—Swindon—Chippenham—Bath—Bristol	25

WESTCLIFF MOTOR SERVICES, LTD.

London—Leigh—Westcliff—Southend-on-Sea	30

EASTERN NATIONAL OMNIBUS CO., LTD.

London—Colchester—Clacton—Jaywick Sands	31
„ —Braintree—Halstead—Hedinghams	32
„ —Danbury—Maldon (Essex)	32a
Through-Bookings from London to Essex	32b

6

7

Derby Day

For many, many years, on a Wednesday early in June, Victoria Coach Station would be used as the assembly point for open-top buses. These were to be used by parties (buffet lunch served quite often on the lower-deck; grand-stand view from the upper-deck) visiting Epsom race course for the annual Derby classic horse race. In this view, two Bristols of very different vintages, one from the Crosville fleet abd the other from Western National can be seen, whilst below on of Southdown's utility Guys is seen awaiting Starters Orders to make the relatively short trip down the A24 to this famous Surrey venue. *(AE Jones)*

Christmas Day

As a contrast to the many views of summer holiday travellers seen in this book, this picture (which may not actually have been taken on Christmas Day!), serves to remind the reader that London Coastal Coaches provided services 365 days a year in all sorts of weather. *(AE Jones.)*

Fuelling

For many of the coaches visiting Victoria Coach Station, certainly those from further away than the south-east of England, a re-fuelling visit was often necessary before the journey home commenced. Quite often this facility was one of those provided by Samuelson Transport, whose garage was across the road from the Coach Station. *(AE Jones.)*

Servicing – routine and less so

Samuelson's Garage was also used for the servicing and, where possible, the running repair of coaches. In the upper view a Midland Red CM6T waits across the road from the Coach Station, having been fuelled and serviced, prior to taking up a return journey to Coventry. If 'Sammy's were not able to repair the windscreen on this North Western Leyland Leopard (a replacement screen would probably have been sent down in the boot of the next coach from Manchester), it would have been returned empty with a volunteer driver to central works in Stockport for repair, much to the frustration of the Victoria-based North Western Inspector. *(Upper GHF Atkins © John Banks collection. Lower AE Jones.)*

Appendix 4 –After Coastal

At long last! The most important development a Victoria Coach Station in the immediate post-Coastal days was the installation of canopies over the bays at the top end of the yard. Now most passengers could board their coaches undercover. *(Peter Scammell collection)*

Huge and extensive alterations were planned during the first half of the 1990s, and upheaval was inevitable, but it was worth all the inconvenience, as it would ensure that Victoria Coach Station would remain a vital centre within the coaching industry. *(Peter Scammell collection)*

INDEX